MICHAEL GRADE: SCREENING THE IMAGE

Also by Mihir Bose

The Crash

The Lost Hero

Money: An Illustrated
Guide for Young People

Fraud

The Aga Khans

A History of Indian Cricket

MICHAEL GRADE

SCREENING
THE IMAGE

Mihir Bose

To Kalpana, with love

First published in Great Britain in 1992 by
Virgin Books
an imprint of Virgin Publishing Ltd
338 Ladbroke Grove
London W10 5AH

Copyright © Mihir Bose 1992

The moral right of the author has been asserted

A catalogue record for this book is available from the British Library

ISBN 1 85227 208 2

Typeset by Phoenix Photosetting, Chatham, Kent
Printed and bound in Great Britain by
Mackays of Chatham PLC, Chatham, Kent

CONTENTS

ILLUSTRATIONS

AUTHOR'S NOTE

This book has been an unusual experience for me. Although my previous books cover a reasonable range from politics through biography and business to sports, I have never written about television before. Also, while it is the biography of a living person, it is written without the help and cooperation of that person. Michael Grade was approached but chose not to help. One or two others, while helpful, wondered whether it was not a bit too soon to write his biography. After all, he is only forty-nine.

But many, many others helped provide information that justified the need for such a book and also made it possible. I must, in particular, thank his sister Lynda Davidson and her husband Arthur, who were particularly generous with their time and insightful with their interpretations of the life and times of Michael Grade.

I am also grateful to Bernie Delfont, Bill Cotton Jnr, Paul Fox, John Bromley, Aubrey Singer, Brian Wenham, Adrian Metcalfe, Sue Stoessl, Mike Bolland, William Rees-Mogg, Carmen Callil, John Gau, Anthony Smith, Roger Graef, Michael Bunce, Pamela Reiss, Justin Dukes, Ken Trodd, Mark Lawson, Dennis Van Thal, James Larcombe, Ian Watson, B. D. Dance, Tim Bell, Winston Fletcher, Hunter Davies, David Dein, Rabbi Steven Katz, Hyman Wolanski and Harvey Mann. There are others whom I cannot acknowledge publicly to whom I am also indebted for information and views on Michael Grade. They know who they are. Thank you. David Docherty, the historian of the LWT, and Ian Curteis deserve special mention for the time they were willing to give me and the information they readily parted with. None of these men or women are in any way responsible for the book, although without their help my task would have been immeasurably more difficult.

The book could never have been written without the inspiration of Derek Wyatt who often has the most marvellous ideas even if he does not always stay around to see them through. As ever, I am grateful to Sue Caincross for all her help, which amounts to much, much more than mere typing or secretarial assistance. Kate Shanker helped with additional typing at very short notice. My nephew Abhijit and my sister Panna provided me with information from distant parts of the world at remarkable speed.

I cannot adequately thank Peter and Ann Fletcher for providing a haven when my own place became rather too chaotic and for being such wonderful surrogate parents to Indira – an immense relief to me and a boon to my wife, Kalpana, who found this book, on top of coping with a one-year-old, perhaps the most trying of all, but nevertheless managed.

Lastly but by no means least, my thanks to the staff of Virgin Publishing who have been both patient and understanding.

PROLOGUE

Grady is better at the short game than the long one
JOHN BROMLEY

THE EVENING OF 9 NOVEMBER 1978 saw the House of Commons conclude a debate on the Labour government's legislative programme that had been presented in the Queen's speech nine days earlier. Such occasions are often predictable but Jim Callaghan's minority government was just entering the winter of discontent that was eventually to destroy it, and seasoned political observers had begun to sense that an era was coming to an end. Callaghan had, astonishingly, failed to go to the country in October when Labour might just have won; now Labour was falling behind Mrs Thatcher's Conservatives in the opinion polls and in the House it had lost the support of the Liberals who had propped it up for two years. Few thought the government would survive long enough to put the programme through; the Conservatives hoped they would not survive the night. They had tabled a motion of censure which was virtually a vote of no confidence and the government knew it would have to rely on support from the ragbag of minor parties like the Ulster Unionists and the Scottish Nationalists to hold on.

At about 7 p.m., as the debate proceeded, a young man emerged from his office in the South Bank complex next to the National Theatre, hailed a taxi and, in the almost classical fashion which draws crowds to moments of high theatre, asked the driver to take him to Westminster. But this young man was not rushing to the Commons to witness the possible fall of the government. He was going there to create his own drama, one that would have such impact that for a few days politics would be pushed off the front pages.

That young man was Michael Ian Grade, then thirty-six years old and Director of Programmes at London Weekend Television. He was acting, as he sometimes did (or said he did), purely on an 'off chance', but in fact the chance was finely calculated. Grade knew he had to do something to rescue his Saturday night schedules. In the eighteen months since he had become Director of Programmes he had been unable to dent the massive BBC advantage over ITV. LWT was an odd station. It broadcast for only three nights in the week, from Friday evening to Sunday night (the other nights belonging to Thames), yet these were the most high-profile, critical viewing nights, where success or failure was glaringly advertised. And the BBC, with shrewd tactical sense, had targeted these nights, particularly Saturday, for special attention.

Almost everything Grade had done to try to combat the BBC had failed. His mix of game shows, situation comedies and drama, cobbled together from the various ITV regional companies, always seemed to come second best to the BBC. When he had sought to promote LWT's own home-grown show *Mind Your Language* he was accused by critics at the Edinburgh Film Festival of purveying racism and had been forced to withdraw. In this era before remote control television or videos, television executives worked on the 'inheritance theory' of television: the belief that once a viewer was hooked on a channel by a programme then that viewer stayed glued to that channel for the rest of the night. And Grade had only to look at his own schedules to realise why the BBC would always inherit the majority of viewers on a Saturday night.

BBC 1 started with a very successful game show, hosted by Bruce Forsyth, called *The Generation Game*, continued with the Edwardian drama *The Duchess of Duke Street*, an American police series *Starsky and Hutch*, rounding off the evening with *Match of the Day* and the Michael Parkinson chat show. Grade just could not see how to break this. ITV's alternatives such as *The Incredible Hulk* or *The Professionals* made no serious dent in the BBC schedules. Even when LWT took a chance and presented *Saturday Night Live*, a late-night show supposedly in the genre of *That Was The Week That Was*, it generated more controversy than it did viewers. Just three weeks before he hailed that taxi to Westminster, the research team on *Saturday Night Live* had threatened to leave because Grade had censored an item about the *Daily Mail*.

The ITV company contracts were up for renewal in 1981 and there were suggestions in the press that LWT might lose its franchise.

Grade had decided that the only alternative was to fall back on the maxim 'If you can't beat them poach them', and he had tried to get some of the BBC performers to defect to ITV. Six months previously he had made his first attempt to break the BBC stranglehold by luring

Bruce Forsyth to LWT with a chat/game show, *Bruce's Big Night*. But the move, seen as Grade's big idea, had backfired. The ratings, after the first week, plummeted and, as can often happen, the show began to suffer from a vicious circle of virulent press criticism leading to even more viewers switching off the moment Forsyth appeared.

The *Sun*, in characteristic style, ran stories which suggested that the show's failure was affecting Forsyth's marriage to Anthea Redfern. Nor did Forsyth help matters when, in only the third show, trying to provide an upbeat introduction for Pam Ayres, he managed to offend Patience Strong. Forsyth, having described Ayres as England's most prominent poetess, then made a throwaway remark about Patience Strong claiming she had 'packed it in'. It was not long before a letter arrived from Miss Strong's solicitors claiming that the remarks were defamatory and that, far from 'packing it in', Miss Strong was continuing to publish poetry in various magazines and periodicals. Forsyth had to apologise and have her on the show to make amends. ITV continued to bill *Bruce's Big Night* as the jewel of its Saturday programmes, but the BBC just counteracted by moving Larry Grayson to host *The Generation Game*, creating a new star in the process, and Saturday night was still part of the patrimony of the BBC.

It was then that Grade had come up with the idea that was now taking him to Westminster. The other plum in the BBC Saturday schedule was football and Grade was on his way to meet the man he hoped would help him carry out the most audacious coup yet in British television history. That man was a Labour backbencher called Jack Dunnett, hardly known outside Westminster but a shrewd choice for the plan Grade had in mind.

As Grade's taxi made the short journey to Westminster, Dunnett was drinking a cup of coffee and wondering when he should enter the chamber to listen to the debate. That night, as on so many nights, he was lobby-fodder for the government, a mute witness to the political drama where his only act would be to vote. However, in fourteen years as a Labour MP he had become the classical backbencher, the man who never made the news but was extremely busy behind the scenes: busy in the committees, busy in his Nottingham constituency; shrewd, ambitious and always looking for a deal. A solicitor by profession, with extensive business and property interests, he was also one of the few Labour MPs involved in the football hierarchy, as chairman of Notts

County and as a member, albeit quite junior, of the management committee that ran League football.

Grade had first met Dunnett almost fifteen years before when he was a director of Brentford Football Club and Grade a reporter for the *Mirror*. Both men shared a passion for the game: Grade had been taken as a child to Charlton; Dunnett had fallen in love with Chelsea as an eleven-year-old. There were similarities in their backgrounds, too. Grade's family had emigrated to England to escape Jewish pogroms in Russia; Dunnett, whose middle name is Jacob, came from a family that had fled to Scotland from Poland and Lithuania.

Grade was aware both of Dunnett's ability to make deals (he had tried to gain tax relief for football clubs forced to make ground improvements) and of his restless desire to change football. Indeed, in the stuffy, closed world that was English football Dunnett was close to being classed a dangerous revolutionary. In 1967, as chairman of Brentford, he had tried to merge the club with neighbouring Queen's Park Rangers, the first such move in English football and one that made financial and economic sense. But it so outraged both clubs' supporters that it never got off the ground and led to Dunnett's resignation from Brentford.

At about 7.15 p.m. Grade arrived at the vast sepulchral Central Lobby and presented his little green card to the policeman, requesting him to forward it to Jack Dunnett. Within a few minutes Dunnett emerged and, although he had seen little of Grade since his Brentford days, greeted him with rare warmth. He ushered him to the Strangers' bar, where most Labour MPs prefer to drink and which has acquired the nickname of the Kremlin. The two ordered large brandies and sat down to talk.

Grade very quickly came to the point. Would the League listen to a proposal to give the ITV companies exclusive right to televise soccer?

To most people Grade's question would have appeared outrageous. For even as Grade spoke to Dunnett, the BBC and ITV were jointly negotiating with the Football League to renew the contract to televise soccer, a deal the clubs were due to vote on the following week. But Grade knew the marriage was far from happy. The BBC showed recorded highlights on Saturday night, ITV on Sunday afternoons, which to many appeared an immutable pattern of life. In the early seventies, the BBC's *Match of the Day* had attracted up to 14 million viewers, ITV's *The Big Match* nine million, but now viewers were switching off when football came on and the clubs were worried both by the amount of football on the box and the money they received for it. Their advertising consultants had told them that televised football kept people away from the games and they felt television was getting football on the cheap.

The BBC and ITV were paying £500,000 a year between them for the recorded highlights, which meant about £5,000 for each club, hardly enough to pay the wages of a reserve team player. The League wanted a 30 per cent rise but the BBC pleaded poverty, an argument that did not much impress the clubs when they learnt that it had paid £2.5 million just to screen one movie, *The Sound of Music*.

Football felt boxed in, more so as the BBC and ITV had what was called a 'concordat', in which they agreed always to negotiate jointly with the football authorities, never separately. So the League could never pit the BBC against the ITV companies.

Grade was well aware that his question to Dunnett bypassed all that and from Dunnett's initial reaction he could sense he had timed his tackle perfectly.

For the next hour, as the Commons debated the fate of the government, Grade outlined to Dunnett his new plan for televised soccer. Although it was a decade since he had reported on soccer, Grade still kept in touch with the game, going as often as he could to Charlton matches, and in his various informal talks with football directors and officials he had sensed that the Football League would not accept the BBC–ITV joint deal. Many clubs felt that if that was the best television offered, they should just turn round and say, 'Scrub television.' Dunnett confirmed that Grade had gauged the mood of the clubs right. Dunnett himself intended to vote against the new TV soccer deal at the League meeting due the following week.

But, encouraging as this was, Grade feared the power and the reach of the BBC. His luring away of Forsyth had already made him unpopular with the mandarins of Wood Lane and he was aware that when it came to sport the BBC zealously guarded its empire. Despite numerous ITV pleas, it refused to alternate major broadcasts such as the Cup Final, claiming that on such occasions the British public expected to see BBC cameras there. ITV had tried for years to televise soccer on a Saturday and had never succeeded. The BBC's football expert, Jimmy Hill, who had made the journey the other way from

LWT to BBC (usually BBC executives moved to the commercial net-work), was also managing director of Coventry, a First Division club. As a player he had helped smash the maximum wage of £20 a week clubs paid to players, ushering in the days of plenty for top players. Now as a pundit on the BBC his pronouncements on the game had the ring of papal utterances. Grade feared that if Hill got wind of the plan it would never get off the ground. If Grade's smash-and-raid plan was to succeed, secrecy was of the essence; the BBC must not get any inkling of the approach. Grade made Dunnett promise not to tell the BBC that an ITV company had made an independent offer and to tell nobody, not even his football colleagues, where that offer had come from.

Dunnett agreed and promised to ring Grade the next morning and let him know what the reaction might be. As Grade returned home, Dunnett quietly slipped into the chamber and dutifully voted with the government which, with the help of the Ulster Unionists, survived to fight another Commons battle.

Next morning at 11 a.m. Grade's phone rang.

'It's Jack,' said Dunnett. 'I've talked to a few colleagues. We'll listen to your proposals. But you'll have to come up with something big.'

So far Grade had told no one else about his plans. But now he slowly started searching for allies who would help him launch the coup. His first port of call was John Bromley, Controller of Sport. When Grade had started at the *Mirror* as a trainee, Bromley was a star columnist and had helped him find his feet, recruiting him as his assistant on the column he wrote for the paper and then bequeathing him the column when he moved to ITV to start the *World of Sport*. Now Grade was Bromley's boss and, as if to emphasise this, Grade had his offices on the twelfth floor of the LWT complex while Bromley was on the sixth floor. But neither this change in the relationship nor the fact that the younger man lorded it over the older one did anything to affect the warmth the two felt for each other. Every evening at about 6.30 p.m. Bromley would take the lift up to the twelfth floor, make himself com-fortable in Grade's office suite and have what he called a 'snogging ses-sion', a couple of jars, while Grade and he set the world right, planned or fantasised about future events. That Friday evening the snogging session turned out to be very different.

Grade told Bromley, 'I think we can get the Football League exclusively.'

Bromley had had a hard day. He had just spoken to Gerry Loftus, the ITV man negotiating jointly with the BBC about the television contracts, and knew how difficult they were proving to be. A funny idea like this was the last thing he wanted. 'Grady, please, don't start.'

'I am telling you,' persisted Grade. 'I've met with Jack Dunnett in the House of Commons. He is on the management committee and he has rung and told me the League will listen to any proposal we make. It will cost us a lot of money and we have got to get everybody on our side. But it can be done.'

Bromley, who likes playing things by the book, thought for a moment that Grade did not really know or had forgotten about the joint negotiations. 'Grady,' he said, 'we have got a formal position here. Discussions, joint agreements, this concordat, the ITV–BBC concordat. Don't you know we are at this moment sitting round and discussing football jointly with the League? We have made a joint offer. We don't go it alone, we cannot.'

Grade waved his cigar imperiously, a trait of his uncle's he had recently acquired, and said, 'Bromers, we are competitors and we have got to get up there and get cracking.'

That evening, as the jars flowed, Bromley gamely tried to play the conservative, seeking to cool the younger revolutionary's ardour, but in the end he could see that Grade, provided he got the backing, had the making of a sensational deal. They departed bubbling with anticipation but agreeing to keep a very low profile over the weekend and vowing not to tell anybody. As it happened, the press did get on to Grade that weekend but it was over rumours about conflict between the stars of *Saturday Night People* and Grade fobbed them off, saying he could not talk as it was the Jewish Day of Atonement. Nobody got a sniff about the real story.

Over the weekend Dunnett was a bit busier. Returning to his Nottingham constituency he spoke to two men. One was Lord Westwood, president of the League and chairman of Newcastle United, whose silver hair and patch over one eye gave him a rather piratical look. The other was Alan Hardaker, for more than twenty years secretary of the League and the man who, in the public eye, personified both its obduracy and its tenacity. At first Hardaker could not make out what Dunnett was talking about. He was himself involved in joint negotiations with ITV and the BBC. Some clubs had spoken about holding separate talks, but in a circular to the clubs that he had sent out only the previous week he had doubted if that was possible. The BBC said it had no money and Hardaker had told the clubs he was not sure ITV could take on the entire burden. So where was this exclusive, higher offer coming from? Dunnett assured him it was genuine and on Monday Hardaker, who lived next door to the League's offices in Lytham St Anne's, travelled down to London.

As always, Hardaker stayed at the Great Western Hotel in Paddington, the League's favourite London watering hole. There on the Tuesday morning, over a breakfast of prunes, kippers, bacon and eggs, Grade explained to Hardaker and Dunnett what he had in mind. It was not merely more money that he dangled in front of them, although that was, of course, an inducement. He also shrewdly capitalised on the feeling among football clubs that there was just too much football on the box. Don't you see, he pointed out, an exclusive deal with ITV means there will automatically be fifty per cent less football on television? Hardaker was convinced the deal was worth looking at and it was agreed that Grade, Bromley, Hardaker and Dunnett would meet the next afternoon at Dunnett's flat in Whitehall Court.

Grade returned to his offices in the South Bank and began preparing a formal offer. It was now time to widen the circle of knowledge. ITV, unlike the BBC, is a federation and a loose federation at that, made up of regional companies who come together at certain times for certain programmes, such as the news broadcasts of ITN. But while in theory all the regional ITV companies are equal, some are more equal than others. Grade knew he needed the backing of the major networks: Thames, Yorkshire, Granada, ATV. Their support would drive any deal through. The first person he contacted was Paul Fox, managing director of Yorkshire. Not only was Yorkshire a heavyweight ITV company but Fox himself was now a crucial player in the ITV hierarchy. In television he had a reputation for being forthright, something of a bruiser, the man who almost a decade before had been dubbed part of the 'new priesthood of television'. As Fox recalls, Grade presented his plan as a *fait accompli* and Fox was happy to back him. Grade knew half his battle was won.

On Wednesday morning Grade organised a telephone conference which included Fox, the other major networks, the chairman of the network controllers group representing the smaller regional companies, and the director of television at the Independent Broadcasting

Authority, the ITV watchdog. They not only unanimously backed Grade, but also gave him their blessing.

Only one man, Gerry Loftus, was kept in the dark, but if the plan had to be kept secret – and secrecy *was* essential – then Grade felt the deception was necessary. Bromley agreed.

It wasn't cricket, thought Bromley, but there was no way they could tell Gerry. Poor Gerry. He had been slogging up and down from London to Lytham St Anne's talking to the League. Both Grade and Bromley felt very sorry for him but what could they do? They couldn't help it, could they? When it is all over, Grade reassured Bromley, we'll talk to him, buy him lunch at the Savoy.

At about 2.30 p.m. that afternoon Grade and Bromley arrived at Dunnett's flat. Hardaker and Dunnett were already there and the four sat round in comfortable leather armchairs. Dunnett had provided coffee, digestive biscuits and plenty of ashtrays. He had also got two secretaries from his office to type up drafts of the agreement. For nearly four hours they haggled over the terms of the deal. Hardaker, realising he had a splendid chance to break the television cartel which had so often frustrated him, negotiated hard, at times so hard that Grade felt the deal would slip away. But in the end they came to an agreement. ITV would pay £5.5 million over three years to televise soccer exclusively. It still meant that each club would get only about £17,000 a year but it was a major advance on what had previously been on offer.

As Grade and Bromley emerged from Whitehall Court it started to rain, making the cold, chilly night even more miserable. For a few minutes, as they waited for a cab, they huddled together on the steps of the building. Grade turned to Bromley and said, 'Do you realise what we have done, Bromers? We have killed *Match of the Day*, the biggest programme BBC had for Saturday night.' It was only then that Bromley fully appreciated the enormity of their achievement and as he looked at Grade he felt a sense of pride and a new respect for his protégé. Grady had cut corners, certainly, but without him this momentous development would not have been possible. Nobody else would have even thought about it.

There were still hurdles to be negotiated. Dunnett and Hardaker had to get the League to agree to the terms – first the management committee, then the full meeting of the League. As it happened, an extraordinary general meeting of the League had been scheduled for the next day to consider the television contract being proposed jointly by the BBC and

ITV. Hardaker assured Grade that the deal would go through and, what was more, LWT's name would be kept secret. He was as good as his word.

On Thursday morning at 10 a.m. the ten-man management committee met at the Wembley Conference Centre and unanimously approved the deal. At 2.30 p.m., in the Centre's Avon Room, fifty-one men representing the entire Football League met and began discussing the proposal. It was, perhaps, the strangest meeting in the League's already strange and convoluted history.

Hardaker and Dunnett told them few details of the proposal. LWT's name was not disclosed, nor were any financial details given, nor even any idea of how the deal would work. Hardaker emphasised how it would mean much more money for the clubs, and much less football on the box.

Few questions were asked. Most of those present were in awe of Hardaker, who commanded the League then as few men have done in its history, and they were glad to trust him. As one representative would later describe it, 'Grade had passed us a fast ball and we put it in the net.'

By 3.30 p.m. just an hour after the meeting had started, the clubs voted 50 to 1 to accept the deal. The one vote against was by Coventry City, although managing director Jimmy Hill was not present at the meeting.

As the League debated, Grade and Bromley were in the difficult position of men who knew they were about to make history but who were unable to share their precious knowledge with anyone. Grade was not convinced Hardaker would get the League to agree and his great fear was that there would be a leak, the BBC would intervene and the whole deal would blow up in his face.

The wait was excruciating: Grade chewed on his cigar; Bromley was almost tempted to chew his fingernails. What added to the tension was that until they knew the deal was approved they dared not talk about it to anybody else. Round about them preparations went ahead for LWT's *Big Match* soccer programme to be shown on Sunday. Great was the temptation to tell staff that within a few months everything would change and ITV would get Saturday night soccer, as it had so often wished. But the two men had to keep silent.

At 3.45 p.m. the tension broke. The phone on Grade's desk rang. It was Jack Dunnett.

'You've got yourself a deal,' he said. 'I'm coming round to see you with a letter from the League agreeing to the terms.'

Bromley quickly gathered his *World of Sport* personnel in Grade's offices. With an appropriate sense of theatre Grade waited until the last person was in before slowly unfolding a piece of paper, the one he, Bromley, Dunnett and Hardaker had signed the previous day.

'There is something I'd like you all to hear,' he said. Then in measured tones he read out the deal. For a few seconds there was a hush in the room; everybody seemed numb. Then somebody uttered 'Bloody hell' and as if the sluicegates of a dam had been opened the excitement suddenly burst forth. Champagne was ordered and the next few hours were quite the most hectic Grade had ever known.

Peter Coppock, LWT's press officer, set about organising a press conference for 7 p.m. that same evening. A few minutes later, Brian Moore, ITV's leading football commentator, made a routine check call about the weekend matches and discovered his world was about to change. At 6 p.m. Dunnett arrived at Grade's office. Grade took out his wallet, extracted a pound note, pinned it to the letter from LWT outlining the deal and handed it to Dunnett. Dunnett smiled, accepted a glass of champagne and everyone cheered as he and Grade toasted this symbolic gesture which meant there was now a contract. In strict legal terms LWT had a fourteen-day option on the deal but this was a minor detail on such a night of celebration.

The BBC was still completely in the dark and was only alerted when a reporter from *Broadcast* magazine phoned a contact and asked, 'Did you know they are popping champagne corks down at LWT?' Within the hour the BBC knew the reason.

Hardaker felt no qualms about pushing the deal through, although he was still formally negotiating with the BBC. However, he did feel he ought at least to warn Alan Hart, head of BBC sport. Just before he left to join Dunnett and Grade at LWT he called him. It made Hardaker feel better, but he knew that by then the BBC could do nothing about the deal.

Grade's coup was now proceeding like clockwork. At precisely 7 p.m. Grade, Hardaker, Dunnett and Bromley filed into LWT's fourth-floor press room. Coppock had assembled all the journalists there, having promised them 'a major announcement'. Grade did not disappoint.

'Gentlemen,' he began, 'London Weekend Television have secured the option, on terms which have been agreed with the Football League and with the full endorsement of the clubs, for the exclusive coverage of all Football League and League Cup matches for three years from next season.'

Again there was a moment of numb silence in the press room. Then, with typical eloquence, somebody uttered 'Fucking hell' and the journalists began to realise that, unlike so many press conferences that promise more than they eventually deliver, this one indeed gave them a major story. As Grade well knew, the timing of the announcement was just right. This was the moment when the back bench of the newspapers, the men who ran the paper, would decide what went on the front pages, and his story had just the right populist touch, blending football and television with a dash of intrigue to spice it up. For the next few days the story dominated the papers. 'SNATCH OF THE DAY' proclaimed one tabloid across its front page, and even the qualities devoted acres of newsprint to detailing Grade's coup. Grade revelled in the publicity.

Michael Grade was not unaccustomed to publicity. As director of programmes he had had his fair share but that was mainly from television and showbiz reporters. And he was always the nephew, the nephew of Lew Grade, one of the most successful men in British entertainment; the nephew of Bernard Delfont, Lew's equally successful brother, the famous impresario. The Grades have been pictured as the First Family of British entertainment, not quite as handsome as the Kennedys but luckier, not quite as talented as the Redgraves but much more sensible. Their spectacular success in show business had an added romance because a generation before they were part of the surge of almost destitute Jewish immigrants that had crowded into the East End of London from Russia and eastern Europe. Michael's grandfather had arrived at Tilbury docks from Odessa in 1912 with little more than the hope that England would provide a better home than Tsarist Russia, where the historical disease of anti-Jewish pogroms was once again gaining strength. By the time Michael was born, the family was not only well established and integrated into mainstream English life but was making a reputation in show business. As he was growing up, the show-business achievements of his uncles Lew and Bernard made them almost household names. Until this moment Michael had lived in their shadow. Now, in one audacious move, he had emerged from under their tutelage and into the spotlight.

Robin Lustig in the *Observer* hailed Grade's move as a 'tactical masterpiece' and described it as 'one of the biggest coups in broadcasting history'. James Lawton in the *Daily Express* could barely contain his enthusiasm for Michael Grade: 'There is a new phrase in the language of television power these days. It says: Whatever Mike Grade wants, Mike Grade gets.' Lawton spoke of Grade's 'ruthless brilliance' which had made him 'a giant in the industry at thirty-five', 'a legend in the corridors of big-time television'; he speculated that BBC chiefs had 'nightmares about him'.

That was, perhaps, understandable hype. Although the BBC chiefs were furious, their fury was all the greater for their feeling that they had played the gentlemen's game, stuck to the concordat, and had been beaten by raw parvenus. Hill was particularly incensed, describing Grade and Bromley as 'hooligans'. Cliff Morgan, head of outside broadcast, saw it as an unfair fight: 'We thought we were still in bed, so to speak.' Alasdair Milne, managing director of BBC television, got himself invited on to *Nationwide*, BBC's news magazine programme, to denounce Grade's coup as 'Mafia with chequebooks very much in evidence'.

But this was not just impotent rage; there were some aces up the BBC's sleeve. The football clubs had not realised that the small print of their previous contract forbade them from dealing with other companies before first talking to the BBC. The BBC sued the League for breach of contract and sought an injunction to stop the deal with LWT. Gordon Borrie, head of the Office of Fair Trading, began an investigation to determine whether the contract violated the Restrictive Trade Practices Act. Labour and Conservative MPs in the House of Commons temporarily forgot their battles to denounce this piracy. The European Commission also got in on the act and said it would examine whether the contracting parties had flouted the rules of competition as laid down in the Treaty of Rome.

Initially Grade felt he could ride out the storm. He had played the publicity of the coup brilliantly. To non-football journalists he would retail the wider considerations that prompted the deal, what it would do for broadcasting and television choice. To football writers he would speak of his love for the game, so much so that one of them went off thinking he was a reluctant TV tycoon who would like nothing better than to go to Charlton's dilapidated football ground in south London every Saturday.

Grade's optimism was such that it proved infectious and Bromley shared it fully. In the middle of the controversy he was invited to be a guest speaker at an insurance lunch at the Savoy. Gordon Borrie was on the top table and Bromley made jocular remarks at his expense about the OFT getting involved in this affair. The insurance men lapped it up.

But Borrie had the last laugh. He had been carefully scrutinising the small print of the existing contract the clubs had entered into with the BBC. This was quite clear. It meant they had to talk to the BBC before talking to other companies. Grade was hardly aware of this clause and to him it had seemed a matter of no consequence. In the euphoria of the deal, he could not believe that such a small legal matter could derail him. He had not anticipated the furore his audacious move would create and he believed the sheer momentum would carry him through. Borrie thought otherwise.

On a technicality he ruled the deal was void, the technicality being that insufficient notice had been given to the OFT. The BBC relentlessly pursued its legal action against the League and in the end ITV just had to capitulate. A new four-year deal was signed whereby the two channels would alternate Saturday night coverage every year.

Bromley ruefully recalls, 'Nothing has ever hit the BBC harder. When they heard our news Portland Place rocked. But we didn't envisage the power of the BBC. This was the establishment of the country we had taken on and we just didn't realise how hard they could hit back. Grady is better at the short game than the long game. He is instinctive. He didn't envisage the Office of Fair Trading, the MPs in the House. He just didn't anticipate that sort of reaction. In the end we had to capitulate. We did something we didn't plan to do. We got the alternating of the schedule but we confused the viewers. The nation had been brought up on *Match of the Day* on Saturday night and *Big Match* on Sunday. Now one year they would have *Big Match* on ITV on Saturday, the next year *Match of the Day* on Saturdays on BBC. It killed *Match of the Day*, which had not been our objective. It also opened up live coverage for football and destroyed recorded highlights. But that was not what Grady had wanted. He hadn't even thought about all that. All Grady wanted was *Match of the Day* and to switch it to ITV. He just didn't realise what he was taking on.'

Grade, with that outward cheerfulness which rarely leaves him, claimed victory, asserting that alternating of schedules was what he had wanted all along. For years the BBC had thwarted ITV's plans to televise soccer on Saturday; now Grade had delivered them that. But even when ITV got football on Saturday, Bill Cotton, Grade's counterpart at the BBC, merely put up a big movie against it and ITV's Saturday soccer never won anything like the 14 million viewers that the BBC's had achieved. At the height of the controversy Cotton had rung Grade and said, 'You're off your head. Remove *Match of the Day* from the BBC and it will get no more than 8 million viewers.' He was proved right. The success of his ploy of screening a big movie as an alternative to recorded football underlined the fact that interest in soccer, at least of the recorded variety, was waning.

Only the Football League could claim victory. It received £10 million over four years, a fivefold increase over the money it had been receiving before Grade took that fateful taxi trip to Westminster. Grade had wanted to improve his ratings; he had ended up helping football and quite inadvertently bringing about the death of recorded football. In a way, the affair sums up the Michael Grade story.

The Grade deal was breathtaking. Nobody but Grade could have conceived it. Its weakness lay in the fact that he had not thought through the implications. He had been mesmerised by the agent's dream: the BBC has a wonderful programme, let's snatch it away from them. He had not sat down and asked: If I do this what will it mean for televised football? The result was that when the deal collapsed the world of televised soccer could never be put together again. Probably the changes to televised soccer would have come in any event, but before Grade boarded that taxi to Westminster nobody had predicted that *Match of the Day* was a dying institution. The audacious nature of his move gave Grade the reputation of being 'American' in his dealings, but as the British system is not American, this merely made him the odd guy of the small screen: his deals had the stamp of Hollywood but he could never quite remodel a system or an institution. His actions often had consequences he had not even imagined.

Publicly Grade never accepted defeat. More than a year later, when the BBC had to announce cuts, he cheekily suggested that they might think of alternating sports coverage. Surely that would save money? It would prevent axing orchestras.

Privately, the experience left Grade, as Bromley recalls, 'shattered. In the end he said to me, "We've got to go away."'

The only cure, Bromley decided, was golf. More than six months had passed since Grade had hailed that taxi. It was April now; the US Masters, one of the great golf tournaments in the world, was about to start in Augusta, Georgia. Bromley and Grade decided that two weeks there would help them calm their nerves and forget the frenzy and disappointment of the past few months in London.

'Bromers,' said Grade, 'you look after the hotel and the baggage, I'll look after the travel.' So, early in April 1979, the two men took the Concorde flight to New York. Soon after they were airborne, an air hostess came round offering cigars. Concorde is the only flight where you are allowed to smoke cigars. Grade took one, lit up and as he blew the smoke away he seemed to try to blow away the past few months' stresses and strains. Bromley looked across at his friend and thought, 'He'll be all right. In our business, you take a knock and then you get up and go.'

I

THE WANDERING CHILD

We had rather a strange childhood
LYNDA DAVIDSON, Michael's sister

MICHAEL GRADE'S WHO'S WHO ENTRY suggests he had no mother, or at least not one he would like to acknowledge. It mentions his father, Leslie, and then in the space where you might have expected his mother's name, Winifred, you find Olga, his father's mother. It is not unusual for the famous to edit out unwelcome aspects of their lives, but generally this is something to do with their career. It is rare to find someone who omits his mother's name in favour of his grandmother's. This omission by Grade provides the most revealing clue to his childhood and early life.

Winifred Smith was the daughter of a journeyman plumber from Wales, Charles Smith. She had met Leslie Grade through her brother George, who was Leslie's partner in his theatrical agency. Much older than Leslie, George looked the senior partner and played to the full the role of the gentleman he aspired to be. He had come into some money from an insurance claim after a road accident and a few months before the war had invested it in Leslie's business. As a sleeping partner he was required to do little except give an air of being in command. He proved so convincing at this that at meetings people would often address him first, thinking he was the more important of the two, until they discovered that it was Leslie who ran the agency.

It was perhaps natural that Leslie should have been drawn to Winifred. Their friendship had some of the qualities of a wartime romance and wars have produced stranger alliances, although their decision actually to marry was due to the panic that the pre-pill generation suffered. Winifred was three months pregnant when Leslie married her at the Hackney Registry Office on 6 January 1940, with George and Charles acting as the two witnesses. It had been a year since Leslie had set up business with George.

For some time Leslie kept the marriage a secret from his family, terrified not only by its circumstances but also because Winifred was not Jewish. But while he eventually told his brothers Lew and Bernard, he could not bring himself to tell his widowed mother, Olga. She might accept that conventions of the day required that he marry Winifred, but could she live with the fact that she was not Jewish? Olga had set her heart on her sons marrying Jewish women. Leslie was her youngest and favourite son, the first child to be born to her since she emigrated to England from Russia and the first to get married. Leslie knew that his marriage outside the faith would devastate his mother.

Initially it was not difficult to keep Olga in the dark. The war had made her a bit of a nomad. At its start Lew Grade, her eldest son and the head of the family, had wanted to send Olga and his sister Rita to Australia to get away from the expected bombing. But Rita, although only fourteen then, refused to go and so Lew settled on the alternative of moving them as far away from London and the major industrial centres as possible. So, in the early years of the war, Olga and Rita had shuffled about a series of South Coast seaside resorts. First Bognor Regis but after a bomb fell there Lew moved them to Bournemouth and finally to the pretty village of Lynton in North Devon. It was while they were in Lynton that Leslie married and word of it reached Olga only some months after her first grandchild, Lynda, was born.

As often happens in such situations, the birth of a grandchild proved to be a healer. Olga immediately rang Leslie and invited him to visit her in Devon with his wife and daughter. In the Jewish religion, the family lineage continues through the mother, not the father, and so Olga was desperate to see the little girl Winifred had produced. The moment of reunion, at least as pictured by Rita, was just as any Hollywood scriptwriter would have wished. No prodigal could have asked for a more forgiving parent. As Leslie entered the little cottage in Lynton with Winifred and Lynda, Olga embraced him.

'What is done is done. We can't alter that. Leslie is my child. I love him,' said Olga to Rita. But although having a grandchild eased some of Olga's pain, how much she accepted Winifred remains debatable. Olga could never quite understand why her son should have wanted to marry a *shiksa*, the less than complimentary Yiddish word for a Gentile woman. As Lew and Bernard followed Leslie's example by marrying *shiksas* this pain was to endure and Olga was only able to assuage it and celebrate a proper Jewish wedding many years after the war when Rita married Joe Freeman.

Leslie's concern over how Olga would react was understandable.

She was the rock on which the Grades had built their family. Then in her late fifties, mother of four children, two of them born when she was in her late thirties, her life had mirrored their struggles and was the story of one of the greatest migrations of people ever seen. Between the middle of the nineteenth century and 1930 something like 62 million Jews moved from Europe to various parts of the world. Olga and her family were part of the Jewish migration from Russia that saw 150,000 come to Britain between 1870 and the start of the First World War.

That journey to England changed everything in Olga's life. Born in Alexandrovsk in the Ukraine either in 1887 or 1888 (she never had a birth certificate), she was originally called Golda Mary. In a previous century she might have lived out her life as many Jews had done in Russia but in 1912, just turned twenty-four, she arrived at Tilbury docks after a perilous journey – by train to Berlin and then on an onion boat from Hamburg – with two little sons, the elder, aged six, the other just turned three. She had come to join her husband Isaac, who had arrived in London just three months before, convinced that there was no future for Jews in Russia. It was in the East End of London, then as much of a traditional Jewish immigrant areas as it is now a Bangladeshi one, that she changed her name to Olga. However, the family never discarded their surname of Winogradsky. Family folklore holds that it would have been more appropriate if Olga had never surrendered her maiden name. Winogradsky, meaning the 'town where the wine is made', gave a misleading clue to her personality, whereas her maiden name, Eisenstadt, meaning 'iron city', more accurately summed up her life and style.

It was this toughness that was to see Olga's family through the early, grim days in the East End, coping both with the upheaval from Russia and a feckless husband who could never resist the lure of the gambling table; at times all she had to feed her three sons was some bread and cocoa. But while Isaac never overcame his ability to lose money, Olga proved to be the nucleus around which the family would first survive and then prosper. And the sons she had brought from Russia, following the example of other Jewish immigrants eager to be accepted in their new country, soon acquired completely new names and identities.

The immigration officials at Tilbury, where Olga was met by Isaac, had already taken it upon themselves to change the names of her two little sons. Lovat, aged six, was too complicated a name for them and the identity cards, so they called him Louis. Boris, the three-year-old, became Barnet, later Bernard. In the mid-1920s, as the Charleston craze crossed the Atlantic, Louis, who took it up very successfully, felt he could not spend the rest of his life entering dance competitions with a name like Louis Winogradsky. He had to shorten it. But which part of it should he choose? Louis Wino did not sound right, so he just took the middle part of his surname and became Louis Grad. Sometime later in Paris, while appearing at the Moulin Rouge, he was interviewed by the *Paris Midi*. The article was fulsome but his name was misspelt as Lew Grade. Louis Grad liked the sound of it and Lew Grade he became.

Grade became the family's anglicised name; everyone used it except for Bernard. He was advised by his agent that two Grades was one too many in show business. An American group called the Dufor Boys were doing very well; the agent worked on some permutations, came up with Delfont, and the child who had started life as Boris Winogradsky became Bernard Delfont. Olga always preferred to call Lew Louis, though in her later years she would sometimes sign herself Olga Grade or Olga Delfont, depending on which son's hospitality she was enjoying.

By the time Leslie got married, the Grades were quite anglicised and had left their East End past, both literally and metaphorically. They had physically moved away from Brick Lane to Pullman Court, a 'luxury' flat in Streatham with its own swimming pool, tennis court and even a miniature golf course: a world removed from the tenements of Spitalfields. They were also making their way into show business. Lew, who had taken over as head of the family on Isaac's death, had decided that his dancing career, which had seen him become the champion Charleston dancer in the country and travel round Europe, was getting nowhere; he would be much better off as an agent.

It is a modern myth to think of show business as something uniquely Jewish. True, Hollywood, as the writer Neal Gabler says, was a Jewish creation. By the mid-1930s, as Lew Grade was seeking to make his way as an agent in London, in Los Angeles Adolph Zukor, William Fox, Louis Mayer and the sons of Benjamin Warner – all Jews from Eastern Europe – had made Hollywood what Scott Fitzgerald once described as 'a Jewish holiday, a Gentiles [sic] tragedy'. But in Britain show business was still a very English affair, shaped and dominated by men like Sir Charles Cochran, who had roomed with Aubrey Beardsley at Brighton College, and Sir Oswald Stoll, who owned the Stoll theatres and had set up Moss Empire. Lew Grade had to work hard to make his way slowly in this Gentile world and he only got his foot on the ladder in 1936 when he finally persuaded Joe Collins, father of Jackie and Joan, to take him on as partner, forming the Collins and Grade agency. Lew changed the nature of the business. Before he entered the scene it was a small-time profession which had little contact with theatrical management, providing the agents with an easy-going lifestyle. Collins, who had been in the business for twenty years, starting as an office boy at fourteen with Moss Empire, rarely came to work before ten or eleven and always enjoyed a three-day weekend: fishing on Friday, football on Saturday, the family and visits to the country on Sunday. On his first day Lew came in at 7 a.m. and by the end of the first week had worked all seven days. The hyperactive agent was being created.

Lew was soon joined by Bernard, whose show-business career had followed a very similar path to that of his brother. Bernard had also taken to dancing and although this had its desperate moments, including performing, quite unwittingly, in a sex show – as he made love to a blonde woman in her house in Berlin, an audience in an adjoining room watched through peepholes – he had achieved some success by teaming up with a Eurasian dancer called Toko. But eventually Bernard realised that, like Lew, his forte would be managing artistes rather than becoming one.

Lew and Bernard, like many brothers who are close in age, were rivals rather than buddies and Lew set stiff terms for Bernard: 'We won't pay you a salary but you can have fifty per cent of everything you bring in.' In 1939 Bernard decided to set up on his own. Lew, after some tough negotiations, lent him £300; he found a one-room office in Leicester Square where the landlord did not bother to collect the rent and the cigar-shop owner below gave him credit. He met his great benefactor, Carl Heinmann of Mecca, quite by accident. One evening Bernard had gone to Streatham Ballroom for a dance, was told Heinmann was there and quickly persuaded him he should become Mecca's sole booking agent.

Leslie was always determined to be different from his two older brothers. He was just as keen to get out of the East End and, like them, did not see liberation through the schmutter business, as the East End Jews called the rag trade. He loved show business as much as Lew and Bernie did, but did not want to be a showman. Unlike them, he had never performed in front of an audience – nor wanted to. While not shy, he did not have quite their extrovert nature and preferred to work backstage. If there had to be performers, he reasoned, then somebody had to act as their agent and it might as well be him. He had started working as an office boy for Lew and Collins and then just before the war set himself up as an independent agent. As a business, it was no more than a grand title, West End Varieties, amounting to two little rooms in Charing Cross Road, a secretary paid 30 shillings a week and a couple of artistes on the books, but it was to lead to the fateful partnership with George Smith and the meeting with George's sister, Winifred.

With Olga away in Lynton and Winifred expecting Lynda, the couple moved into Pullman Court, the family's new headquarters, but within a few months of Lynda's birth, on 25 November 1940, Leslie was called up by the RAF and almost immediately sent to Preston. Fortunately for him, the exile in Lancashire did not last long. He was soon posted back to Hendon in north London and he moved the family there. For most people during the Second World War such call-ups proved the end of any peacetime activities but Leslie adapted so well to the war that his business prospered. As Leading Aircraftsman Leslie Grade he began to lead an extraordinary double life, arriving for parades in Hendon a few minutes after arranging shows in the West End. He began to show the flair for agency business that would make him a legend in the industry.

This was helped by the fact that Leslie was most adept at creating his own legends. He told Bert Knight, the producer, how he would often sit in his dug-out on the airfield and try to book acts. So impressed was Knight by this story that on his birthday he presented Leslie with a big blotter and a folder to help him do just that. Even before the war he had shown his flair when he had booked Paul Robeson to appear in a concert at the Royal Albert Hall. Alas, that was the very day war was declared and the concert was cancelled.

Leslie's coup in getting George Formby, then one of the greatest entertainers in the country, to perform for a RAF charity show again revealed his genius for the agency business. Leslie was not Formby's agent, nor did he know him, but he convinced his commanding officer that he could get him. The officer gave him special time off to make the arrangements but it seemed unlikely he would succeed when Formby insisted that Leslie come up to Blackpool to meet him. With travel difficult and petrol rationed – what cars there were were mostly locked up in garages – this was a near-impossible demand. However, Leslie, who loved cars and still drove his Armstrong Siddley, somehow managed to gct petrol and, after a ten-hour drive, arrived in Blackpool. He found Formby and his wife in a café near the theatre. It did not take long for Leslie to persuade Formby to sign, although he was quickly made aware of Formby's legendary meanness. As Leslie was leaving the café, Formby called, 'What about the money for the tea?'

Leslie's gift as an agent was that he saw a deal when others saw only an empty stage. The normal agent sold his client to the theatre. Leslie sold the show first and then worried about getting the stars. Pre-war agents were content to send producers lists of their clients' available acts and the weeks they were booked. They also conveniently indicated the weeks they were free and Leslie, who got hold of these lists, used this information to generate business for himself. Leslie contacted the theatres that had a free week and promised them he would get a big name with a supporting cast. Often the big name he would promise was not his client or even known to him. But once the theatre had made the booking he would contact the star and with war forcing many of them out of work they were only too eager to appear. This war-induced shortage of work also persuaded Leslie to think up his most audacious gimmick.

The war had seen a collapse of the West End shows as people stayed at home, frightened by the air raids of venturing out in the evenings. Leslie persuaded theatres to have more than one star name on the bill. With such a dearth of work, four or five big names would happily appear on one bill and this profusion of riches quickly attracted crowds back to West End theatres, including Stoll's 2,500-seater in Kingsway. By 1943 Leslie had built up a successful agency: he had five shows touring the country, money in the bank and clients such as Billy Cotton and his band and Troise and the Mandoliers, both major attractions. To add to his joy, on 8 March 1943, Winifred gave birth to their second child, a son whom they called Michael Ian Grade. The child had startlingly blue eyes that everybody commented on and Leslie's and Winifred's world seemed complete.

The Grades had had a very lucky war. Lew had been invalided out of the Army because of water on his knee, Bernard had never been called up because he was a stateless person (he was classed as a Russian alien which meant travelling with a permit but no great inconvenience) and Leslie was leading as normal a life as any man could expect to do during wartime. Then suddenly, four months after Michael's birth, Leslie's world was shattered.

*　　*　　*

In the summer of 1943, with the war turning the Allies' way, things started going wrong. For three years he had had an extraordinarily lucky show-business war when, while supposedly serving the country, he spent more time around Shaftesbury Avenue than on the parade ground at Hendon. The RAF seemed prepared to provide Leslie with a very liberal amount of leave. Quite why the RAF was so generous with Leslie remains a mystery. One story, believed by his secretary Dena, was that Leslie had made friends with a corporal who, in exchange for a share of the business, kept giving him leave. Dena recalls a visit to the office one day by a corporal clutching a piece of paper which claimed that he owned half the firm. Leslie was far from happy to see him but in the end agreed to pay and thereafter the corporal regularly returned to collect money from Dena. Perhaps this arrangement broke down. Whatever it was, in July 1943 Dena was holidaying in Bournemouth when she was suddenly rung up to be told she must immediately return to the office: Leslie had been posted abroad. He would have to leave Hendon and head for Tripoli in North Africa.

In a sense, the arrival of the real war for Leslie was providential. While he had been making money he had also been paying no taxes. Anxious to protect his agency while he was away, he persuaded Lew to look after it. Lew's way of doing business was somewhat different from Leslie's; Lew preferred to book acts into theatres rather than handle famous names, but the request from Leslie came at just the right time. Lew's business relationship with Joe Collins was turning sour and he was more than glad to become Leslie's partner. With £10,000 borrowed from Sid and Phil Hyams, two cinema owners, the Lew and Leslie Grade agency business was set up.

It was only after Lew had moved into Leslie's offices – success had enabled Leslie to move to an office overlooking the Queen's and Apollo theatres – that he discovered his little brother's habit of avoiding the Inland Revenue. It took Lew almost two years of hard work to clear up Leslie's tax affairs. A more persistent problem was coping with Leslie's temperamental stars. However, it did introduce Lew to what was to become the Grade trademark. His wife Kathie, worried by the effect their tantrums were having on Lew, gave him a box of cigars and suggested he offer them to the stars to put them at ease. Lew took her advice and discovered the cigars gave him such a sense of security when dealing with top stars that he decided to make them his speciality; a habit that, in time, the other Grades, including Michael, have copied.

However, in a personal sense, the posting abroad was a disaster for

Leslie and his family. He was being forced to leave Winifred when she needed him most and if his departure made a classic wartime picture – a woman with a baby in her arms, a toddler by her side, waving goodbye to a husband going to war – it was also the recipe for a common wartime tragedy: the woman left on her own seeks fresh pastures, the marriage splinters, the children are scattered.

Even before Leslie's departure and Michael's birth, the Grades, like so many during the war, had become something of a wandering family. Lynda vaguely remembers being evacuated to Bognor Regis just before Michael was born. Now with Leslie gone, Winifred took Lynda and Michael back to her relations in Wales. Leslie provided generously for them and they had two Welsh nannies to look after them. For about a year Winifred was the devoted wife. When Leslie's secretary Dena got married, Winifred travelled to London to be at the wedding, although Olga and Leslie's sister Rita did not turn up. They appeared to have changed their minds when they heard who was invited and Dena got the impression Olga did not want to see Winifred. Shortly after Michael's birth, Winifred had been involved in a bad car accident which had left her with a limp, to which Olga often made reference.

It was some time after this that Winifred met the man who was to take her away from her children, a Canadian airman called Kenneth Walton Beckett. One day she unexpectedly came back to London and asked Lew to give her money from the firm. Dena was told she had 'met some bloke' and she wanted her fur coat and her Savings Certificates. Dena and Lew, despite all the wartime restrictions, managed to ring Leslie in North Africa; he agreed to let the fur coat go but not the certificates. Lynda believes that Olga drove Winifred away into the arms of this other man, having made it clear she thought Winifred was not fit to be her son's wife. Winifred let herself be seduced by a man who had a higher rank than Leslie, a captain as opposed to an aircraftsman, and who could buy her nylon stockings which in wartime deprivation meant a lot.

'She is a whore, she is no good,' Olga often told Lynda, when she asked questions about her mother. Lynda and Michael grew up hearing their mother referred to as a *kurra*, Yiddish for a fallen woman. With Leslie away there was no way the breach could be healed.

Towards the end of 1945 Leslie returned from war, literally a shadow of his previous self. He had nearly died of typhoid in Tripoli, lost most of his hair and weighed no more than six stone. But, far from having an opportunity to recover, he was almost immediately confronted with trying to rescue a doomed marriage. Lew and Kathie vacated their flat in Cavendish Square, moving temporarily to the Savoy, in the hope that this would provide Leslie's fractured relationship a bit of breathing space in which to heal. For the first time in three years the whole family were together and a room off the kitchen that Lew and Kathie had used as the staff sitting room was made into a nursery for Michael and Lynda.

But it required more than a spacious flat to rescue this marriage. The attempt at reunion lasted less than a month. Winifred had become too involved with Kenneth Walton Beckett for there to be any way back. She left and, literally, vanished from Michael and Lynda's life. So, not yet three years old, Michael lost his mother and has never seen her nor even heard from her since.

In February 1946 Leslie filed a divorce petition naming Kenneth Walton Beckett as co-respondent. Beckett and Winifred admitted adultery, Beckett had to pay £1,000 in damages plus costs, Leslie was awarded custody of the children and the decree was made absolute on 20 June 1947. On 19 December 1947, Winifred, who by now had changed her name to Lynn Walton, married Kenneth Walton Beckett. By then whatever impression his mother may have made on Michael had completely faded, as if it had never existed.

Periodically stories reached them about how Winifred had had another son, Lee, but she never again contacted either Michael or Lynda. Many years later, at a football match, Michael passed his mother. He knew immediately that it was her and the urge to say something must have been enormous, but he did nothing. When Lynda got married she received in the post Leslie and Winifred's wedding photograph, but she thinks this was sent to her by one of her former nannies. Many years later, Hunter Davies, researching his book *The Grades*, contacted a man called Kent Walton who was then a TV wrestling commentator employed by Michael Grade, but he denied any knowledge of Winifred. In 1991, after the disclosure of golden handcuff payments for Michael Grade, the *Daily Mail* tried to get Michael, and Lynn together, but the attempt failed. Lynn Walton, now living in Haslemere with an unlisted number, said, 'I can't talk about it. I've got nothing to say. Michael is nothing to do with me.' Forty-five years had passed since she had seen her son but the wounds had not healed for mother or son.

Michael and Lynda were, of course, never going to be the classical victims of a broken home, but there was the problem nevertheless of who would look after them and where they would live. For a while they stayed on with Lew and Kathie. But although Leslie had the money, and the tradition of Welsh nannies started by Winifred continued, it was not quite that easy to decide who was actually going to bring the children up. Leslie could hardly play house father. He was also still not very well. There was the business to consider and he was neither equipped for such a role nor did he have an appetite for looking after two small children. In any case, the times were not right; the concept of the single father had not yet been invented. The only obvious candidate was Olga. It was to prove a fateful choice.

Of course, bringing up grandchildren would be very different to raising her own four offspring through the poverty and despair of the East End, now that her sons were prosperous and could afford most things, but Olga was sixty years old and it was still a demanding task.

Lynda has no doubt that it was a mistake to make Olga the surrogate mother. 'She was much too old to be looking after two such young children. She had already had two goes at being mother. There was a great age gap between Lew and Bernie and then my father and my aunt Rita. They were her second family; even then, she was rather old to bring them up. Now she was another twenty years older and just very, very difficult. We had a succession of nannies because my grandmother was so difficult. I have been told they used to call my grandfather the white mouse because he had my colouring, very pale, and was terrified of my grandmother. I can well understand that. She was just a tyrant.' This did mean, however, that Michael and Lynda avoided the fate common to children brought up by grandparents: overindulgence.

Lynda may sound a trifle unkind and her recollection may be coloured by what happened later. Michael appears to have enjoyed his grandmother's rule rather better. References to Olga form a leitmotiv in Michael's life. Whenever he is in trouble or perceives himself to be in trouble he has a story or a joke to tell about Grandma Olga. In 1991, as the row over the golden handcuffs given to him by Channel 4 broke about his head at the Royal Television Society conference, Michael tried to defuse the situation with a joke about Olga.

It was 1962 – the Cuban Missile Crisis. Olga asked, 'Babula, what does this mean for Jews?' Grade shook his head at the recollection and to uproarious laughter said, 'I was twenty-seven before I realised my name was not Babula.' Olga provided the comforting frame of references for Michael that his mother should have done but did not.

Yet for Olga suddenly to have to mother two small children did bring out her own contradictions. Although she was Jewish, deeply disappointed that all her sons had married *shiksas*, and keen to bring the children up in the Jewish tradition, she never kept a kosher home. She would light the candles on Friday night to mark the start of the Jewish sabbath and she would not use lard when cooking, but there was no general ban on pork. On Saturday mornings she served bacon and eggs to Michael and Lynda because she felt it would build up their strength.

'After the war,' recalls Lynda, 'you were lucky to get anything good to eat. So she served ham and cooked liver and bacon when we came home from school in the evening. We used to stay at Jewish hotels in Bournemouth but we were just as likely to stay at the Imperial in Torquay, and that was not kosher.'

Olga had the Jewish Momma's obsession with food. Lynda would be forced to drink milk in such quantities that when she grew up she found she could no longer stand it. Worried that Michael was skinny, Olga told his prep school, Norfolk House in Bognor Regis, that he was undernourished and made them give him raw eggs and milk every morning at 11 a.m. There was always a lot of chicken soup, known as the Jewish penicillin and offered to any sick child. Apart from the obsession with food, bringing up children meant giving them a set of instructions and Olga's favourite was, 'If you have a bath you can't go out for six hours in case you catch a cold.'

Lynda and Michael found these restrictions irritating. Lynda, three years older than Michael, led the resistance.

'Michael used to follow me and often it was a case of Michael and I sticking together against our grandmother.' Michael was more biddable than Lynda and did not take things quite so hard. In any case, he was away at prep school and apart from suddenly being confronted by raw eggs did not often feel the full force of Olga's mothering.

Sometimes the task of bringing up Lynda and Michael would prove too much and then Olga would ring up her brother Moshe and, speaking in Yiddish, say that the children were a couple of *mamser*, Yiddish for bastards. Moshe knew this was part of the by-play with his sister, but then he had a running joke of his own. He would go round saying, recalls Lynda, that he was Lew, Bernie and Leslie's father and that they didn't give him any money. Not only was he not their father but they did give him money every week. Yet Olga also showed resilience. Like many Jewish immigrants of her generation she couldn't read or write English (although she spoke it well enough even if with a Russian accent), but she could read Russian, so if somebody phoned for Lynda or Michael she would write down any message phonetically in Russian and then try to work it out.

In many ways the strangest part of their childhood was the nomadic existence forced upon them by Winifred's desertion. Olga may have replaced Winifred as 'mother' but there was no settled home and Lynda and Michael spent the first post-war years wandering all over the south-east.

This might have been avoided had Olga taken to Quies, the house that Leslie bought from Bill Cotton Snr, soon after the final break with Winifred. It was a purchase which emphasised his growing affluence, a huge seven-bedroom house with a large garden, lily pond and a full-sized billiard table. For about a year Michael and Lynda lived there with Olga and Rita, making a sort of alternative family to the one that might have been had Winifred not left. Leslie would come down only for the weekends, preferring to spend weekdays in a small bachelor pad in Kensington.

Michael had his first taste of show business at Quies. Bernie would use it for parties and Richard Tauber, the famous singer, was a frequent guest.

But Olga did not like living in the country. Most of the time since she had arrived in England she had lived in teeming cities and after about a year Leslie was persuaded to sell the house, back to Bill Cotton as it happened, and Michael, Lynda and Olga were on the move again.

For about six months they stayed at Leslie's flat near the Royal Garden Hotel in Kensington. He had taken it over from one of his artistes who kept seals in the bath there. Soon after Leslie moved in, one of the seals escaped and flapped down Kensington High Street but they were long gone by the time Olga arrived with the children. The flat was far too small to accommodate nannies; it had just two bedrooms with Michael and Lynda sharing a room while Olga and Rita shared the other.

It was when they were living in this flat that Leslie remarried. Much to Olga's regret, Audrey Smith was another *shiksa* although, unlike Winifred, she had converted. This helped make the wedding an open family occasion and Olga herself attended. But she would not let Michael and Lynda go to the wedding at Caxton Hall, insisting that it was against her religion to let children watch their parents getting married. They were left at the flat with George Perry, the manager of Leslie's costume store. Michael and Lynda retaliated by locking themselves in the bedroom and throwing the key out of the window.

'George, who was a lovely man,' recalls Lynda, 'was terrified what would happen if we were still in there when they came back but he managed to get us out before they returned.'

Leslie's remarriage should have solved Michael and Lynda's accommodation problem, particularly when he set up home with Audrey at Tiptoes in Chiselhurst, Kent. But it did not happen. Here again Olga appears to have intervened. Audrey was not Jewish, although she converted on marriage, and while Olga had accepted her she still did not want the children to grow up in a non-Jewish home. In any case, Audrey had little time for children. Olga continued to look after them and their wanderings along the South Coast continued. The first stop was Bournemouth where Leslie fixed them up with a seafront flat. He also found places for Michael and Lynda in a day school run by the Gittings sisters. Leslie would come down once a month and ask, 'How are the Gittings sisters doing?' which would be the cue for Lynda and Michael to go into hysterics.

Rita continued to live with them but in 1949 this cosy relationship ended when she also married: much to Olga's great delight, her husband was Jewish. It produced the first great family photograph of the Grades: Olga, looking matriarchal and stern, all in black, standing next to her daughter; Lynda as the coy bridesmaid; and Michael, looking a trifle nervous in a white sailor's suit. If Michael was really overawed it was understandable, for the reception showed the growing power and influence of the Grades: nearly every show-business star from Maurice Chevalier to Arthur Askey and Sophie Tucker was there. Lew did the Charleston and Billy Cotton Snr and George Formby wished the new couple luck. Rita's marriage, however, meant another move for the children, this time back to London.

Clearly Lynda and Michael could not be kept moving about; they needed a place they could call home and good schools. Leslie decided that the best place for Olga and the children would be in a flat and so he moved them into Grosvenor Court Mansions, a twenties-style block which was both spacious – three bedrooms and two reception rooms – and central: on the Edgware Road, near Marble Arch. For the first time Michael and Lynda had a home they could call their own. Lynda was almost eleven by then, Michael about seven.

There was some talk that Michael should go to the Arts Educational school, run by Fosters and well known in theatrical circles. But Olga was appalled at the thought that Michael might have to learn ballet there; she feared exposure to such influences might make him a 'nancy boy'. Instead, both Lynda and Michael were sent to Mitford Colmer but left after a term when Olga became convinced that the school had something to do with the Mitford sisters, one of whom had married Oswald Mosley, the wartime fascist leader, and another had championed Hitler. When Olga got an idea it was difficult to shake her out of it and Leslie was forced to move the children yet again. Lynda got a place at a school called Town and Country and for a couple of terms Michael also went there.

Already the childhood experiences of Michael and Lynda were different from those of most of their contemporaries but now they also acquired an exotic touch. Every morning as Michael and Lynda went down the stairs of Grosvenor Court on their way to school Olga would shout, 'Wrap up warmly, keep warm, make sure you eat your lunch,' as if they were embarking on a perilous journey. At the front door of the flat there would be a limousine from International Car Hire waiting to take them across London to their school in Swiss Cottage. So while a nineteenth-century grandmother's warning rang in their ears they would step into the most luxurious of twentieth-century cars to go to school.

Life with Grandmother was relieved by parties. When George VI died and Leslie discovered that the procession to take the King's body to Paddington would not go past his office but would go past the Marble Arch flat, he decided to have a party there for which Kathie did all the catering. Lynda recalls seeing that one of the soldiers had brown boots when all the others had black.

The Swiss Cottage school was no more than a stopgap for Michael. Leslie had by now established himself as the country's leading agent and was enjoying great wealth. He had just acquired his first Rolls-Royce, although the family outing he planned to celebrate the occasion, a drive to Blackpool where he was making bookings for the Winter Gardens, was ruined by Lynda and Michael being sick in the car. Within a week he had got rid of the Rolls and did not buy another one for years. This did not, however, dampen his determination to see his son Michael have the education he had himself missed – he had been educated at the Stepney Jewish school – and this meant a boarding school. Within a year Michael was back in Bournemouth at a boarding school run by Miss Gittings's brother. A year later he was moved to the Norfolk House in Bognor Regis, not far from where Bernie had his home. It was the first school which left any impression on Michael, partly because of the forced diet of raw eggs and milk, but also because he had the opportunity to slip away to Uncle Bernie's place and sit at the feet of the great names of show business.

Michael was now nine years old and for the first time spent more than a year at one school. Between the ages of six and nine he had moved school four times; at Bognor he stayed for four years. The stability showed through in his exam results. He worked hard, sat the Common Entrance and did sufficiently well to get a place at Stowe.

Just before Michael went up to Stowe he had his bar mitzvah at the New West End synagogue at St Petersburgh Place in Bayswater. It is curious that Michael should have had his bar mitzvah. Amongst Jews the lineage comes through the mother and Winifred had not converted, so Michael was not strictly speaking Jewish. However, Leslie had kept the faith, felt strongly about it and, in any case, St Petersburgh was almost a family synagogue for the Grades. It was where Rita had married.

For Jewish males their bar mitzvah is probably the most crucial ceremony of their youth. It can be the occasion, as the writer Chaim Bermant says, when the boy becomes a man and the father becomes a bankrupt. There was no fear that Michael's bar mitzvah would bankrupt Leslie, although he did not stint with the celebration and the occasion is remembered more for the party than the ceremony.

Curiously, given the social significance it has acquired, bar mitzvah is not required by Jewish law and came into existence only in the Middle Ages. The ceremony Michael went through, like all bar mitzvahs, was redolent of that time. He watched in fascination as the Torah, the hand-written scroll which contains the teaching of the five books of Moses, was removed from the ark at the end of the synagogue. Then this rolled-up parchment was ceremonially carried by two members of the congregation and handed over to the Rabbi who walked with it on his shoulders round the congregation before getting up on the bima, a raised platform in the middle of the synagogue. This is all part of a normal service on the Sabbath; it was Michael's participation in it as the bar mitzvah boy that made the whole day special.

Some time during the service, Michael, dressed in a dark suit, was summoned up to the bima where he first chanted some six or seven lines from the Torah. He had already learnt the lines by heart but as the scroll does not have any vowels it gave his chant a certain rhythmic feel. Then he repeated the exercise reading from the Haftarah, a printed book containing the words of the prophets, but this time with the vowels included. Then, after the Rabbi had given his sermon and addressed Michael, praising him for how well he had learnt the Torah, he was once again summoned to the bima to collect his certificate which testified that he had passed his bar mitzvah test. The Rabbi also presented him with a prayer book. The service lasted nearly the whole of that Saturday morning and at the end of it Michael and the other Grades adjourned to the synagogue hall to have a sip of kiddush wine.

If the ceremony at the synagogue was standard, no bar mitzvah boy could have had a more glittering lunch. As ever, Kathie had organised the catering and the guests who gathered that day at Grosvenor Court Mansions included nearly all the great show-business stars of the day. The singer Alma Cogan, whose song 'Dream Boat' had got to Number One in the hit parade, came in a brand-new mink coat which the ladies could not take their eyes off – for days afterwards Lynda could think only about the mink coat. Arthur Askey was there, plus a whole host of other show people. It seemed the ideal send-off for Michael as he prepared to go to Stowe. But although the bar mitzvah may have made him a man in the eyes of the Jewish world, it was hardly the right preparation for the very different challenges public school would present.

He may have been too young at three to appreciate Winifred's desertion; now at thirteen he was suddenly confronted with the horror that a public school can be for some boys and it proved too much. Michael Grade was at Stowe for only two terms but there is no doubt it proved the most traumatic period of his young life.

Stowe should have been a good choice. Founded in 1923, its first headmaster, J. F. Roxburg, saw it as a different kind of public school, providing greater freedom for the boys, development of artistic and literary appreciation and above all a proper respect for the individual whatever his capacity. Its ambience and history, as Noel Annan has said, had both beauty and liberty, with the spirit of the school embodied in the eighteenth-century mansion rebuilt by the Temple family who had originally acquired it in the Elizabethan age. They had used architects and landscape gardeners to rebuild the house and surround it with elegiac scenery, providing a setting that was, probably, the most sublime of any school in England. Throughout the gardens are scattered *temples d'amour*. Bridgeman had started the revolution of landscape by surrounding the park with a ha-ha, a sunken fence which acts as an invisible barrier, and it was here that Capability Brown had begun his career as a under-gardener. In its heyday, long before the school was conceived, it was the place where the arts met politics; it had been the political headquarters of that Whig faction called the Grenville cousinhood and the meeting place for writers such as Pope, Vanbrugh, Congreve, Thomson and Chesterfield. All this, combined with its landscape and temples, made it a monument to the English Enlightenment.

The boys at Stowe could hardly escape this history and were constantly reminded of the beauty. They gathered for assembly in the Marble Saloon which had a white marble floor and pink marble pillars carrying a classical frieze of three hundred figures moving in procession above the cornice. However impressive all this looked in the school prospectus, it meant little to a thirteen-year-old who had already changed schools far too often and found this latest move quite the most unsettling. As a school, Stowe needed leadership; as a boy, Michael needed warmth and reassurance. Neither was available. By the time Michael arrived, Roxburg had long gone and the sense of leadership he had provided had begun to dissipate. Reynolds, who succeeded Roxburg as headmaster, had never really recovered from a severe fall while climbing in the Cuillins in 1951, and although he carried on for some years he was very much a lame-duck headmaster.

Olga may have had her limitations as a parent figure but there was no denying the warmth with which she enveloped Michael. Stowe took him away from this, replacing it with a cold, almost monastic, formality. Richard Strange arrived at Stowe a couple of terms before Michael and was in his house. 'The main problem at Stowe was that it was isolated. We were allowed to go out into Buckingham but there was nothing there apart from a couple of cafés. It was not like other public schools such as Harrow or Eton or Rugby that have major towns attached to them. So it became a very monastic place; you did not rub shoulders with other people.'

For all little boys, going away to school is an unnerving experience. Stowe added to it by making Michael learn a new language. The toilets were known as Egypts, because of an Egyptian entrance at the basement of the mansion, and when he wanted to go to the toilet he had to say, 'Sir, can I go to Egypt?' Stowe attracted those who were not quite good enough to get to the major public schools. Strange had failed Rugby where his father had gone and Stowe was very much second choice. It also had many pupils who were from an army background, which could not be further removed from the show-business world with which Michael already identified and felt so much at home.

Public schools in the fifties still reeked of dank, cold dormitories and a regime of fear built on petty rules and restrictions. Stowe, despite its intentions, could not quite escape that. Michael had to fag for the older boys, which meant polishing their shoes, making toast, running errands and, most probably, letting them share his tuck box. Corporal punishment was very much the order of the day. If the caning by the housemaster, an Irishman called Bruce Barr, was not too unpleasant (he administered it on bended, trousered bottoms), that given by the seniors could be cruel.

'This would,' recalls Strange, 'be administered in the head boy's study. He always had the grandest study in the house. And it would be done on a naked bottom. Not very nice. What was worse was a horrific form of physical P.T. You had to do a knees-bend and then hold the position, with your knees half bent, for a couple of minutes. It was quite horrific and Michael, like the rest of us, had to go through it. This extraordinary punishment could be given for a whole range of what were called misdemeanours, like walking on the grass in the North Front [the grand entrance to the main building at Stowe] or walking with your hands in your pockets, or talking in prep, or being late for assembly.'

Michael was assigned to Grafton, a house whose old boys included David Niven, Peregrine Worsthorne and Jack 'Union Jack' Hayward. Their sepia prints stared at him from the walls as he climbed up narrow stairs to the third floor and the Ipswich dormitory, the topmost dormitory in the house and traditionally assigned to newcomers. After Grosvenor Court this could not have been less inviting: a room with no curtains, metal bars across the high windows, metal ex-National Health Service beds, with little wooden tables next to them, and sleeping about twenty boys. The bathroom next door had long pipes from which it was not uncommon to suspend naughty boys. The privileges of the house increased as the boys grew older but at that stage privacy was extremely limited and escape from tyranny by the seniors difficult. Harry's Hole, where Michael, along with the other boys, kept his tuck, was a small cramped place where he was always likely to be confronted by a senior demanding food.

'A lot of that undoubtedly happened,' said Strange. 'It was a case of if you were a newcomer you had to prove yourself to your peers. I did not mind that because I was good at sports and that counted for a lot at Stowe.' Even here Michael was cut off for, although the school was strong on sports, it did not play the one sport Michael loved: soccer. Rugger and hockey were Stowe's main winter sports. The only time the school played soccer was when the Pineapple Club, a charitable institution that supported a boy's club in London, either went up to London or entertained the boys from London at Stowe.

Michael had started in Stowe in Remove D which, based on his high marks in the entrance exam, meant he was actually put in a form with people who had arrived there a year earlier. But by the end of that first Christmas term in 1956, Barr was beginning to sound the first alarm bell. He wrote in Michael's house report for that term: 'He is certainly in a high form for a new boy but that is no reason why he should make such a weak start in it.'

Michael's one joy was singing in the choir and Stowe also gave him a chance to take to the stage, the first time he had given expression to the show-business side of his family. His form master, Joe Bain, put on *The Government Inspector* as the Congreve Club play on 7 and 8 December and Michael had two small parts. Bain had few experienced actors to work with and the *Stoic*, the school magazine, thought it was brave of him to put on a foreign play for the second year with such inexperienced actors. We do not know how well Michael performed, although the *Stoic* complimented Bain for getting the best from his inexperienced boys. Michael's acting career, however, did not please Barr. 'He must see that his work is satisfactory before he acts again.' But Barr was reassured that 'he has settled well in the house, and with his several interests should find plenty to keep him occupied at Stowe.'

Perhaps Michael did give that impression to Barr; perhaps this shows how easy it must be to fool housemasters; or maybe something happened during the Easter term, because by the time he came back to Grosvenor Court for Easter, Michael knew he could not face Stowe again. A few days before he was due to go back Lynda found him crying in bed one night with the blankets pulled tightly over him. Worried and anxious, Lynda asked, 'What's wrong?'

Michael, between sobs, replied, 'I don't want to go back.'

'Don't want to go back to Stowe? Why?' asked Lynda.

Michael refused to elaborate and kept repeating, 'I can't go back.'

Lynda knew it was unlike Michael to make such a fuss. 'He wasn't that kind of child. I knew something was seriously wrong. Slowly it came out. He had been beaten up, bullied. The reason he wears glasses was because of the beating he received at Stowe. He was miserably unhappy there and couldn't face another term.'

Lynda cannot remember whether she told her grandmother or Rita, probably she told Kathie to whom she was already very close, but

Michael was taken out of Stowe. Michael's recollection of how he escaped Stowe is somewhat different. Here Lynda plays no part and, according to the version he gave Sarah Lawson, his second wife, when he had decided he could not take it any more he rang up Leslie and said, 'I am not having a good time.' It was this phone call which prompted Leslie to remove him from Stowe.

The Grades' suspicions of Stowe was confirmed when seven or eight months after Michael left there was a big shake-up at the school: several masters left, Reynolds retired and some boys were even expelled, although none of this had anything directly to do with Michael's departure. That came as a complete surprise to Barr, who wrote in his house report for Easter 1957, 'He seemed to be making his way satisfactorily, to be showing promise in his many interests and to be friendly and happy.' This only confirms that Stowe of the fifties was not a sensitive place and, probably, shows how well Michael concealed his unhappiness and dislike of it. None of the school authorities knew how tormented he was by the anti-Semitism of the type sadly then all too common in public schools or how affected he was by a vicious form of public-school bullying which verged almost on homosexuality. Bernie gained the impression that Michael was both frightened and repelled by this.

How far this homosexuality went is hard to determine. 'If there *was* homosexuality,' said Strange, 'then it was not overt. I suppose a bit of it was going on. I think a lot more was spoken about it than physically occurred. The young new boys, who were, in quotes, 'pretty', were talked about. I had no personal experience of homosexuality. But a year later some guys were expelled from another house, although I cannot recall whether this was for homosexuality. The fact was that Stowe was a place for misfits. My memory of Michael was that he was not very bright, what we used to call thick, which is perhaps unfair as he was clearly a late developer.'

Michael himself has never referred to the homosexuality, latent or otherwise, as the reason for his leaving Stowe, preferring to stress anti-Semitism. Indeed, his experience there deepened his faith and made him aware of the traumatic history of his people. Before Stowe he had heard from his grandmother about her Russian anti-Jewish experiences, but that had been like a history lesson. Stowe made them come painfully alive. It was at Stowe that he came across *The Diary of Anne Frank*, one of the most remarkable books to emerge from the Holocaust, and many years later, when asked to contribute

to the *Independent on Sunday*'s feature, 'A Book that Changed Me', he
chose that one:

'I probably changed schools more often than was good for me, or
the schools. To get through my first day at yet another school (mostly
boarding), I developed a simple survival routine which never failed,
namely 'spot the other Jewish boys'. I knew from experience I could
rely on making some first-week friends in this way. At expensive private schools such as these, there are but a handful of "us" and it was
comforting to seek each other out and establish a bond. Anti-Semitism
was rife, particularly at my [first] public school [he means Stowe], and
you needed friends to help you grin and bear the periodic outbreaks of
Jew-baiting. It was around then that chance, or fate, handed me *The
Diary of Anne Frank*, one teenage girl's eye-witness account of what it
felt like to be hunted by the Nazis, to be caught and to experience the
horror of the concentration camp. I devoured the book faster than anything I had read before or since, and the memory of my feelings on
reading it lives with me today: I was moved as never before in my
young life. Her simple, accessible narrative offered a vivid testimony of
the indescribable, of the unimaginable.'

Anne Frank's book had such a devastating impact on him that he
has never been able to reread it or go to Israel to visit Yad VaShem, the
memorial to the six million Jews who perished in the Holocaust. It also
provided him with a tool to cope with the experience of Stowe.
'Michael', says second wife Sarah, 'has never been one to turn round
and fight back. He would take quite a lot before he would retaliate.
One of his forms of retaliation is to shut off the aggravation.' He had
shut out his mother's desertion by wiping her from his records; he did
the same with Stowe, omitting it also from his *Who's Who* entry. He
has never publicly concealed his dislike for Stowe and over the years
has resented old Stoics coming up to claim his friendship and bask in
his fame. In 1986, as Controller of the BBC, he did visit the school to
talk to the boys about careers, and had tea with James Larcombe, the
current housemaster of Grafton. When Larcombe, a gentle, sensitive
man, asked whether his son might go to Stowe, Grade sidestepped it by
saying that as his interest was football he would never be happy there.

Michael's ability to sublimate his feelings helped him recover from
Stowe. Outwardly he did not display any marks of the experience and
Lynda does not believe Stowe affected his ebullience. 'Children are
resilient and Michael did not let Stowe dampen his spirits.' If anything,
Stowe may have taught him how to cope with adversity and at his next

school, where he acquired a reputation for being a bit of a wag, he developed a technique of defusing situations by making some remark that would make people laugh, a technique he had since found very useful in meetings.

In some ways it was easy taking Michael out of Stowe, but it was hard finding another school for him. For a whole term he wasn't at any school, just left with his grandmother at Grosvenor Court Mansions. His lack of formal education so concerned the Education Department that they sent an inspector round to find out what was going on. Olga saw them off, explaining he was having private lessons. Then Leslie managed to get him into St Dunstan's.

In his *Who's Who* entry St Dunstan's College is the only school Grade acknowledges and with good reason. After all the turmoil of his education so far it was indeed a haven. Located in Catford it was a boys' day school which could trace its origins back to the fifteenth century and served south-east London as an independent grammar school. It considered itself to be in the middle of the first division of schools and was usually among the top fifty schools in the Oxbridge scholarship league table for open scholarships, sometimes in the top thirty.

St Dunstan's was very proud of the fact that it was a school in the Head Masters' Conference, which gave it a social cachet. Although a Church of England school, it always took a few Jewish students. Michael came into the fifth form, the O-level year, in September 1957 as a fee-paying student, as almost half the students in his form were. His school record suggests he did well enough without being brilliant. He played all the major games – cricket, rugby, athletics – appearing for his house though not school. He also reached the rank of corporal in the Combined Cadet Force.

Being at St Dunstan's meant that Michael could also enjoy the comfort and warmth that Grosvenor Court Mansions provided, such as the impromptu fun he had with Lynda. They would team up to present Michael Grade Productions, starring Lynda Grade.

'We used to perform on the windowsill in my grandma's bedroom. It was a very broad, white sill about one and a half feet long and it had the right windows and the right curtains. Michael and I would do whatever was popular at the time and Grandma would go potty.'

Michael's fascination for show business, not surprisingly, grew and he began to see the London Palladium as the ancestral home of the Grades. Leslie booked the variety bills there and on the opening nights, every other Monday evening, the whole Grade clan would gather at

Leslie's office just across the road at about 5 p.m. for the first show at 6–15 p.m. It gave Michael the habit of being early for everything. Then they would go to the theatre sandwich bar where a boy called Tom carved out smoked salmon sandwiches. Leslie, a creature of routine, loved it. Michael was always smartly turned out for such occasions with his hair slicked and his clothes neat and tidy. The Grades always had the same seats: 13, 14, 15 and 16 in row C in the stalls. Even then Michael realised that being a Grade was different, because of the way they were welcomed and the publicity about the family. Although the Palladium was huge, Michael felt an intimacy between its performers and the audience.

The shows at the Palladium gave rise to his first fantasy. He was mesmerised by the conductor in his evening suit and would lie in bed dreaming of becoming one. Comics were his next great love. The first show he saw featured the Ink Spots topping the bill with a set pattern: first dancers, then a comic and then a speciality act. Michael was much taken by the comic who fell into the orchestra pit as part of his act. If anyone came late he'd do it all over again and Michael now wrestled between becoming a conductor or a comic. Lynda is convinced Michael 'would have made a very good comedian. He loved the old Max Miller jokes. He had all the old books.'

These heroes were later superseded when the recording era arrived by Johnnie Ray, Guy Mitchell and Frankie Laine. Johnnie Ray gave what Michael thought was the most exciting performance he had ever seen on stage. And, like so many teenagers growing up in the fifties, Michael was not immune to the attraction of Buddy Holly. When the family moved into television and *Sunday Night at the London Palladium* arrived, Michael would spend hours watching rehearsals.

The London Palladium was all the more special for Michael because the Monday shows were some of the few occasions he saw Leslie. Leslie had always rationed his time for his first family but now they were settled in Grosvenor Court he followed a set ritual. When the children had been in Bournemouth he had seen them once a month. Now once a fortnight he would come to Sunday lunch at the flat. For Lynda and Michael this did not seem strange. 'When you are young,' says Lynda, 'you don't think it is different, because you don't know any different.' This routine Leslie never varied except on one occasion when he arrived on a Sunday night.

Lynda had just been given a car by Leslie, a Hillman Mini. One Sunday night while returning from a Hampstead tennis club she was involved in a serious accident. Lynda, lucky to be alive, was rushed to the Royal Free Hospital which contacted Leslie to get him to sign the consent form for the anaesthetic.

'I was coming round from the anaesthetic and I could hear my father on the phone to the man he had bought the car from. "It is all your fault, you should never have sold me this car. It is coming back to you tomorrow." He then drove me home in his Roller and I was violently sick by the side of it. When we got to Marble Arch, he said, "Wait outside, I'll break the news to your grandmother." That was the wrong thing to do. Grandma was most surprised to see Daddy. "Leslie, Leslie, what are you doing here on a Sunday evening?" Daddy said, "Well, Lynda has had an accident." Grandma exclaimed, "Oh she is dead," and passed out.'

Leslie made up for his remoteness by being generous and although Lynda was not allowed another car he did let her have an account with a car-hire company that operated from the bottom of Grosvenor Court. 'We never lacked for anything. He kept my aunt Rita in the lap of luxury, meeting with a string of demands: Leslie, I need a new dress, she would say, I have a dance to go to. Leslie, I have seen a fur jacket. He was always buying her things.'

Despite the fact he saw so little of his children Leslie still tried to play the role of father as protector. He refused to let Lynda go to see Johnnie Ray. He kept saying, 'I haven't got a free seat for the first night.' One night Lynda decided to go and see him on her own. 'Harry Claff was the manager and I persuaded him to let us stand at the back. Then I found out why my father didn't want me to see Johnnie Ray. There was a comedienne who closed the first half with lesbian jokes. Nothing to do with Johnnie Ray but Daddy thought this was not suitable for us.'

Apart from the Palladium nights, and lunch every other Sunday, the only other occasions Michael saw his father were alternate Saturday afternoons when he would take Michael, Lynda and Billy Cotton Snr to the Valley, where Charlton Athletic played their home matches. As a young man growing up in the East End, Leslie had been fascinated first by West Ham and then by Herbert Chapman's Arsenal. As he grew more affluent he had moved from standing on the terraces to the comfort of the directors' box at Leyton Orient where he persuaded Bernie to become a director and invest over £25,000. At some stage he had become very friendly with the Gliksteins who ran Charlton and this club now claimed his allegiance. Michael fell in love with Charlton almost as much as he did with the Palladium and when he had children of his own he initiated them in the rites of the football tribe. So, in a curious way, although Leslie (remote, his visits to his children rationed) could not have been more unlike a conventional father and it was only towards the end of his life that Michael got close to him, he did make two very conventional gestures to his son. As fathers are supposed to do he took him to football, albeit not on the terraces but in the directors' box, and he also took him to the Palladium, igniting a passion for entertainment and football that children who see their fathers every night may not have.

In the summer of 1958 Michael passed three O levels: English language, Maths and Latin. It was not remarkable that he didn't take more O levels; three was pretty standard for St Dunstan's then. In the Sixth Form he took English, French and Latin for A level, before leaving school in July 1960. He had no desire to go to university, or to follow his father's business; for the moment there was satisfaction enough that school had at last worked out all right.

All this was overshadowed, however, by an undreamt-of domestic crisis. The two constants in Michael's world had been his grandmother and his sister. Now suddenly, just as he was preparing to leave school, there was another fracture in his life which, in many ways created a far greater shock wave than either Winifred's desertion or the horrors of Stowe.

By 1959 Lynda was a young girl in need of a career or a husband. She was nineteen, a strikingly good-looking girl, blonde, with blue eyes and a personality that was both forthright and bubbly. Three years earlier, her school career had come to a dramatic end when, irritated by her being kept late at school to finish something, Leslie had arrived, had a row with the teacher and taken Lynda away. Lynda never returned. One day she was at school, the next day she was not. She wanted to go into show business but Olga did not like the idea, although she did manage to appear on Hughie Green's *Opportunity Knocks*. Rita had been similarly discouraged by her brothers from going on the stage. The Grades evidently followed Noël Coward's advice to Mrs Worthington not to put one's daughter on the stage. Lynda ended up by helping out in Leslie's office. Then one evening after a Jewish committee meeting she went into the Boccaccio, a coffee bar in Baker Street, and her life changed.

The man she met there was called Arthur Davidson. For the first few weeks it was a blissful romance. Arthur was twenty-four, came from a good Jewish family, and was doing quite well as a sales manager for a company that sold peanuts and processed food.

'When I first met Lynda,' recalls Arthur, 'Michael was still at school. I got to know Michael and Grandma very well and there was no problem for about the first seven weeks.'

Lynda and Michael went away to the south of France for a week and Arthur, desperate to hear Lynda's voice, made his first overseas call. Arthur seemed to be getting on very well with Grandma but while Lynda and Michael were away he met Aunt Rita and the problems started.

'She had a tremendous influence on my grandmother, a typical example of Jewish mothers and daughters,' Lynda remembers. 'My aunt was a hyperactive and hypernervous woman. When I take out an insurance policy and they ask is there any lunacy in the family, I do think about whether I should put her down or not.'

Arthur believes what followed was cooked up between Rita and the grandmother. 'In Jewish families you are not obliged also to fall in love with the person your son or daughter is marrying. But in this case the two women got together and it gradually got quite out of hand. Leslie was got at by these two women, they put it into his mind I was after the Grades' money.'

Arthur's job was described as a peanut salesman with all that that implied; stories about his lady-killing activities were circulated. Arthur had once pinched a girl's bottom and this was built up to make him appear a Casanova. Yet Arthur was far from impoverished; his parents were comfortably off and his father, who was born in Britain and had fought in the First World War, had his own business. Arthur could also claim to be better educated than most of the Grades, having been at The Hall prep school in Hampstead, then the City of London school, 'but I was pictured as a gold digger out to get the Grades' fortunes.'

As it happened, when Arthur met Lynda he had never heard of the Grades. 'I had heard of the Bernsteins. But I had never heard of Leslie or even of Lew Grade. I never used to go to the cinema or the theatre, never mixed in Jewish society. I just went to the coffee bar and met this pretty girl. It kind of exploded after that.'

Faced by this family opposition, Lynda and Arthur thought of eloping. It was a time when Gretna Green was rather fashionable. Jimmy Goldsmith had eloped with his South American heiress, Tessa Kennedy, and Dominic Elwes had eloped to Gretna Green, but Arthur was advised not to go.

'They were waiting for us to run to Gretna Green,' says Lynda. 'Arthur's cousin who was a barrister said don't do that. Lynda is nineteen. They will make her a ward of court and you won't be able to marry until she is twenty-one. So we decided to go to court to get permission to marry.'

What followed would have shaken any family. In a close-knit Jewish household it was sensational. Lynda rang up Leslie and said, 'I need the name of your solicitor.'

'What for?' Leslie replied.

'To issue the writ for permission to marry,' said Lynda.

'Don't be silly,' retorted Leslie and put the phone down.

Two days later he was served with a writ when turning into Regent Street and *Grade* v. *Grade* was launched. Lynda had already moved out of Grosvenor Court. One of her schoolfriends was the daughter of Ted Allen, the Canadian writer hounded out of America by the McCarthy witch-hunts. The Allens took Lynda in and she lived in their Swiss Cottage home for about four months. Fortunately, Lew did not share his brother's misgivings and he provided Lynda with enough money to rent a small flat in Brunswick Square.

A Jewish daughter was not meant to take her father to court, that is how Gentiles behaved, and the press built it up as the first such case of its kind. It generated such interest that Lynda and Arthur's engagement picture was in the *Daily Telegraph*. This added extra spice to what was already a story made for the popular press: a millionaire's daughter versus a father who was the biggest agent in the country, with an uncle who owned a very important television company.

'When we went to court,' recalls Lynda, 'the judge, Kenneth Thomas, wouldn't hear the case because there were too many pressmen there. He postponed it until the following Tuesday. On that day he took Arthur outside and talked to him. He took me outside and talked to me. Then he turned to this very smart gentleman sitting in his cashmere coat and said, "Mr Grade, what objections have you got to your daughter marrying this young man?" The gentleman got up and replied, "I'm not Mr Grade, I am Mr Davidson." Judge Thomas asked, "Where is Mr Grade?" The clerk said, "Mr Grade hasn't the time to attend the hearing today." Judge Thomas said, "Permission granted." Then he turned to Arthur and asked if he wanted costs but Arthur declined as our lawyers had had such marvellous publicity and the costs, in any case, were only four guineas.'

Lynda and Arthur had a registry office wedding at Caxton Hall on

3 March 1960, twelve years after Leslie had married Audrey in the same small room. Kathie came but with the place packed with the press she was forced to hide, spending the whole of the reception in the toilet at the home of Arthur's parents. The second wedding, seven months later, was a more conventional Jewish affair. Lew gave Lynda away at the synagogue and the wedding reception was at Lew and Kathie's flat. But no other Grade attended, not even Michael.

It was Michael's absence that hurt Lynda the most. 'Michael took Grandma's side. He was probably more dominated by her. I think it was difficult for Michael to keep an even keel with my grandmother, but then you would require to be a Kissinger or Perez de Cuellar to do that. I expected Michael to stick by me and he didn't. When you are young you get very hurt. By the time my grandma and my aunt finished telling the story you would have thought that I had one leg and a hump and Arthur was a fortune hunter. I felt very bitter about Michael.'

Michael had initially been bewildered by the turn of events. He found himself having to choose between the two people he knew best and loved most: Olga and Lynda. He chose Olga, accepting her argument that Lynda had dishonoured the family by taking Leslie to court and making public a family quarrel. Just before her marriage he wrote Lynda an angry, bitter letter denouncing her for bringing disgrace to the family name, words that would ring in Lynda's mind for years. As with any situation he could not cope with, Michael's answer was to shut it out and he shut Lynda completely out of his life. He was not unique in this. The rest of the Grades did the same. Although three of the Grades have written books about their family, providing engrossing details about their East End upbringing, Lynda's marriage just does not figure. Not even Lew, the only Grade who has continued to maintain his relations with Lynda, has a word to say about her wedding. It was as if it had never happened. For Michael it is a past, like his mother and Stowe, that he does not want to know about.

Just as he was learning to talk he had lost his mother; now, just as he was about to embark on his first job, he lost his sister. He could do nothing about his mother deserting him; he could have found his sister but chose not to. It was to leave a void in his life that has never been completely filled.

How big a gap his mother's desertion left can only be guessed at.

That it has left an emotional vacuum can hardly be denied. Friends and amateur psychologists are bound to speculate that his subsequent search for female companions – wives and girlfriends – shows his desire to find strong women almost as substitute mother figures.

But his rejection of his sister shows how he copes with a fraught emotional problem. His answer is to shut it out.

11

THE TRAINEE IN THE ROLLS

It was bloody tough, the worst way to start
JOHN BROMLEY

Michael was not your average junior reporter. He was
very sophisticated, had a kind of West End confidence,
like someone who knew his way around
ADRIAN METCALFE, sports personality and friend

ONE OF THE MOST ENDEARING of Michael Grade's qualities has to be his ability to tell a story against himself, making gentle fun of the Grade power and influence. His favourite story, one that he willingly retells, is how as a seventeen-year-old he walked out of St Dunstan's College straight into the *Daily Mirror* as a journalist.

The story, as Michael has so often told his friends, goes like this. It is the summer of 1960, he is just about to leave St Dunstan's and one day he tells Leslie, 'You know, Daddy, I am leaving school next week, what am I going to do?'

'Why not come into the company?' offers Leslie but Michael does not fancy that. 'All right,' says Leslie. 'Let me think about it.' A few days later he says to Michael, 'Right, next Thursday you are going to meet Arthur [Leslie's chauffeur] and he is going to take you in the Roller to see this chap.' He then hands a card to Michael, who does not even look at it, just casually puts it in his pocket.

Thursday at ten o'clock, Arthur arrives at Grosvenor Court Mansions with the Rolls-Royce and Michael is driven to the *Daily Mirror* building at Holborn. The doorman rushes up expecting to find a dignitary, only to see a snotty-nosed seventeen-year-old kid emerging from the back of a vast limousine. Michael walks up to reception where he is received rather dismissively: What does this kid want? Kids like these are always coming up to the reception and are a pain. Michael does not seem to be sure who he wants to see, then, fishing the card Leslie has given him out of his pocket, says, 'I have come to see someone called . . . Cudlipp.'

At the very mention of this name the receptionist seems to come alive as if an electric current has been passed through her. Michael has given the name of the man who is like a god at the *Mirror*. There is now a new respect for this snotty-nosed kid and he is escorted through thick-piled carpets and offices containing secretaries to the eighth floor where Cudlipp holds court. Cudlipp wastes little time on preliminaries. 'Come in, young Grade, sit there. You have got yourself a job on the *Mirror*. What do you want to do?'

Michael says, 'I don't know.'

Cudlipp says, 'You interested in sport?'

Michael replies, 'Yes, I support Charlton.'

Cudlipp resists the temptation of saying supporting Charlton hardly qualifies him to know anything about football but grunts, 'Right.' He then buzzes his secretary and says, 'Get me the sports editor, what's his name, Jack something.'

Meanwhile, Jack Hutchinson, a quiet, nice man, much respected by his staff, is sitting on the third floor, which houses the sports desk and the other editorial staff of the *Mirror*. The phone rings. It is Cudlipp's secretary. 'Mr Hutchinson, Mr Hugh Cudlipp wants to see you.'

Hutchinson, who only ever sees Cudlipp twice a year at the odd cocktail party, immediately suspects the worst. 'What! Oh crikey.'

Racking his brains to try to anticipate the problem, Hutchinson arrives at Cudlipp's offices.

Cudlipp says, 'Come in, Jack, sit down. This is Michael Grade and he has just joined your department. I hope you are very happy together. Goodbye.'

Grade accompanies Hutchinson down to the third floor; they walk along the editorial floor past the news reporters, the back-bench, the picture desk to arrive finally at the sports desk where Hutchinson motions him to an empty space at the end of a long table. Less than an hour ago he was another school-leaver, now he had a job on one of the most powerful newspapers in the Street.

Like all stories, this has an element of hyperbole, and with every retelling it gains an extra twist, a further dash of colour, but its essence is correct. Hugh Cudlipp was an old friend of Leslie, they knew each other through Leslie's involvement with Leyton Orient and Grade's job on the *Mirror* was a case of Daddy fixing it up for him. Without Leslie's influence, Grade would indeed have been dismissed by the doorman as a snotty-nosed kid and not got past reception.

In 1960, the *Daily Mirror* was at the height of its powers. It sold more than five million copies and it was rich and powerful, if already infected by the touch of complacency that led to its downfall. Whenever John Bromley, who had joined the *Mirror* from the *Daily Herald* to cover football and athletics, would come up with an idea for a new story he would be told, 'John, we are selling five million copies a day. We don't want too many ideas.' The *Mirror* had replaced the *Express* as the paper every journalist wanted to join. The sports desk of the *Mirror* was a highly prized, highly competitive place, a mixture of seasoned hacks who had seen it all and the aspiring journalists who had fought and scrapped their way to it from provincial papers. Different Fleet Street papers have different catchment areas. On the *Mirror* sports desk quite a few recruits came up from the *Portsmouth Evening News*, or from Hayters, a sports agency run by Reg Hayter, the doyen of Fleet Street sports writers. John Bromley had been at Hayters. Ken Jones, then the *Mirror*'s star football writer, had come from Dicksons agency, which Hayter bought out. The *Mirror* then had the added attraction that it was almost the only tabloid newspaper – others like the *Express*, *Mail* and the *Daily Herald* still being broadsheets and the *Sun* did not exist – and the popular journalist who got on to the third floor of the *Mirror* felt he had at last arrived.

Many of those who worked on the *Mirror* sports desk had known each other for years, shared a camaraderie, were proud of their journalistic craft and also jealous of it. Their heroes were such *Mirror* stars as the urbane, witty cricket writer Brian Chapman, and the sports feature writer Peter Wilson, who epitomised modern sports journalism and whose column appeared under the heading 'the man they couldn't gag', a title bestowed on him by Cudlipp. Grade's arrival was a challenge to this system. Here was this kid without any training walking into one of the most sought-after jobs on the Street just because his old man knew Cudlipp. When the story of his arriving in the Rolls-Royce became known it only added to the feelings of resentment.

Nothing could have prepared Grade for Fleet Street. Lacking the traditional journalistic training he also lacked shorthand, which in the days before the portable tape recorder was quite a handicap. Almost everybody on the third floor had a joke about the millionaire's son who couldn't do shorthand. Grade also had to cope with the *Mirror*'s unique systems. The *Mirror* had recently moved to this building, popularly known as the Wedding Cake building, Holborn Circus. In the old offices a lot of typewriters had gone missing and now the upright Imperial typewriters, hardy beasts of burden, were chained to the desk and padlocked to make sure nobody could walk away with them. Grade had slowly, painfully slowly, to learn to type with two fingers, then master the *Mirror*'s peculiar system of producing an article. Now, in the age of modern technology, it seems primitive, but then it was the state-of-the-art technology. Each typewriter had a roll of continuous, specially treated paper attached to it. After Grade had written his article he would tear off a length, put it on a rotary machine and have several copies made to provide the precious 'blacks', as they were known in newspaper jargon. These would then be read by the sports editor and the sub-editors. All around him there were cynical writers and sub-editors willing him to fail.

It would hardly have been surprising if Grade had failed. But with a shrewdness that belied his years he handled the situation brilliantly, making a deep impression on John Bromley.

'It was bloody tough, the worst way to start. But he just sat and listened. Didn't open his mouth. So when the old cynic from the *Sheffield Star* made remarks he said nothing. They would chuck him the old greyhound results, ask him to put them in some sort of order, or chuck him a little paragraph about reserve team injury. He would do what he was told. He would come in every day, keep his mouth shut, always be very polite and follow the motto: Look, listen, learn, don't say too much. In the end they got to like this guy. The cynics who had been so critical of him were soon saying "smashing bloke".'

Ian Watson worked on the sports desk and watched in admiration as Grade handled the pressures of the job:

'He may have been journalistically green but he was very much aware, he wasn't naïve. There was a little resentment by some of the staff that somebody should suddenly walk into a Fleet Street job. The *Mirror* didn't take trainees. But he overcame that by buckling down and working hard. One copytaker who resented taking his copy because of the way in which he had joined the *Mirror* very quickly learnt he was a good writer who could put over good copy. I have to take my hat off to him. He was a pleasant, cheerful character, who got on with everybody.'

Although the job was a grind and he was paid only £10 a week for the first year, Grade gave the impression he enjoyed it, quickly becoming one of the lads, proof of which was provided when, like the rest of the sports department, he became quite a devotee of the White Hart just across the road. Known as the Stab (short for stab in the back, because legend had it the *Mirror* editors would do their plotting there) the pub has an almost deliberately cultivated image of decrepitude to create the impression that this is just the sort of scruffy drinking place a news-paperman would frequent: a long dirty railway-carriage-style interior relieved only marginally by photographs on the wall of various sportsmen and journalists. Michael's fellow journalists would some-times gossip about his family's fortunes and name but, as Watson recalls, 'he never showed any side. He mixed extremely well with everybody and never gave the impression he had been brought in by Cudlipp.'

About a year after he had started, Grade was suddenly rescued from the subs desk by Bromley. Bromley had just started writing a daily column called 'Sportsline', a sort of Nigel Dempster-style sports diary full of offbeat stories with Bromley's name and picture on top. A daily column like that is probably the most demanding job in journalism. Two columns down a page consisting of seven or eight items, it required a great deal of time and lots of telephoning, and after a time Bromley felt he could not do it on his own and needed an assistant.

'I told Jack Hutchinson that I needed help; if I got ill or flu, who was going to write the column? I need someone who knows what I am chasing or following up for the next day's column. He said, "Who do you have in mind?" I said, "What about the chap sitting right at the end of the subs table doing the dog results? Why don't you pull him in?" That was Michael Grade. I had met him but I didn't know him all that well. He pulled up a chair next to me, helped me on the column and got to know what I was doing. I chose him because he was young, begin-ning to get a little confidence and the respect of the subs. Also, the job of assistant was not a top job. You couldn't pull in another reporter. He was perfect: made cups of coffee, helped me with chasing stories, fielded my telephone calls. Michael is not a man of great intellect but he is well read and learns very quickly and is very sensible.'

Bromley was already known as Bromers and Grade soon became Grady. Adrian Metcalfe, then at Magdalen College, Oxford, had already made a name for himself as one of the country's leading middle-distance runners, having been ranked Number One in the world in the 440 yards in 1961. He was often used by Bromley as a Varsity stringer.

'Bromers would ring and say, "We need a quote, old darling, we are struggling for the column today, for Christ's sake tell us something."

So I used to think up a quote and he would say, "Ah, well done." Then every so often Bromers or Grady would come down to Oxford and we would have lunch. I was always good copy for a guy desperate to fill a daily column.'

Metcalfe and Grady made an unlikely partnership. The two men's backgrounds could not have been more dissimilar and Grade's chief interest was football not athletics, but their relationship blossomed. Metcalfe was taken by this 'very funny, entertaining guy full of snappy one-liners'. What struck Adrian was that, 'Michael was not your average junior reporter. He was very sophisticated, had a kind of West End confidence, like someone who knew his way around.' Part of the sophistication was that his range of stories culled from the showbiz world of the Grades was always different and he was so much more enticing then the people Metcalfe normaly mixed with. Also, with the cult of youth just beginning (the Beatles had recently emerged from the Cavern Club), Grade had the sort of café showbiz glory that gave him an edge. 'He always had a few girls, of course. He also had one of the very first Volvo sports cars, one of those low-slung jobs, and a very interesting mix of friends. There was Lenny, a nightclub owner who ran a club called Kilt in Soho. He was a Jewish fellow, very short, five foot four, and he always had Swedish models, tall, blonde Nordic types, who all seemed to be six foot one and towered over him. It was always great fun to be with the short Lenny and his leggy Swedish blondes. Lenny seemed to have an inexhaustible supply of them. He eventually married one of them, Gundy, a spectacular Brigitte Nielsen-style Swedish blonde.'

Michael also let his friends glimpse some of the fabled wealth of the Grades. Leslie had two villas in a development just outside St Tropez. He would let Michael and his friends use the smaller of the two villas and Adrian, along with other friends of Michael, often holidayed there during the summer.

'We use to muck about as you do on holidays. But I remember one occasion when Michael wanted to prove he was the great yachtsman. There were these dinghies on the bay at St Tropez and we decided to sail. So we bung this bloke a few francs and climb into the boat. Michael says, "I know boats." He wants to play the helmsman and I am the crew. In about three minutes we are almost in Algeria, winging along brilliantly, and St Tropez is the size of a thimble, a pimple on the horizon. This is great. We fool around a bit in the middle of the Mediterranean, then decide we had better get back. We turn the boat round and nothing happens. Grady, this genius, says, "We have to tack." I say, "What do you mean, tack?" He says, "When you tack the boom comes down," and as he says "boom", crash, he hits me on the head. So we start tacking and we make about a hundred metres in an hour. There is rising hysteria by now, a sort of sailing version of *Dad's Army*. "Sit down, don't panic," we are shouting at each other. But we can't get this boat to move. Gradually we edge our way back towards St Tropez. All around us these young guys are hanging out of the sides whipping backwards and forwards, crisscrossing us at thirty knots in their bloody boats while we have dropped the sail and found a paddle. We come back like Saunders of the river, paddling back to the shore. Humiliating, absolutely humiliating.'

A young man enjoying such pleasures of the twentieth century could have been expected to turn away from the nineteenth-century world Olga offered, even feel a bit embarrassed by it. But it is to Michael's great credit that he never shunned Olga for his new-found friends. Michael still saw Olga as the centre of his life and friends like Adrian were often encouraged to meet Grandma. Olga was the only secure thing in his life, the only source of affection he was really sure about, and he was not going to abandon her. Olga and Michael had now moved from Grosvenor Court to a flat in Wimpole Street, just off the Marylebone Road, much more upmarket, a larger flat than the one in Grosvenor Court, with half a dozen good-sized rooms. When Adrian visited Michael there Olga would insist on treating him as an under-nourished child, just as she did with Michael, and there would be lots of lokshen soup and chicken and a variety of good Yiddish cooking. She would also happily entertain them with stories of Russia and her arrival in the East End until Michael, who had heard them so often, would interrupt and suggest they went out. But even if he was going out he would have to eat with Olga before she would let him go, which often meant that on his jaunts with Adrian, Lenny and the others he would have to eat two dinners: soup and chicken with Olga, then a meal out with them at a really smart place.

Olga did not mind how long Michael stayed out or the state he returned in as long as he had enough to eat. Once while Michael was out the flat was burgled. The thieves removed the front door and left it outside the common entrance of the block. Michael, returning from a late-night drinking session, saw this and thought, 'I must be drunk,' and went up to the flat and fell asleep. It was only the next day he realised that the door he had seen was their own front door and that they had been burgled.

Michael retold this and other stories with relish and as ever Adrian could only admire the impeccable timing of his jokes and one-liners, but, as he looks back, Adrian cannot recall any one of the one-liners that so enthralled him then. As John Bromley says, Michael is good fun, great to be with but you do not remember any anecdotes. And always there was the hint of a deeper sadness. In the midst of his showbiz stories there would sometimes be talk of the mother he never knew, the English (or, strictly speaking, Welsh) side of his family that had gone for ever and even of the wounds that Stowe had opened and never healed. Like the comedian whose laughter often hides his tears, Michael sometimes gave friends the impression that behind the marvellous one-liners there lay a deeper vale of tears. An evening with him was always brilliant. Adrian would come away thinking how lucky Michael had been to have had years of practice honing his skill as raconteur by watching the great showbiz artistes at first hand, but although he was very close to him, Adrian never got to know the inner man.

'I knew him very well in those years. We saw a lot of each other. But did I really know him? I don't know. Behind the bonhomie there was a deeper reserve which I don't think I ever pentrated.'

As Grade gained more prominence as Bromley's assistant, he was also acquiring a reputation as a football reporter, impressing *Mirror* subs with a nice turn of phrase, and his fellow reporters with his style. Few reporters than had cars, certainly not junior reporters, and Michael used his to take his fellow football journalists to matches. They enjoyed the novelty; also the fact they they could still claim train expenses from the *Mirror* and other papers, and sometimes half a dozen or so journalists would travel with him, in comfort and in pocket. To add to this Grade style he would, at least at Leyton Orient or Charlton where Leslie had made him familiar with the directors' box, sometimes report from there. What impressed his fellow journalists was that the style was matched by substance. Grade quickly became adept at doing the football 'runners' where instead of waiting to file a report at the end of the match, the reporter starts filing his copy as the match is being played, so that even with the match finishing very near the edition time the report can still make it into the paper. Such 'runners' are a specialised skill and Grade became very adept at filing about two hundred words at the half-time of a football match, another hundred words at three-quarters time and a fifty-word 'top and tail' as soon as the whistle went. The trick here was to write the various segments of the report in such a way that in the following day's paper the reader would not be able to discover the join.

In August 1964 Bromley left print journalism to join television, convinced that his prospects at the *Mirror* would always be blocked by Peter Wilson. Wilson, who had joined the *Mirror* the same day as Cudlipp and Cassandra, the legendary columnist, was the biggest name in the *Mirror*'s sports department and a close friend of Cudlipp's. Wilson had been less then happy with Bromley's column, which he saw as a threat, and although Bromley had joined the *Mirror* on the promise that for the major world sporting events like the World Cup and the Olympic Games he would be Number Two to Wilson, at the Tokyo Olympics, the first great television Olympics, the promise was not kept. Wilson went to Cudlipp and persuaded him that Bromley shouldn't attend; instead the man who did the pools and who was also assistant sports editor, went. So when ITV came to Bromley with an offer to help them start *World of Sport* he was glad to leave. It was a risk, he was leaving an established media for a new one, but in years to come he would be grateful to Wilson for engineering his departure. It also benefited Grade, who now took over Bromley's column. Just twenty-one, he had his own daily column in the country's biggest-selling paper, complete with by-line and picture. It also meant more money, about £2,000 a year, and things did seem to be knitting together again. Even Lynda was back.

For five years now Michael had made no contact with Lynda. Then she had given birth to her first child, Simon. This should have been the cue for a grand reconciliation; the birth of a child often makes even the most estranged parents forgive and forget. But this time events did not follow the script. When Arthur phoned Leslie and said, 'Lynda has just had a little boy,' Leslie retorted, 'So what?' and put the phone down. There was no help from Leslie's wife Audrey, who had long ago washed her hands of the whole affair, claiming it was nothing to do with her. Michael appeared to be still wedded to the family line on Lynda but, recalls Lynda, 'When we started making a bit of money it thawed. Then Michael started popping in to see the children and a relationship was re-established.'

Michael was drawn back to Lynda partly because Penny Levinson had come into his life. He had plenty of girlfriends but this one was serious and one Olga would approve of. For years Olga had hoped that her sons would marry Jewish women. Now Michael, her favourite grandson, was fulfilling her deepest wishes. Born of a *shiksa* woman and so strictly speaking not even Jewish, he was now deeply involved with just the sort of north London Jewish girl that even Olga could not fault. Penny could not have been more Jewish: her father was a director of Lyons; her mother, a delightfully extrovert woman, was a great friend of the family, and they lived in the right part of north London, St John's Wood. So for Olga, Michael going out with Penny seemed both natural and right. Penny worked as a librarian with the BBC and Michael met her in the most conventional fashion: at a dinner party thrown by friends eager to act as matchmakers.

Penny also formed a bridge with Lynda. 'We lived,' recalls Lynda, 'in St John's Wood. Penny was a local girl and we became very friendly for a while. She got very fond of Simon and all of us and she would often come and babysit for us.' Once Penny and her mother took Lynda's children to a Lyons corner shop but created so much noise that all of them, including Penny and her mother, were thrown out.

Michael's happiness appeared to coincide with his father's reaching the pinnacle of his career. Leslie was now not only the country's most successful agent but an increasingly successful film producer, making *Please Sir* and films such as *The Young Ones* and *Summer Holiday* with Cliff Richard, and *The Servant*, directed by Joe Losey. Having started off proving that he could match Lew's capacity to be a seller, he was now showing signs of becaming an impresario like Bernie. Ultimate proof of Leslie's success came in 1966 when he bought a four-bedroomed flat on an eighty-year lease in Kensington Palace Gardens, popularly known as Millionaires' Row, for what was then the fabulous sum of £100,000. Unlike Lew or Bernard, Leslie rarely made the papers and he liked it that way. But the purchase of such a flat was news and there was much publicity about Leslie's purchase and the fact that his yearly outgoings in rates and services of £2,000 exceeded most people's income. As ever, he was working almost round the clock, if not on the telephone then on the plane as he crisscrossed the Atlantic in search of shows, stars and deals. It took Leslie and his family some time to move into the flat, which was in a brand-new block, but on 19 April 1966 the delays about furnishings and fittings were resolved and they moved in.

On 21 April 1966, a Sunday, Leslie came back from hectic business meetings in New York, had lunch and then began complaining of pins and needles in his hand and an excruciating backache. Audrey got alarmed by the mention of pins and needles and feared the worst. Very soon he was sick and collapsed. Audrey summoned Rita's husband, Dr Joseph Freeman, who was soon joined by Dr Charles Joiner, a specialist from Guy's Hospital. It was clear that Leslie was very seriously ill and while Dr Joiner thought there was little point in moving him, Freeman felt they should try to get him to Guy's Hospital. Joiner was very reluctant: 'You know this man is going to die, don't you? He will never survive an ambulance journey to the hospital.' But eventually it was agreed that they should try to move him. Joiner accompanied Freeman and Audrey as they took Leslie to hospital. It was clear he had suffered a massive stroke and there was no certainty that he would ever emerge from his coma.

Michael was devastated by Leslie's stroke and it hit the Grades like a thunderbolt. As the family gathered in the waiting room adjoining the public ward where Leslie had been taken, they wondered about the fate that had dealt them such a hand. Lew and Bernard had a more pressing problem to solve: who would run the Grade organisation? The next day, a Monday, they met at Leslie's office. Denise Parkhurst, Leslie's secretary, who knew nothing of the stroke, came in to find Lew, Bernie and Billy Marsh, who ran Bernard Delfont's agency, sitting in Leslie's office. She looked at their sombre faces and immediately thought: Leslie is dead.

In business terms he was. It had always been assumed that if anything happened to Leslie, Lew would take over. But Lew was now running ATV, a paid employee of a major public company, so he could hardly do what he had done in 1943 and step in to take charge. Robin Fox, father of Edward and James Fox, who was a director, would have been the logical successor but he, too, was very ill and was dying of lung cancer. That left Bernard. Two years previously he had merged his Delfont agency with Leslie's Grade Organisation whilst remaining a senior director of the company. Bernard knew that even if Leslie recovered he would not be back for a long time. Bernard himself had had heart trouble and he reckoned that Leslie would lose a year off work for every month he spent in hospital. As an independent who worked for himself, Bernard was able to adapt his working life, so it was decided that he would take over. But he saw it only as a temporary move; he had neither the inclination nor the health to be a full-time agent. He was far too much of an impresario, a man who liked putting on a show, to try and become another Leslie, even if he could. There was only one person who could become a long-term successor to Leslie: Michael.

Rita Grade claims that it was at her suggestion that Michael was thought of as a successor. According to her, Leslie and Bernie agreed and one day as Michael and Rita sat in the car outside Nuffield House at Guy's she tried to persuade him to leave the *Mirror* and join the Grade Organisation. It took, says Rita, a considerable amount of persuasion. 'He loved his job and was doing well. However, after I'd used a bit of emotional blackmail, and as soon as Michael realised he would be doing something that would help his father, he agreed to think about it.'

In Bernard's recollection Rita had no part to play and it was his idea that Michael be approached.

'The one person I could think of who would do it well was Michael. I rang him up and took him to lunch at Verry's, next door to Leslie's offices in Regent Street. I suggested he leave sports writing. It couldn't lead him to much. I pressed him very hard on the virtues of the agency and said, "I would like you to come into the business and run it for your father." He said he would think it over.'

Clearly Michael was under family pressure to do the right thing by his father and the family business. As it happened, the call came at just the right time. He had been thinking of a move away from journalism into becoming a sports promoter. Despite the regard the *Mirror* sports desk now held him in, Grade did not think he was that good a sports writer and further promotions at the *Mirror*, particularly to the top job of chief sports feature writer, were blocked by Peter Wilson. He had got just about as far as he could.

But did he really want to be an agent? Michael had always had a desire to distance himself from the family business. He wanted to make a name for himself on his own and he feared he might not be able to match his father's skills. Although he had seen little of Leslie over the years, his admiration for him was immense and he would often tell people how he thought his father was the most brilliant man he had ever met. Could he fill his shoes? Adrian sensed he was torn, that Leslie's illness was forcing him to become something he did not want to be. 'Leslie's illness dragged him off to become an agent; he never really wanted to do the agency job.'

For about a week Michael wrestled with his options. He was flattered when Bernard told him he was being asked not because he was a

Grade but because the family felt he could do the job. In any case, Bernard reassured him, Billy Marsh, who was not far behind Leslie as an agent, would help.

Then there was the question of money. The *Mirror* salary was comfortable but not great. Michael had decided to get married to Penny and he knew he could do with the money. Not for the first time, Michael Grade was strapped for cash. The bitterness created by Lynda's marriage had been erased, partly due to Leslie's illness. It was just like their old childhood days and he turned to his big sister for help.

'He did not have a bean in the world,' says Lynda. 'I lent him the money to buy a bracelet as an engagement present for Penny. He had got engaged to Penny while Daddy was in Guy's Hospital. Daddy had an account at Gerrards but we didn't have access to that and his cheque from the *Mirror* had not come through. I rang up his bank and said I would stand guarantee for him until his cheque from the *Mirror* had been cleared. It was not a lot of money but he needed it to buy the bracelet.'

After a week of much thought Michael finally rang Bernard and told him he would accept. The family welcomed the decision as if this was the return of the prodigal. Their fears about Leslie had been confirmed. Doctors at Guy's Hospital diagnosed that Leslie had suffered a cerebral haemorrhage. Although there was no brain damage, they expected him to remain frail and Bernard sensed that he would never fully return to normal. In time, although his left side remained paralysed, Leslie recovered sufficiently to return to work, but he was never really the same again.

Michael's decision to accept the job was the one thing that cheered Leslie up. Even though he had got him the job on the *Mirror*, he had always seen it as only an interlude. He had been less than pleased when his son's column in the *Mirror* appeared under the byline Mike Grade. 'Don't ever let them call you Mike,' he had said, clearly upset by the shortening of the name. Now the name Leslie had given him could be restored, he would never again be called Mike, and he could become a full subscriber and contributor to the Grade business.

Grade told the *Mirror*, 'I am sorry, I have just go to go and run my father's business,' and in the summer of 1966 he moved from Holborn to Regent Street, a short taxi ride away but one marking a complete revolution in his life. He gave some of his *Mirror* colleagues the impression that he might come back. But most knew he would never return.

Journalism had taught him cynicism but also the worth of deadlines and publicity – both of which would be of immense value to him in the future. He would find he worked best when given a deadline and his use of publicity would set him apart from his colleagues.

The move may have been logical, even inevitable, but Metcalfe believes Michael Grade missed his metier. 'I think he was made for journalism and had he stayed he might have ended up like David English or Nick Lloyd, editing a tabloid. He would have enjoyed that more than anything else.'

We will never know.

III

A Buyer in a Seller's World

*Michael did not enjoy being an agent. It is a selling job.
Michael is fundamentally a buyer. A buyer is one who
goes to a lunch and lets someone sell him something. A
good salesman is only interested in selling the thing to you*
BILL COTTON JNR

*Michael was very good. He's a clever fellow. But I don't
think being an agent was an important part of his life*
DENNIS VAN THAL, Grade's partner in the agency business

A FEW WEEKS BEFORE Michael Grade moved into the offices in Regent Street, *The Sunday Times* had run a story called 'The Show Business Octopus'. The Insight team, then reaching the height of its glory, produced an elaborate chart to show how the Grades ruled the entertainment world, calling the family 'probably the most powerful entertainment network in the world'. The chart showed the interconnecting maze of companies which linked the three brothers, and how between them they had an interest in virtually all the major show business, film and theatre stars of the time.

The Sunday Times warned of the dangers of what they described as a 'virtual monopoly' and confidently asserted that Harold Wilson, then the Prime Minister, would bring in legislation to restrict the Grades' powers. This theme was picked up by the rest of the media, with columnists and pundits either mocking the powers of the Grades or expressing alarm.

Leslie's Grade Organisation, which had become a public company in 1964, was very much in the centre of the *Sunday Times* 'octopus'. The Grade Organisation owned or had a majority interest in more than fifty cinemas and half a dozen agencies, whose list of clients *was* the British stage and screen: Laurence Olivier, Ralph Richardson, John Gielgud, Noël Coward, Julie Christie, Susan Hampshire, Albert Finney, Dorothy Tutin, Sarah Miles, Kenneth Moore, Dirk Bogarde and Ian Carmichael.

If Leslie had the performers, then Lew, the majority shareholder in the Grade Organisation, had the places where their talents could be displayed. As managing director of ATV he had the means of putting Leslie's clients either on television or in some of the prestigious theatres in the West End, including the Palladium, Drury Lane and the Lyric, all owned by ATV. The 'octopus's' reach was completed, or so said *The Sunday Times*, by Bernard Delfont, who was deputy chairman of the Grade Organisation, owning a string of theatres and putting on his own shows.

The greatest concern was that Leslie would book the stars for the Palladium, the live show would be sold to ATV for *Sunday Night at the London Palladium*, then, feeding off the television publicity, it would do the Stoll–Moss circuit, owned by ATV and covering the major London and provincial theatres, with the brothers raking off their ten per cent all the time. The Grades insisted with just a touch of righteousness that the competitive instinct of the brothers was so great that there could be no monopoly; Bernard laughed it off as a monopoly of goodwill. Leslie claimed he had found it difficult to sell his shows to ATV and both Lew and Bernard presented evidence to suggest they had never quite got over their sibling rivalry. Lew, for instance, had not known for some time that Bernard had changed his name to Delfont; the two hardly ever socialised together, and Bernard was a little hurt when Lew, moving into television, gave Leslie but not him the chance to buy shares. Twenty years earlier, just after the war, when Bernard had opened the Casino in opposition to Val Parnell and the Palladium, Lew and Leslie continued to favour the mightier battalions of the Palladium and Bernard's Casino failed. But not everyone believed the brothers' protestations, although in 1968 Lew won a court action against Emile Littler who had implied that ATV had colluded with the Grade Organisation to try to stop one of his shows.

To an extent Michael's arrival confirmed critics' fears that the Grades were building a show-business dynasty, with Michael pictured as the second generation taking over a vast, well-connected family monopoly. But it hardly felt like that to him and any thoughts of inheriting a family empire were far from his mind. His priority was simple: he had a business to learn.

It could not have been more different from the third floor of the *Mirror*. There he had been taught an early lesson in cynicism: death was a useful space filler. 'If so-and-so pops off, we'll be OK for page three.' The agency, which now occupied several floors in Regent Street, thrived on an excess of optimism, everybody was a darling and there was always a glass of pink gin. That would be poured out by Dennis Van Thal at precisely twelve o'clock every day. If this pink gin routine set him just that bit aloof from the rest, then Dennis quite liked that. Of Dutch extraction, he had grown up in Hampstead, trained to be a classical musician and had been a conductor for many years before the war. He would still have preferred to have carried on conducting but somehow found himself drifting into agency business and by the time Michael joined he looked after clients who were on 'the straight side of things': the actors and actresses of the stage and screen.

Michael had an office on the floor just below Dennis Van Thal and his brief was to look after the variety artistes: light entertainers such as Morecambe and Wise. The two sides of the business needed very different skills and Michael found the transition to this new world bewildering and strange. Although Bernard's reassurances that he had the qualities to become a successful agent were comforting, they did not quite still the doubts he had. Even when he had convinced himself he merited the job, it was quite another matter to follow a father who was on his way to being immortalised as the greatest show-business agent of his generation, if not of all time. It is always difficult for a son to follow a famous father, but everywhere Michael, the tyro agent, went he was preceded by a story of Leslie, the super agent.

Almost everybody Michael met had a Leslie story. They were often told with affection to help the young man and ease his path in this new, unfamiliar world, but they succeeded only in putting up more hurdles for him to clear. So he was told about Leslie, the great promiser. He did not always manage to keep his promise but never failed to make one and his opening pitch when talking to a producer was legendary: 'Have I got an act for you!' Overbooking is an agent or a producer's nightmare but Leslie never worried about that; indeed, he thrived on it. One of Bill Cotton Jnr's favourite stories, which he now told Michael, was how Leslie converted overbooking into an art form to exploit the fame of his own father, Bill Cotton Snr:

'Leslie would book my father into four theatres for the August bank holiday week. Just before the bills were due to go out he would ring up three of the four theatres: "I don't know what has happened but Bill Cotton doesn't want to come, but I have got Troise and his Mandoliers." August bank holiday week was always full anyway and they had to accept. So Leslie got four bookings on one name.'

Had Leslie been by Michael's side, the jokes and the stories would have helped with the tutoring, but with Leslie lying ill in Guy's Hospital they only made him all the more of a distant, unattainable legend and Michael badly needed a mentor to guide him. Fortunately there was one man, Billy Marsh, who could step in to become a sort of alternative Leslie for Michael. Marsh, a farmer's boy from Kent, had been attracted to show business some years before the war when he had seen Bernard Delfont perform as a dancer. In 1942 Delfont had signed him to run his agency business. Although he started on only £4 a week Marsh had proved so skilful that Delfont, who had never much cared for the grind of agency work – booking artistes, massaging their egos – let Marsh handle this side of the business while he developed into an impresario. Marsh, given a free rein in the light entertainment field, made the Delfont agency one of the most successful in the business. By the time Michael appeared in the business, Marsh provided a role model for any aspiring agent.

Michael Grade, looking for somebody to lean on, fell in love with him.

'Michael,' recalls Metcalfe, 'just worshipped Billy Marsh; he thought Billy Marsh was one of the greatest geniuses of British entertainment, signing up everyone and signing them up for nothing and selling them for fortunes. He used to love telling us all those Billy Marsh stories.' The stories of Marsh's success were legion: how on seeing Frankie Vaughan finish his act with a weak impersonation of Al Jolson, he persuaded Vaughan to put on a top hat, sing 'Give Me the Moonlight' and become a star; or how he spotted Norman Wisdom at the Victoria Palace and exploited his comic genius. Marsh had acquired a reputation among his clients for just the right blend of persistence and reserve. Perhaps his greatest success was helping Morecambe and Wise become a television success. In 1954 Morecambe and Wise had made their first appearance on television to almost unanimous derision. Their variety act had just not transferred to the small screen, with one critic writing, 'Definition of the week. TV set – the box they buried Morecambe and Wise in'. Eric Morecambe became so depressed he thought of packing TV in for good and for years all the television they could manage was the odd comedy appearance on a variety bill televised from the London Palladium or the Hackney Empire.

Then they changed agents to Billy Marsh who slowly, successfully, engineered their reintroduction to television, never too much, but enough to get noticed. In 1961 he negotiated a thirteen-week television series with ATV. Morecambe and Wise came on performing to the theme tune of 'Two of a Kind' and in the best traditions of show-business stories, lived happily ever after on the box – or at least until the next series.

It had been decided that as an introduction to the agency Grade would share an office with Marsh, the idea being he would drink in the magic of the agency business from one of its best practitioners. In a way, something similar had happened to him at the *Mirror*. But what works when you are a down-table sub on a busy paper does not work so well in an agency where you are required to be on the phone all the time selling. Things seemed to go on around Michael, he never seemed to be part of it. One story goes that during that first year sharing Marsh's office, Grade hardly ever spoke, and followed his early *Mirror* practice of look, listen, don't say anything to such an extent that Marsh despaired of teaching the young man anything.

Marsh confessed to friends, 'He never seems to learn anything. How can I make him into an agent if he never opens his mouth?' Marsh, a polite, dapper man who insisted on calling everyone sir, racked his brains to figure out how he might turn this apparent mute into an agent and, in that first year, all his skill and patience was put to the test by Michael Grade. Witty and even voluble as he could be with friends, the agency and its routine were proving too much. Michael was not sure what he had landed himself in.

Grade was, clearly, overawed by his situation, although to be fair he had other preoccupations. That first year at the agency was also one of the most crowded in his life. For a start he was again homeless. Leslie's illness had forced Lew and Bernard to consider Olga's future. Their first concern was how Olga would take the news; clearly it had to be broken to her very gently. Kathie undertook to do so. The day after Leslie's stroke she drove Olga to Wimbledon where her own mother, with whom Olga got on well, lived, and it was Kathie's mother who told Olga about Leslie. But not quite the full story. She was given the impression that it was a heart attack and that Leslie would recover. The papers conspired in this, describing his illness as a heart attack and writing about Leslie 'resting in Guy's Hospital'. Lew and Kathie did not think it was right for Olga to go back to her Wimpole Street flat, so she was taken to their own flat in Cavendish Square and stayed there until Leslie improved.

This, of course, meant that Michael now had to look for another place. Trevor Chinn of Lex Garages and his wife Susan, who were old friends of Leslie's, offered to put up Michael in their Chelsea home. And so, as he tried to cope with his new job, he was also fitting into a new home – both very unsettling events in their own ways.

Leslie's illness had, of course, cast a shadow over everything. Although he defied the gloomy predictions made immediately after his stroke, he did not emerge from Guy's Hospital until almost Christmas. Michael, now drawn closer to him, visited him regularly and the only light moments were provided by Olga's visits. She did not visit her son that often, as it was distressing for both her and Leslie, but when she did she always brought along some fairy cakes she had baked. Or at least, that is what Olga called them, although they were more like rock cakes. Leslie could not eat them and kept stuffing them into his bedside cupboard. He did not have the heart to tell Olga this and the more he pretended they were wonderful, the more cakes she brought. Finally came the day when it was time for Leslie to leave, the bedside cupboard was opened and a whole heap of 'fairy' cakes came tumbling on to the floor.

As if all this was not distracting enough for Michael during that monastic year with Marsh, he was also busy arranging his marriage to Penny. It was meant to be a major family occasion to make up for the secrecy of his father's marriage to Winifred and Lynda's to Arthur, and was billed as the first great wedding in the Grade family since they had been anointed the royal family of British entertainment. To Olga's great delight, the setting completed the story of the perfect Jewish wedding. The Liberal Jewish synagogue at St John's Wood, exactly opposite the Lord's cricket ground, was the almost automatic choice of venue.

The night before the wedding, Adrian, Lenny and seven or eight other friends organised a memorable stag night for Michael, with a meal at a restaurant followed by a visit to Raymond's Revue Bar. Such events are usually characterised by the amount of alcohol consumed and the complete inability of the participants afterwards to recall what happened.

Appropriately, the only memory Adrian has was, 'We got pissed and laughed a lot. Raymond's Revue Bar was considered naughty but not too naff.' So, in an age when the young looked to be revolutionaries, Michael bid a fairly traditional goodbye to bachelorhood. But then in some ways Michael Grade was always conventional. When a good many of his peers were smoking joints, he inhaled tobacco. About a year before his marriage, as he recalled later, he had 'tried my first and last joint of cannabis at a party. It made me silly and giggly and I decided never to take any drugs again because I was worried about losing control.' Like all children he had faced peer-group pressure to be daring but this had never gone beyond putting a little extra brandy in the orange punch and thinking it was very wicked.

The wedding was a lavish, society affair with Trevor Chinn acting as the best man. Although Chinn was his father's friend, Michael felt grateful to him for giving him a home after Leslie's stroke and this was his way of showing gratitude. The picture of Michael and Penny in the papers as they left the synagogue caught the moment well. Michael combined the look of any young man of the late sixties Beatles generation: long sideburns, long hair contrasting with top hat and tails; Penny looked very much like the models who graced the cover of *Brides* magazine. Lynda's daughter acted as bridesmaid and the family seemed whole and established. All the three brothers, Lew, Bernard and Leslie, posed outside the Dorian columns of the synagogue in top hat and tails for the definitive family picture. In subsequent years it has been this picture which has represented the Grade dynasty. In 1981, when Hunter Davies wrote his book about the Grades, this photograph, with a suitable tint, was chosen for the jacket illustration. The photograph also appeared in Lew Grade's memoirs with the caption, 'a show-business dynasty', and the one of Olga and her three sons taken at the wedding appeared in Lord Delfont's memoirs. The wedding marked the high tide of the family's recognition by a wider world. The only moment of embarrassment came when an usher introduced Bernard Delfont as Val Parnell, the man who ran the Palladium and had been his rival.

Even before the wedding Michael and Penny had decided on their home – a modern spacious house with five bedrooms and two bathrooms on Dulwich College Estate. All his life Michael had been a north London person and Penny was very much a north London girl, significant classifications in a city where the river is so important. But now for the first and only time he was lured south of the river. The attraction was the house. If it was not as fashionable as Leslie's Millionaires' Row dwelling it did mirror it to an extent. Like Leslie's house, it was on a private road barred by a gateman who had to be paid six old pence before he would let non-residents through, making it one of the few toll roads in London. Michael setting up home with Penny meant the brothers had to find a permanent home for Olga. Leslie's illness had led to her moving in with Lew and Kathie, but that could not be called home and nor could she continue living on her own. They decided it would be better for Olga to live in a hotel and she was moved to Grosvenor House.

The year had already been busy for Michael Grade, with a new wife, a new home and a new job, which, say psychiatrists, are just the combination to create stress. To add to all this, the business changed hands. A short while before Leslie had had his stroke, EMI had approached Delfont with an offer to buy the Grade Organisation. EMI then was the world's leading music record company with stars such as Frank Sinatra, Nat King Cole and the Beatles signed to them. Soon after Leslie had his stroke, Sir Joseph Lockwood, chairman of EMI, personally approached Bernard: if EMI made an offer, would he sell? The Grade Organisation had just had an outstanding success with Michael Caine and *Alfie* but Bernard was not so sure they could maintain it. This, he felt, was the right moment to sell, at the top of the market, and he told Lockwood that if the price was right a deal could be done. Leslie and Lew agreed. For two months there followed some judicious press leaks, then a final price was agreed which valued the business at £12 million – almost double its worth before EMI had made its offer.

Leslie, now much recovered, insisted he would be as good as new but EMI were not convinced and they agreed to do the deal only if Delfont joined EMI to run the business. Delfont, jealous of his independence, agreed but refused to move to EMI's offices in Manchester Street, keeping his own in Piccadilly. Bernard and Leslie signed five-year service contracts and along with Lew shared £3 million. The deal meant a lot to Bernard, who experienced a sense of financial security for the first time and felt he could at last look Lew in the eye.

The change also suited Michael. He had always been unhappy about working for his father and could now claim that in strict theory he had worked for the family business for only a few short months. He was now an employee of a public company. But there were still no signs that he would make an agent. The spark of originality and independence so valuable in an agent seemed to be entirely missing in him. Indeed, he was prepared so slavishly to follow Marsh that once it meant losing a month's wages. This happened when, as Marsh and Grade were talking to a famous American agent, EMI's PAYE girl came round with their wage packets and tossed the envelopes on their desks in that impersonal style so beloved of the petty tyrant. Marsh, she called out, and tossed a packet on to his desk. Grade, she called out, and tossed another packet. Marsh was so embarrassed to be treated in such a fashion in front of an important visitor that he tossed it away in the waste bin pretending it was nothing; Grade followed his example. But while at the end of the day Marsh remembered to pick up his wage packet, Michael forgot and that evening his salary cheque was swept away along with the general rubbish by the cleaners.

It was almost two years before Grade began to show any signs that the intensive tutoring from Marsh was paying off but, significantly, his first public forays as an agent proved that whatever skills Marsh had taught him, he certainly had a touch for publicity. Like Leslie, Marsh was quite happy not to bask in the glare of publicity and allowed Michael to take the glory. He was still being introduced as the son of Leslie Grade but almost from the beginning Michael showed a flair for dealing with the press, for providing just the right quote to make a headline. In May 1968 he organised what the press called 'OPERATION MADCAP' to try to take the London Palladium to the O'Keefe Centre in Toronto. It was to cost £40,000, a colossal sum in those days, and involved Millicent Martin, Morecambe and Wise, plus the usual plethora of chorus girls, carpenters, sets and props. The headline came from a vivid quote that Grade provided: 'Everyone who has heard about it thinks we are mad.' There were hopes that if the two-week run proved successful it could start the Palladium touring season. The pre-Toronto publicity worked brilliantly but few papers took much note of what happened in North America, where the idea did not work, proving to Grade that what matters in publicity is getting your story in first; there is seldom a follow-up.

Morecambe and Wise were soon to pose a greater challenge to Grade. Not long after this they were back in North America, taken there by Ed Sullivan to appear on his own show. But they returned almost as depressed as after their first British television appearance. Eric Morecambe hated it; the critics slated it. The *New York Daily News* wrote after their appearance on a show to celebrate Irving Berlin's eightieth birthday; 'There was one curiously out-of-place vaudeville team called Morecambe and Wise which should remain England's problem, not ours.'

That experience forced Morecambe and Wise to give up on America. Lew Grade believes that had they listened to his advice and slowed their pace a little they would have succeeded. Soon Lew Grade was to have an even bigger problem with Morecambe and Wise as they refused to listen to his advice even about shows in Britain. Wise, who looked after the business side of the partnership, was less than happy with the terms Lew Grade had offered: £39,000 for a three-year contract, tying them to thirteen shows a year. The talks ended in a furious row. Lew Grade shouted at Wise, 'Why do you boys want all this money?' Wise replied tartly that 'We all wanted the money.'

Normally the negotiations with Lew would have been handled by Marsh but as he was away Michael found himself in the middle of this row. He had heard a great deal about his uncle's selling power but this was the first time he had confronted it in a business setting and he felt Lew was being stubborn. He could not really believe, however, that Morecambe and Wise would leave ATV and felt sure a familiar compromise could be arrived at. But even more than the money, Wise was particularly upset about Lew's refusal to shoot their series in colour and whatever Michael said and Lew did he was determined to go. Suddenly Michael Grade had to find their most important stars a new home.

For the first time, Michael's agency mettle was on test and in a deft move he showed he had learnt well the lessons Marsh had taught. He rang Bill Cotton Jnr, who was now head of light entertainment at the BBC. Cotton had seen Michael grow up and regarded him as a younger brother, the son of a man who had been his father's agent and intimate friend. He immediately offered Morecambe and Wise a summer season on the BBC. It would be on BBC2, then a relatively new channel, but it would be in colour. The deal, quickly done, occupies a minor niche in the Grade story. Morecambe and Wise's move to the BBC got them the national exposure they needed and another legend of the competitive Grades was born. In years to come, when people spoke of nepotism amongst the Grades, Michael, and for that matter Lew, would retell the story of how Michael took Morecambe and Wise away from Lew and sold it to his bitterest rival, the BBC. It helped make Morecambe and Wise, it helped to still criticism that the Grades colluded with each other to build up a monopoly in show business. It also proved that Michael had the makings of an agent. If not quite a Leslie, then still good enough.

By the autumn of 1969, Michael Grade, his tutoring at the hands of Marsh complete, was ready to be unveiled as the fully grown agent. EMI's purchase of the Associated British Picture Corporation, the result of the open cheque given to Delfont to build their leisure interests, had made the IBA and the Board of Trade twitchy. ABC also owned half of Thames Television and the IBA was concerned that fifty per cent of a television company could just change hands as part of a commercial transaction. The Board of Trade was worried that EMI could now operate a cartel of theatre, television and agency interests. The agencies had to go and Delfont devised a scheme whereby Marsh, Van Thal and Michael Grade could buy out London Management, one of three agencies in the Grade Organisation. EMI were happy to sell for £250,000 and Michael became joint managing director with Van Thal and Marsh.

The announcement was made in appropriate style on 28 October 1969 at the Café Royal. In an air laden with the whiff of cigar smoke, Michael Grade was introduced as 'one of the world's most powerful Mr Ten Per Cents'. This was, perhaps, Grade's first major, formal encounter with the press and it set the tone for much of the subsequent publicity he has had. Cigars featured prominently and there was a punning headline about 'making the Grade'. The *Daily Mail* declared, 'Mike makes the grade – agent to Lord Snowdon', over a picture which showed Michael puffing a cigar almost as long as his sideburns while Leslie looked on indulgently. Underneath there was a gallery of the stars the agency handled: Frankie Vaughan, Bruce Forsyth, Ian Carmichael and Brigitte Bardot. They were, said the paper, 'Some of the stars in the Mike Grade sky'. Even the *Financial Times*'s normally staid 'Men and Matters' diary, which rarely strays outside the activities of sober company chairmen, devoted a paragraph describing the 'Grade magic' and enthused about this tall, bustling twenty-six-year old with bushy sideburns who had spent three years 'learning the business from the bottom'.

In many ways, the buy-out of London Management marks the start of Michael Grade's life as a proper agent. He now had enough confidence to go looking for clients. At times this could mean trawling the West End searching for them. On one occasion he found himself at the Stork Club at one-thirty in the morning watching a comic in a drag show. The comic was Larry Grayson and he became one of the first clients Grade signed. Finding Grayson was easier than getting him a booking. Almost nobody wanted to touch him, not even the BBC, and it was only the faith of the booker at ATV that provided him with an opening. He was prepared to have him on every third week on *Saturday Variety*. Grade insisted: 'Every week or not at all.' Grayson was offered one three-week run and that was enough to launch him.

This was followed soon after by the signing of Freddie Starr, a comic who was later to be immortalised by the *Sun* in the classic headline 'FREDDIE STARR ATE MY HAMSTER'. Grade was now beginning to show that he could be an inventive agent, even if not all his ideas took off. He saw Michael Crawford in *No Sex Please We're British* and thought he would be ideal for television playing an accident-prone husband whose well-meaning efforts always ends up by wrecking his home. But Crawford was not quite ready for television, Grade didn't persevere and it was the BBC, some years afterwards, who made Crawford famous in the role of the endearingly clumsy Frank Spencer.

Much as Grade enjoyed some aspects of being an agent he had neither his father's gifts nor the patience or even the capacity for hard work that the business required. Leslie liked nothing better than to be on the telephone. This was so much a family joke that on his fifty-second birthday Audrey ordered a telephone-shaped cake for him. He would come into work at 6.30 in the morning and start telephoning by 7 a.m.

Michael had inherited some of this work ethic, the much talked-about Jewish guilt drove him on, but he did not have quite the persistence that a great agent requires. The demands of agency work left him frustrated.

'Often', he said later, 'you know what the right thing to do is and you can't make other people see it. You get bogged down with the contracts and the wheeling and dealing.'

Cotton has no doubts that 'Michael as an agent was not as good as his father. Leslie was one of the great agents, the best of the three brothers as an agent.'

The world of show business can be simply divided into those who are sellers and those who are buyers and Michael Grade was proving himself to be a buyer in a crowd of sellers, a great contrast not only to Leslie but also to Lew.

'The difference between Michael and Lew', says Cotton, 'is that Lew is a seller. He is the best closer of a deal you will ever come across. He doesn't get off your back until you sign and you don't know why you sign.'

Once Cotton signed some Barbara Cartland stories from Lew Grade. They were talking for a bit and the deal was nearly done when Lew Grade suddenly said, 'We have been talking in pounds but everything in this film is in guineas.' So the deal was redone in guineas. Sometime afterwards when the video rights were bought and he asked about the price, Cotton quickly said it was the same price in guineas. 'I frustrated Lew then, but he is a seller. Michael is a buyer.'

The media with the greatest modern buying potential is television. Michael's agency work had already brought him in close contact with it and it was this that now provided him a way out of a career that, in the words of a Rolling Stone number popular at the time, gave him no satisfaction.

For some time Grade had been a frequent visitor to an ugly tower block in Wembley, Brent, that bore some resemblance to Stalin's palace of culture. This twenty-storey monstrosity, where static electricity built up to such an extent that it produced electric shocks if anyone touched anything, housed the programme makers of London Weekend Television. As Grade had begun to grow and develop as an agent, LWT had begun to recover from its nightmarish start as a television company. Created in the wake of the Pilkington Report's criticism of the then ITV franchises, it sought to break free of the ITV companies' stultifying wish to give the public what it wanted, even if that was the lowest form of pap, rather than to 'lead public taste to a higher ground'. The predictable result of such television bravery was to lead the station to very stony ground.

British post-war media history is crammed with media launches that didn't work. LWT's launch was a classic among such disasters, resulting in what the company's historian, David Docherty, calls 'an organisation burlesque'. Within a year of coming on air in 1968, it lost nearly all the broadcasters – mainly from the BBC – who had conceived the station, and such were the comings and goings that a popular joke at the time was about an executive being told by his secretary, 'The managing director is on the line.' The executive replies, 'Just find out his name and I will ring him back.'

The task of rebuilding fell to Cyril Bennett, who, having been an original controller of programmes, had fallen victim of the early mayhem at LWT, but was now back. In Grade's working life he has always sought and found a mentor. At the *Mirror* it was Bromley, at the agency it was Marsh, now it was to be Bennett. The former mentors taught him the skills he did not have. Bennett opened the door to a world he coveted: television.

Bennett was everything Michael Grade wanted to be – and he was Jewish. He was, writes David Docherty, 'the archetypal poor but fiercely ambitious East End Jew', who worked tirelessly and through energy, persistence and flair made himself into a formidable television executive. He also enjoyed and revelled in his Jewishness. When he had been made controller of Rediffusion, the London channel out of which LWT had been carved, one of the directors had commented, 'Now we have a house Jew', which made Bennett only more determined to parade his Jewishness.

When a LWT researcher said, 'You know, some of the things Hitler did were all right,' Bennett responded, 'Yeah, he just had a bad press officer.' At times it amounted to a stage Jewishness but it was mightily effective.

Grade was enthralled. He found Bennett, as he told Docherty, 'tough, unpredictable, whimsical, penetrating, charismatic, funny, intelligent and cosmopolitan'.

Bennett was also a hustler and at one of his early pitches as agent Grade had been exposed to Bennett's tactics. As Grade was making the pitch, and he and Bennett had just begun to haggle about the price, the office door opened and Ron Miller, head of sales, wandered in. Miller seemed surprised to find Bennett in a meeting and made as if to go. Bennett said, 'No, no, come and meet Michael Grade. We are thinking of doing this programme with him. How much do you think it would earn?' Miller gave a figure, Bennett turned to Grade and, 'See what I mean? That's why I cannot meet your price.' It was only much later that Michael Grade learnt that this was a familiar Bennett trick. He had arranged for Miller to interrupt the meeting and this was his way of getting the price down on a deal. He did it to all agents.

It was during one such occasion that Bennett was to realise that Grade was different to most agents he met. Grade had never been very successful in making pitches to Bennett but that day things started going very wrong. Bennett was not impressed, wondered if this was all he could sell and was about to ask him to leave when suddenly Grade began to invent a programme on the spot. The programme was to become legendary as the show about impressionists, *Who Do You Do?*. It provided a splendid vehicle for Freddie Starr and Grade's ability to think on his feet made a deep impression on Bennett. It showed he had some of the ability that a successful television executive needs.

Bennett knew he had to shed some of his appalling work load. He was under pressure from John Freeman, who had been brought in as chairman to sort out the chaos of the early years, to delegate. It was not in Bennett's nature to delegate or be organised, but he began to see in

Grade a man a bit like himself, a man who could take over some of his responsibilities. Some time in 1972 he offered Grade the position of head of light entertainment. This is a crucial position in any television company but particularly so at LWT where, because of its weekend franchise, it is competing head-on with the BBC over the crucial Friday night–Sunday evening period. The BBC concentrated all its resources on winning the Saturday night viewing battle and LWT's head of light entertainment was at the sharp end of this war. It was most unusual for a man with Grade's background to walk into such a position but Bennett seemed to have few doubts that he could do the job.

As this Grade story has been presented, particularly by Michael himself, it was as if the ability to think on his feet which he had demonstrated in Bennett's office was all that was needed to prompt Bennett to offer him this vital job. But charming as the story is, and while Grade's improvisation did play a part, it is inconceivable that Bennett did it merely on this one piece of evidence. Bennett was an impatient man, haunted by fear of a second failure at LWT, his sense of insecurity was well known and although he felt Grade matched his restlessness, he would not have given this job to just anybody, however well he improvised.

But Grade was not just anybody. His ability to improvise may have provided the final clinching argument but, much as Bennett valued instinct, there was more to the Bennett–Grade relationship than that of buyer and seller or even of two people who felt a common bond through their Jewishness.

Michael Grade has always maintained that his family did not open doors for him. In a formal sense this is true. Apart from the *Daily Mirror* job, influence did not secure him positions, but the Bennett–Grade relationship blossomed because of a Grade family network. Cyril Bennett had developed an uncle–nephew relationship with Lew Grade and Bennett in turn saw Michael as a sort of nephew. He found him amusing, likeable, felt he could train him and above all admired his chutzpah, that marvellous Yiddish word that may be translated as a combination of flair and cheek. Bennett himself would illustrate chutzpah with the story of the boy who goes into the witness box after killing both his parents and asks the judge for clemency on the grounds that he is an orphan. He saw some of this quality in Grade and felt confident that with his background he would ensure success or, at the very least, avoid failure.

The offer had come at just the right time for Grade. He had had his fill of the agency by then and was feeling very frustrated; almost the only thing he liked about being an agent was thinking up TV shows for clients and selling them to television companies. He did not, however, immediately seize Bennett's offer. He was worried about how Marsh and Van Thal might react. Both of them were in their sixties and for the younger man to leave without making adequate arrangements might seem like a betrayal. There was also the question of money. Agency work may have been boring, but it was secure and it brought him a lot of money; to accept Bennett's offer meant leaving a position where he ran his own show to become an executive at someone else's behest. As an agent he could have lived comfortably all his life. Did he really want to try the unknown? He asked Bennett for time to sort out his affairs.

Above all, Michael needed time to bring Leslie round. He could not bring himself to break the news to his father. He was much closer to him now than ever before but he still did not feel brave enough to ask him. John Freeman volunteered to break the news to Leslie, who was on holiday in his villa in the south of France. Freeman flew there to meet him, and, almost like a suitor asking a father for his daughter's hand in marriage, asked whether it would be acceptable if LWT approached Michael. Leslie, flattered that a former cabinet minister and ambassador to India and the United States should travel down to see him, readily agreed.

It had taken nine months to arrange the move from the agency to LWT and when the announcement was made, in September 1973, Grade joked that it was like having a baby. It was another three months before he was completely free and at Christmas 1973 Grade joined LWT as Deputy Controller of Programmes (Entertainment). At the age of thirty he was ready to start his television career.

The contrast with his contemporaries could not have been more marked. Most of them had started in television much earlier, usually straight from university in their early twenties, and most of them had announced themselves either as programme makers or presenters. Grade's contemporaries could all tell stories of how hard it had been to make the initial break.

John Birt, who was then executive producer of *Weekend World*, the flagship LWT current affairs programme, had seen his application to the BBC turned down before he was rescued by Granada. Brian Tesler, who was then tipped to become managing director of Thames, had struggled to be accepted by the BBC. Grade had never applied for a job in his life, yet he now held one of the most attractive positions in television and seemed on the sure road to success.

IV

THE ENTREPRENEUR IN THE MIDDLE

He was very bright and very energetic and these seemed
to me to be pretty good qualifications
BRIAN TESLER on appointing Michael Grade Director of
Programmes at LWT

ON THE WEEKEND of 4 November 1976 Michael Grade met with his
LWT colleagues at Selsdon Park Hotel in Croydon. He knew that both
the station and he himself faced a moment of truth. LWT was in crisis
and Grade faced the sack. A growing number of critics, particularly
within the organisation, felt that his light entertainment division was
one of the main causes of LWT's current problems.

As he drove through the crowded streets of south London it seemed
a lot longer than three years since the wonderful publicity that had
greeted his arrival at the station. Then he had been hailed with the sort
of fanfare that heralds a new movie: the introduction to Peter Fiddick's
Guardian article, echoing the start to a Bond film, said, 'The name's
Grade.' Fiddick had spoken approvingly of how this 'Grade of the
Grades' had gone quickly off the mark and was bound to make an
impression on the light entertainment field. But ominously, Grade's
arrival had been marked by the return of *Candid Camera*, which was
being resurrected after having been killed off in 1967 by Lord Hill seeking a nobler path; and in the nearly three years since then Grade's light
entertainment division had produced just three pilot programmes.

The future did look brighter; Grade had planned several good
comedies such as *It'll Be All Right on the Night* (which was to prove a
great LWT standby), *Maggie and Her*, another popular programme,
and *Two's Company*, featuring Donald Sinden and Elaine Stritch and
probably as stylish a comedy as any seen on the BBC. But the present
was dominated by disasters like the wretched situation comedy *Yus,
My Dear*. This haunted LWT and was widely regarded as perhaps the
most embarrassing sitcom ever produced by the station.

Grade's job was not, of course, easy. His remit extended to two and
half days from Friday evening to Sunday night and this meant, as he

had confessed to Fiddick even before he joined, that 'there is nowhere to lose a show, no quiet time to try something out or tuck something that didn't quite make it.' The BBC's strength on Saturday evening, to which it devoted so much of its resources, made his task all the more difficult.

What was really worrying was that he seemed to have no vision about his role. Six months into his job he had felt confident enough to give his first proper interview to *Stage & TV Today* about how he saw it. But dismayingly he had come down firmly on the side of those who said television's duty was to reflect public taste. 'The public taste is there and you've got to find it.' The only pessimism he felt was 'about one's failure to reflect taste'. But even with such a traditional, and dispiriting, view of television, which was in contrast to what people such as John Birt were saying, he was not sure of delivering. He spoke despairingly of how variety on television had come to a full stop, how there was a glut of sitcoms with the same writers doing the same rounds, and of his five years as an agent when after seeing all the summer shows and pantomimes he had been convinced that 'There aren't enough stars to go round; those that there are have been over-exposed beyond belief and supporting artistes are hard to find.'

Grade seemed to have no solutions except the belief, in the great tradition of the agent, that 'the stars will come through; they always do'. Larry Grayson had been around for thirty years before he became a star. 'There are another six Larry Graysons walking about England somewhere and they'll get a break when the time is ripe.' Grade himself could do little to hasten this process. When he did try, it did not come off. When Freddie Starr left to pursue his solo career and Grade relaunched the programme as *Now Who Do You Do?*, the *News of the World* ran a campaign against it. Its readers felt it should be 'kicked off the screen' and eventually Grade, recognising that the series was repeating an old formula, confessed that it 'needed a holiday'.

In the autumn of 1974, when he had presented his first line-up to try to challenge the BBC, he did introduce a relatively new star, David Jason, but the comedy series *The Secret Life of Edgar Biggs* was written by 'over-used writers' and in any event it made no dent in the BBC's dominance. Jason did make a name for himself eventually but on the BBC.

Many years later, after he had moved on to fresh pastures, Grade, analysing this stumbling start to his television career, confessed that he had found it a very alien medium and one that had forced him to discard almost everything that Marsh had taught him. He had had to learn to 'redevelop my critical faculties, and to redefine audiences. I was used to filling halls with two or three thousand people or getting a play into the West End for a year.' Now it could take a year or two to make a programme that lasted barely half an hour, yet attracted an audience of fifteen or twenty million. Nothing had prepared him for such an experience.

All this professional disappointment was masked to an extent by the fame that anyone associated with television gets and which had already made him a minor celebrity – or at least worthy of occasional gossip column attention.

On 15 May 1974 Penny gave birth to their son Jonathan James Grade, a healthy, bouncy 7lb 5oz baby, at the Nuffield Wing of Guy's Hospital. Ten days later it made the diary column of the *Daily Express*, complete with the sort of banality that, uttered by ordinary people, wouldn't go beyond the intimate family circle, but in Grade's case was considered newsworthy. Grade hoped his son would became a super athlete, a great conductor or a brilliant golfer and, of course, very rich. Penny just hoped 'he takes his food'. Celebrities, of course, have such status in our world, but what made this interesting is that three years before, in 1971, when his daughter Alison was born, no gossip columnist bothered to report her birth. Then he was an agent; now he was a man who decided what was shown on the nation's television screens and therefore important.

Publicly, of course, Michael was still happy to be billed as the nephew of Lew, now Sir Lew, having been knighted by Harold Wilson. Bernard, too, had received a knighthood, the two brothers keeping marvellously in step. The *Daily Mail* article about Michael's first autumn schedule at LWT was almost as much about Lew Grade, then involved in making his *Life of Jesus*, as about Michael and, far from resenting it, he seemed to prefer that. He presented such a self-effacing image that the writer thought he was the least publicity-conscious of the Grades and was much taken by his confession of the awe in which he held his father and uncles: 'The nightmare about what they may think of me destroyed any self-confidence I ever had.' Grade spoke of the family in the way that Prince Philip speaks of the Royals as a specialist family business, no different, say, from a grocery business. 'Being a Grade doesn't make you a good businessman. But anyone can be a good businessman if you, like me, were taught by the best in the world: Leslie, Lew and Bernie.' There was something boyish and charming in him that the accompanying photograph enhanced by emphasising his fashionable long hair, sideburns that came down well below his ears, and his wide-rimmed spectacles.

The birth of the two grandchildren not only delighted Leslie but came as something of a relief. He had expected Michael, like Lynda, to start a family soon after his wedding, but as the first few years of marriage went by and no news came of his becoming a grandfather again, he got just a little worried. 'I hope,' he told Olga, 'Michael will be starting a family shortly.'

Olga replied, 'I am not sure. He was always lazy.'

Now the two children had proved that he was not that lazy.

This family happiness should have been completed a few months later when his half-sister Anita got married to Brook Land, a lawyer and son of David Land, a West End impresario. Michael's relationship with Lynda was almost restored. Penny adored her children; Lynda had helped Penny choose the wallpaper in their Dulwich home, and even Olga appeared to have forgiven Lynda. Her new abode at Grosvenor House was quite near one of the antique shops Arthur and Lynda had opened, in Mount Street (the other was in Jermyn Street) and she would often pop in.

Although the Grades were by now very well off, certainly more than enough for Olga not to worry about money, she could not shake off the habits of a lifetime. Grosvenor House charged her two shillings for a telephone call, which she thought was exorbitant, and she would come to Lynda's shop to make calls so that it wouldn't go on her hotel bill. Lynda's shop assistant, a girl called Garland, was not Jewish and every time Olga came she would say to Garland, 'I have brought two olives and don't worry, I have brought one for the *shiksa*.' Lynda would cringe at the mention of the word but could say nothing. Olga thought Garland and Lynda looked a little pale and so every two or three days she would bring a bottle of Ribena. 'We couldn't stand Ribena. We had a kitchenette downstairs and after about six months it was full of Ribena. Then one day she went to spend a penny, discovered the bottles and was most upset.'

The bitterness over Lynda's marriage seemed so much part of history that Lynda even held it up as a model to persuade Audrey that Anita should be allowed to get married to Brook Land. When Audrey protested that Anita was too young, Lynda replied, 'I was this age when I got married to Arthur.' Audrey, who had been very dubious, was convinced. Lynda's daughter Laura was to be bridesmaid and the memory of Lynda dragging Leslie to court seemed very far away indeed. Then one evening, about six weeks before Anita's wedding, as Lynda was cooking dinner, Leslie rang.

He wanted to know why she had not replied to the wedding invitation. Lynda replied, 'When is it that one daughter has to reply to her sister's wedding invitation?'

Leslie said, 'I want a formal reply.'

Lynda, getting increasingly angry, retorted, 'You are not going to get one. I can't talk to you now, the dinner is burning.' With that she rang off.

Leslie phoned back and said, 'It's a joke. You are coming to the wedding?'

'No,' said Lynda. 'I've had enough, I am not coming to the wedding.'

Lynda was now really upset. 'The whole incident was minor but it was the straw that broke the camel's back. There had been so many other little things. Arthur would do little things for Daddy. He would come and say, "I've come to thank you but I don't want to thank you. I want to thank my daughter." Little things like that.' Lynda, distraught, had to drink nearly half a bottle of whisky before she could get to bed.

Leslie, worried that his joke had misfired so badly, rang Michael and late that night Michael rang Arthur. But instead of calming things down this only ended in a shouting match between the two. Such family rows are not unusual, even in the best of families, but they usually end there. The morning leads to calmer heads and a reconciliation, but like wars which can start with trivial incidents this was a prelude to the start, or rather resumption, of the War of the Grades.

Leslie's hamfisted joke showed that the deep fissures created more than a decade earlier by Lynda's marriage had never closed. Some of these obviously related to Leslie's money and Lynda's share of it, although that is something that even now she refuses to talk about. Michael's tone and manner were akin to casually tossing a lighted match on a tinder-dry pile of accumulated grievances and problems. By now Arthur had begun to have a great distaste for the Grades and he saw that evening's quarrel as a final decisive break. He had been willing to put up with the Grades for Lynda's sake. But now that she 'was really fed up with it, I said, that's it.'

So, with that one late-night telephone call, Michael Grade lost his sister for ever. He has never spoken to or seen her since except at Olga's funeral. Lynda and Arthur went to the burial, at the Jewish cemetery at Bushey, which they had some difficulty finding and did so only with directions from two nuns. Lew put the first bit of earth on the grave, then Bernie, then the Rabbi passed the shovel to Michael. After he had put a bit of earth in, he did't know what to do and passed the shovel to Arthur. Lynda and Arthur were not invited back to the house and Michael and Lynda parted as if they were strangers.

The years since then have not brought them any closer. Because they move in adjacent show-business circles they sometimes meet, like ships passing in the night. One of Arthur's and Lynda's closest friends owns the Theatre Royal, Haymarket, which means tickets for first nights. 'We see him, he says hello, I say hello and that is all.'

One day, many years later, as Lynda looked out of her Jermyn Street shop, she saw Michael walk past. Not a flicker of recognition crossed his face. He had, as with his mother and his school, just written her out of his life.

Lynda regrets this. 'I would like to have known Jonathan and Alison. My son Carlton was watching television recently and said, "A very pretty girl flashed on the screen."

' "Why are you telling me?" I asked.

'The only problem is she was Michael's daughter. I know he is my brother. I am very proud of him. He is a very clever fellow. He has done very well for himself. He hasn't done very well with his personal life, although he is very critical of what I might have done with mine. My marriage was given six months. Thirty-two years later ours is the only marriage in our generation that is still intact. Can he say the same about his marriages?'

But if Michael Grade lost his sister, he found a replacement. The final break with Lynda drew him closer to Anita. She was, of course, much younger than Michael, more like a niece than a sister. Indeed, when Anita was a child she was under the impression that Michael was her uncle. Nobody had told her that Leslie had had a previous marriage, Winifred's name being taboo in the Grade household. With Lynda's exile, Anita now rightfully came into her own as his sister, so much so that many of his closest friends and associates have never known that Anita is a half-sister or that Lynda is his real sister. Now when this emerges accidentally it always causes surprise.

Not long ago Lynda sat in her hairdresser's between Esther Rantzen and Gloria Hunniford. They, unaware who she was, leaned across her to speak disparagingly about Michael Grade's penchant for publicity, that he would do anything for a mention in the media. The hairdresser, aware of who Lynda was, grew increasingly fraught. After Lynda had gone, they told Rantzen and Hunniford, much to their embarrassment, that the lady who had been sitting between them was Michael Grade's sister.

This instant replacement of Lynda by Anita may explain why Michael has made no attempt to heal the breach. That he needed a sister to turn to, particularly when he had a crucial decision to make, is clear, but with Anita as a ready substitute he could afford to forget the original. To try to repair relations with Lynda would have meant delving in the fractious past, coping with family aggravation, and that is not his way. His way of dealing with such trouble is to shut it out. Michael Grade has patented his own special method of walking away from aggravation when the pain begins to show. It is the only way he can cope with the attendant emotional problems.

The break with Lynda may also have drawn Michael closer to Lew. As their relationship has developed over the years hardly a day has passed when uncle and nephew have not spoken to each other on the phone. Yet this is richly ironic as Lew is the only one of the family who still retains his ties with Lynda. He gave her away when she got married and the uncle–niece relationship remains intact. But this, far from providing a bridge between the estranged brother and sister, merely marks the family divide.

Now, at Selsdon Park in the autumn of 1976, Grade faced what looked like his moment of truth. Brian Tesler, the managing director who had taken over from John Freeman, while sympathetic to the young man wondered whether Michael would in fact, 'make the grade', and there were others at LWT who felt he should go. Grade was not the only one in trouble; the whole organisation felt disturbed and unhappy and desperate for what *Variety* called a 'skull session in a country hideaway'. LWT needed to bang heads.

Selsdon Park was an appropriate place for such head-banging. Six years earlier the hotel had been made famous by Ted Heath and the Conservatives who, again over a weekend, had formulated their policies for the 1970 election. These projected a hard-nosed right-wing slant and led to the phrase 'The Selsdon Man' entering the political vocabulary (although much of the right-wing rhetoric was to be jettisoned by Heath once he got to power). But it had established the hotel's reputation as an ideal place for brain-storming sessions.

LWT, as David Docherty says, was beset by troubles on three fronts: 'Revenue was depressed, the BBC was rampant and the IBA was unhappy with LWT.' The IBA had give 'reluctant approval' to its Saturday evening schedules for the year but David Glencross, the IBA's Head of Programmes, had written, 'I can't believe that you regard it as a very distinguished shop window for ITV in London.' The approval, he warned, did not mean that in future such schedule would be accepted. In the six months leading up to the Selsdon conference, LWT had not broadcast a single Top Twenty show on the great barometer of television popularity; the BBC kept winning the important weekend battles. Eight of the BBC's fifteen top twenty programmes were broadcast at the weekend and *Time Out* had called for Cyril Bennett to be sacked and replaced by Brian Cowgill, the managing director of BBC television. But although Bennett and Tesler outwardly professed not to be worried, several of the young programme makers working at the station, some of whom had been lured by the attraction of working in London, were feeling very frustrated, most notably John Birt.

Birt had been recruited by Bennett to head current affairs on the strength of his achievements with Granada's *World in Action* and *Nice Times*, a mixture of chat show and parlour games. But at LWT he found there was 'no sense of a community or fraternity of programme makers'. Birt occasionally saw programme makers in the lift, but the way Bennett ran the station meant there were none of the formal structures necessary for views and ideas to be exchanged. When Humphrey Barclay, who headed comedy, arrived at Selsdon he looked round and said, 'I have never had lunch with anybody in this room.'

Birt, in characteristic style, had prepared meticulously for the conference and, as Grade joined his colleagues round the conference table, Birt opened with a paper outlining why LWT was 'making less prestigious programmes' and why 'rather fewer people are watching the programmes now than have done in the past'. This was as direct an attack on Grade as any, although Birt's shaft was aimed not just at him. Birt's call, however, that the BBC was catering to the public's growing taste for intelligent programming and that LWT had to follow this example, made it abundantly clear who was meant to bear the point of the shaft.

Everyone wondered how Grade would respond. The contrast between the two men could not be more evident. It would have been very unlike Grade to copy Birt and present a fully researched and carefully drafted paper; Birt's ways were not his. But while Birt had sounded like a civil servant, Grade had his charm and he disarmed his colleagues by a confession of his failings. Yes, he admitted, only three pilot programmes in three years was disastrous. By the end of the weekend, helped by late-night sessions at the bar, the conference, far from leading to a rupture, had produced a camaraderie, a spirit of what Docherty calls a Camelot, which suffused the organisation for years. Despite the sharp criticism he had suffered at Birt's hands, Grade's ebullience was not affected and he felt the conference had brought the barricades down. Grade realised that most of his colleagues were of the same age group as him and the talk, as much as the drinking afterwards, generated an interest in each other's work which had not existed before.

Some of this was due to the reassuring way Tesler had ended the conference. He refuted Birt's suggestion that LWT suffered from 'hardened programme arteries', or that it was 'suffering from age'. It was more like 'relief', said Tesler. 'It had climbed out of the abyss . . . and it had paused to breathe in pure relief.' But he promised changes and Bennett concluded the conference by proposing a vote of thanks to the sound recordist taping the session. There was a final round of drinks, then, in that jovial, upbeat mood that such conferences can generate, the participants departed. Bennett got into his chauffeur-driven Rolls-Royce and headed for his small flat in Westminster. Grade, feeling relieved and rejuvenated, bid him goodbye, little knowing that within a few hours his life would change. In one of those dramatic, totally unexpected moments, Grade, who had driven to Selsdon two days previously not sure what his future at LWT would be, suddenly found himself at the centre of a different, more challenging world.

Bennett had a house in the country where his estranged wife Shirley and their children lived. He preferred his flat in Westminster, the base for an active social life. In the opinion of some, it was a bit too active, suggesting an inner insecurity which often manifested itself in a need to prove his sexual prowess. That evening he had planned to go out again and told his chauffeur to park the car in the yard of the block of flats. But the chauffeur, for some reason, parked it round the corner where Bennett was unable to see it from the window. Bennett's flat was on the sixth floor, the window happened to be unusually low, the sill was covered with debris which had not been cleared for some time, and as

Bennett tried to peer beyond it to spot his car, he fell and was killed instantly.

The press, learning that Bennett's death had come within hours of the Selsdon conference, saw that as a catalyst. He had not died accidentally, they suggested, but had been pursued by the demons unleashed at Selsdon. Selsdon Man had claimed a victim. The coroner, Dr Thurstone, disagreed. 'There is nothing to suggest that it was a deliberate action and it appears probable that he was looking out of the window of his flat to see whether his car was in the yard.'

For Grade, Bennett's death was like a blow to the stomach. In the early hours of that morning he gathered with Tesler and the others at LWT's headquarters in Kent House, trying to absorb the news. Bennett stories were told, but every now and again the tormenting why, why did it happen? kept being asked. (Russell Harty and Ron Miller, who were away for a sales pitch, just retreated to their hotel room with a bottle of whisky and told Bennett stories all night.)

Grade was the most prominent of Bennett's childen, men who owed their careers to him, but he was not the only one. John Birt was so upset by the death of a man he saw as a father figure that he openly wept at the grave.

As can often happen on such occasions, the untimely death led to resentment and both Grade and Birt focused theirs on Tesler. They felt John Freeman's recruitment of Tesler as his successor had meant that Bennett had been frozen out of the top job. Grade could sense such a mood in the entire organisation and he would later tell the LWT historian that, 'there was an underlying feeling that Brian had been insensitive with Cyril – domineering and aggressive'. For almost two months after Bennett's death, Tesler was seen as a sort of scapegoat. Then Tesler invited Grade, Birt and the other senior executives to his office for beer and sandwiches and let them release their pent-up feelings. It was only then that Grade felt himself rising from the pit of despondency which had settled on him ever since the night of Bennett's death. As Grade and the others spoke of their sense of loss, it cleared the air and made a fresh start possible.

It was only now that the question of succession could be tackled. Press speculation had been rife, with the favourite suggestion being that LWT would poach either Brian Cowgill or Bill Cotton from the BBC. But for the moment Tesler himself took it on, trying to gauge which of the internal candidates might fit the bill. In effect, as John Bromley says, 'Brian Tesler conducted some auditions. When he took over from Cyril he had regular meetings with his four controllers: Head of Sport, Drama, Current Affairs, Light Entertainment. Every time you went to a meeting with him you could see he was looking you over, to see who could do what, who could be the best bloke for this job which is such a wild job.' The two front runners were Grade and Bromley. Bromley accepted that 'As Head of Light Entertainment Grady was in the right position. I know my metier, that is sport. That is my business and I love it. I am not too sure I am strong enough in other areas. But I would have liked to have been asked.'

He wasn't asked. Although Tesler was impressed with Bromley's experience and sound judgement, in the end he was swayed by Grade's instinct and enthusiasm: 'Michael had never produced a programme in his life, which for some people may have been a disadvantage, but for him was an advantage because he was not restricted to one technique or one method. He was interested in everything. He had fascinating views about drama, sport and current affairs. His creative interests ranged more widely across the spectrum than anyone else's in the committee. He was also interested in scheduling – in the effect of juxtaposing programmes, taking advantage of what was on the opposition. Finally, he was very bright and very energetic and these seemed to me to be pretty good qualifications.'

Docherty suggests that Tesler saw Grade as Bennett's double, with all the right qualities but without the dark personal side that had frightened some people. Tesler also saw something of himself in Grade. All three formed part of the Jewish show-business heritage. Indeed, Tesler himself shared some of Bennett's show-biz pizzaz, wearing expensively cut suits, always sporting a suntan as if he had just returned from a holiday, and ever able to divert his listeners with stories of his days as a producer.

Like Grade, Tesler had been a sportscaster, although with the British Forces Broadcasting Services in Trieste while doing his National Service. But other than that his life had been very different. From grammar school he had gone to Oxford where he had gained a First in English but had avoided being sucked into the supercilious student intellectual life by writing popular songs. It was this more than his First that had got him his first BBC job, which was producing *Pet's Parlour*, a show starring the singer and actress Petula Clark. Tesler came to variety from a very different background to that of Grade but mastered it just as well. By the time he had the chance to decide Grade's future, he was a giant of the industry. As early as 1970 he had been featured by Joan Bakewell and Nicholas Garnham in their *The New Priesthood*, a book containing interviews with the men (and they were mostly men, only two women being featured) who were supposed to control television. Tesler was Director of Programmes at Thames then and the franchise had been awarded to the company only on the condition that Tesler got that job.

The great skill Tesler had acquired was in the developing art of scheduling. In newspaper terms this would be equivalent to designing the paper, deciding where each article should be placed, or whether a feature should run on a Wednesday or a Saturday. But in television it is far more vital – it can mean the difference between success and failure and Tesler had become a master scheduler.

An ITV scheduler as opposed to a BBC scheduler has special problems. ITV's advertisers need to know what the programmes are, so ITV schedules are prepared well in advance and sent to the agencies. BBC schedulers can play it very much closer to their chests. Both Donald Baverstock and Michael Peacock, when they were at the BBC, used to wait until the *TV Times* came out, which had an earlier press date than the *Radio Times*, and then change their schedules accordingly.

Fairly early in his career Tesler had learnt how hard the BBC could chase ITV in this art of scheduling. Tesler, despite his feel for variety, could also aim for high culture and, attracted by the success of *Monitor*, the BBC's arts programme, he got Kenneth Tynan to do *Tempo*, which he saw as a swinging *Monitor*. Tesler had only two afternoons at his disposal and since Saturday was out, chose 5.15 p.m. on Sunday (*Monitor* went out on Sunday night). The BBC was so outraged that commercial television should have an arts programme that on the opening afternoon of *Tempo*, it scheduled *Bronco*, the first western it had ever shown on a Sunday afternoon. Tesler had to rejig his schedules to avoid being annihilated and, chased aggressively by the BBC, he finally ended up showing it at 2.15 p.m. on a Sunday afternoon, generally reckoned to be the deadest hour on television.

Such experiences had taught Tesler the art of 'hammocking' programmes, 'so that the inevitably less popular programmes are hammocked in such a way that they catch as many viewers as possible, so that those viewers will give them a chance also.' Tesler sees it as one of the basic ploys of scheduling and a test 'that the schedule works as a whole'. Tesler felt Grade could be coached in this, the most obscure, yet most demanding, of jobs and he saw in Grade's youth a reflection of his own rise in the profession: he had been thirty-two when he was

Right: *Michael Grade's parents, Leslie and Winifred, on their wedding day in January 1940*

Below: *The nine-year-old Michael with father Leslie and elder sister Lynda, Christmas 1952*

Above: *Michael* (at left) *at a rare
meeting with Lynda in 1961, after h
marriage the previous year to Arthur
Davidson* (at right)

Left: *Michael and his first wife,
Penny Levinson, after their wedding
in 1967 at the St John's Wood
Liberal synagogue*

The family trademark: the 26-year-old Michael with his father at the Café Royal in October 1969

Michael's redoubtable grandmother, Olga Winogradsky, meeting Princess Anne

Michael in 1977, having just taken over as Director of Programmes at London Weekend Television

Michael and his second wife, Sarah Lawson, at their London wedding in July 1982

Michael and Sarah soon after the move to Los Angeles in 1982

Michael and Sarah skiing at Meribel in March 1985

Michael and Sarah shortly before the break-up of their marriage in 1989

Michael promoting a 1987 BBC series of French and Saunders, *in one episode of which he appeared as himself with Jennifer Saunders* (at left) *and Dawn French* (at right)

Bill Cotton Jr, Michael's mentor and his managing director at the BBC

Leaving Downing Street with John Birt after meeting the Prime Minister in September 1987

With Sir Richard Attenborough at the November 1987 press conference announcing Grade's appointment as the new chief executive of Channel 4

David Mellor with Michael at a Broadcasting Bill conference in 1990

Michael and his half-sister Anita at the Grosvenor House Hotel for the BAFTA Awards

Michael with Patti Marr at the Queen's Club in June 1991, three months before their separation

made Programme Controller on ABC in 1961. Grade was now thirty-three.

Bromley, despite being miffed that he had not been asked, recognised that Grade was the man for the job. 'Without doubt,' says Bromley, 'the right choice was Michael Grade who was born to the job. Grady is the finest director of programmes I have ever known: great scheduler, great feel for popular programmes, knows his audience. He just has an instinct for it, the gut reactions and feel for good shows. He is a very quick learner and, being a very bright man and prepared to listen, learn and watch, he quickly learnt the tricks, learnt how to hammock shows. You have got to keep the viewer all night. You don't want them to switch over to the other side. He did that superbly.'

On 3 February 1977 Tesler announced that as from 1 May Grade was to become Director of Programmes or, as *Variety* put it, 'Michael Grade in PD chair at LWT', which made it sound like a painful visit to the dentist. Even the gods seemed to approve of the appointment. Just as Tesler was giving the news to the press the storm that had been raging over LWT's South Bank headquarters abated, the clouds parted and a brilliant rainbow curved its way over the ghastly modernistic pile. Could it be, one wag quipped, connected with Lew Grade's new television series, *Moses the Law Giver*? But as Michael Grade was soon to discover, it was easier for his uncle to show Moses parting the sea than it was for him to part the BBC from its audience at weekends.

The three-month delay was very useful for Grade. Tesler provided intensive tutorials to coach him in his new job, going along with him to the powerful Big Five Networks controllers meeting where the major decisions about what would work best on ITV were made. It also enabled Tesler to bed down the new system he had designed for LWT. Bennett had run LWT like a functioning anarchy. Tesler now imposed a structure providing programme controllers to whom the producers reported. Grade stood at the head of these controllers: men like John Bromley (Sport) and Tony Wharmby (Drama). In theory, Grade was Bennett's successor but he did not inherit his title (he was Director of Programmes, not Controller); and the structure Tesler had devised meant he had neither his range of responsibility nor his workload.

It has never been easy in British television for a single ITV company to establish an identity which could in any way match that of the BBC.

Paul Fox tried and failed at Yorkshire. Granada probably did the best, particularly during that purple patch in the early eighties when it produced award-winning, critically acclaimed series such as *Brideshead Revisited* and *The Jewel in the Crown*. LWT had been under special scrutiny ever since its disastrous launch and there were a few murmurs in the organisation about Grade's appointment – after all, what had he achieved? The fact that he had never made programmes was held against him. But with a skilful management of publicity, Grade's appointment, coupled with Tesler's other changes, was now represented as the age of the young at LWT: the next milestone on LWT's long slog to respectability. Rupert Murdoch's money, John Freeman's ambassadorial management style and the curious combination of stagestruck enthusiasm and hardnosed impresario that was Cyril Bennett had brought them back from the edge of the abyss. Now the bright young men were to take them forward. The Press made much of the average age of the executives, which was thirty-five. John Birt, at thirty-two, was adding a Features Department to his Current Affairs empire which included *Weekend World*, *The London Programme* and Ms Janet Street-Porter. And, of course, Grade at thirty-three was the youngest member of the ITV's Big Five Network Programme Controllers and the youngest Director of Programmes in ITV's history.

Newspapers still referred to Michael as 'the most self-effacing and least showbizzy of the Grades'. But even before he moved into Bennett's twelfth-floor office, he showed an impressive ability to handle the press. Exuding confidence, he made much of the young crew he was heading: 'We are a young team and we have a young and fresh way of looking at things.' The press had lapped up his confession of being an indiscriminate viewer of everything from *World of Sport* to *Aquarius*, his assertion that London Weekend was strong in all areas and that there was no BBC programme he envied. At that stage the BBC dominated the Top Twenty and Grade got round that by rather disingenuously distancing himself from the television rat race: 'While it is my job to get the ratings, the Top Twenty is pretty meaningless. I won't shed one tear for the Top Twenty.'

Then, the day before he took over as Director of Programmes, Grade showed the sort of chutzpah that Bennett would have admired. He changed his normal tie to a revolving bow tie and went on in front of a 200-strong television audience to act as a warm-up comedian. When the story leaked out the newspapers were swift to mock him. The 'patter', said the *Mail*, 'lacked timing and did not elicit much laughter.

Perhaps he should take lessons from Uncle Lew who was once the Charleston champion.' But Grade had not performed for the benefit of newspapers or of the world at large, he had a more limited but crucial audience in mind – the LWT staff who made the programme – and they loved it. Grade, in one impromptu show of awful jokes, created a bond that would prove extremely useful. That a man who was now earning £20,000 and was the 'governor' could also be so down to earth made a deep impression on people used to more imperious ways from their masters'

This casual style, the ability to mix with the common herd, was all the more impressive as it contrasted so strikingly with the desire to succeed, the need to prove that, although he was a Grade, he would still have been a success if he had been a Jones or a Smith. He had never been quite as much of a workaholic as Leslie or Lew, who in his memoirs confesses that purgatory for him is sitting on a beach in the south of France away from the telephone doing nothing. (Lew had just one holiday, in Switzerland, which ended when he saw a newspaper report about Maria Callas and *Tosca* that prompted an idea of putting part of it on television.)

But Michael Grade was still a man who felt driven. Some years later, explaining his drive, he would say, 'When you have a lot to live up to like I have, you either have to cop out completely or you go for broke. Some unconscious something has made me want to emulate my father and uncles and I'm not happy unless I'm striving.'

Lew had been known to give interviews at 5.30 in the morning in his office; Michael Grade would come into the office at the more civilised 8.45 a.m. but work still absorbed him in a way that dwarfed almost everything else, in particular his marriage.

It is always difficult to chart the breakdown of a marriage but in retrospect it is clear that Michael's elevation to one of the top jobs in British television also marked the start of the end of his marriage to Penny. Many years later, looking back on that failure, he would say: 'I went through my first marriage with a basically nineteenth-century view of women and I now realise it was an empty relationship.' Olga, he felt, had influenced him too greatly for Penny to change him. His grandmother had instilled in him the idea that the kitchen was a no-man's-land and she 'went mad if she saw a man in the kitchen'. He didn't blame her. 'It wasn't her fault – she grew up in the nineteenth century – but it took me a long time to move into the twentieth century.' By the time he did, Penny had long been left behind.

In an age when militant feminism was on the march, Penny, although not a feminist herself, found it difficult to adjust to a mentality that believed that women should kow-tow to their husbands and just accept the situation. A quality in Michael that she had always admired was his ability to make her laugh, but as he got drawn to his new job she found she hardly saw him.

Penny was often left alone in their sprawling Dulwich home coping with the pressures of bringing up two young children with a husband who might get home one night at eight, one night at midnight, but whenever he did he more often than not then watched television. Grade, by his own admission, was never a great communicator. Penny could share some of his television interest, but not when he watched sport, which he did a fair bit. Then she moved to the bedroom to watch something else on a television set there. 'Other people', he lamented years later, 'could manage the balance. Lew has a marvellous marriage but he is probably more thoughful and considerate than I am.'

It was a familiar recipe for a broken marriage and in late November 1977, less than six months after he had moved to the twelfth floor, Grade moved out of his Dulwich home. A measure of his growing status as a celebrity was that this news was leaked by the usual 'friends' to Nigel Dempster who wittily saw it as a case of 'A Grade finds £20,000 but loses his Penny'. For the Royal Command Performance that year Grade escorted Olga.

Grade was acutely aware that of the young men who now ran LWT he was the only one who had never made a programme. But he made a virtue of this and promoted himself as 'the entrepreneur in the middle': he was responsible for everything that went out from Friday night to Sunday night, but it was the creative people around him who made the programmes while his job was to make sure they got the most advantageous position in the schedules.

Tesler's organisational changes had already made Birt one of the most powerful of the young men reporting to Grade and this period was to see the flowering of what has since been called 'Birtism': an attempt to provide television with a theoretical basis. This basis applied particularly to News and Current Affairs and was first formulated in *The Times* where John Birt and Peter Jay had written an article explaining how television news was obsessed with pictures and talking heads, adequate in human-interest stories, disastrous at trying to explain complex political and social issues. Birt and Jay called this television's 'bias against understanding', a phrase that caught on, although in time it was to be wrapped round Birt's neck like an albatross.

But in that early period, working in a medium which has never been strong on theory – or felt a need for it – this was exciting: a case of theoreticians and philosophers becoming one-eyes kings in a land full of men blind to everything but that vital television question Does it work? Birt was determined to show that his theories worked. London Weekend staff mockingly called it Jay-Birt (the term 'Birtism' was coined many years later), but in News and Current Affairs it generated some exciting and very watchable television, especially with *Weekend World* where, for almoist the first time in television, an attempt was made to examine the serious issues of the day yet to do it entertainingly.

Birt's Features Department also produced other good programmes. LWT had started with Humphrey Burton producing a very individualistic arts programme called *Aquarius*. *Aquarius* was often brilliant, but it depended too much on one man and it did not have the analytical quality that Birt looked for in programmes. In 1977 it was transformed into *The South Bank Show*, presented by Melvyn Bragg. Birt held high hopes for it and Grade pushed hard to make sure it had a full network slot. Arts programmes are television's Cinderellas; in ITV they were regarded with even greater disdain than on the BBC and Grade had to fight to make sure his got accepted. If the initial programme was rather like a first novel attempting to do too much, it soon settled into a format which avoided the twin problems of arts programmes of being patronising while trying to explain, and it went on to win major awards.

The success of *The South Bank Show*, now television's major arts programme, illustrated how Grade saw his role of the entrepreneur in the middle and how well the Grade–Birt team could work. As with the best of partnerships, it was one of great contrast. Birt was definitely not part of the Jewish show-biz world that Grade grew up in. His roots lay in Liverpool, in the Irish Roman Catholicism of that city which combined both the desire to succeed in middle-class England, yet contained, says Docherty, the Church's tradition of self-control, austerity and rigour. At Oxford, where he had gone from a grammar school in Liverpool after taking A levels in Maths and Physics, Birt read engineering and his LWT colleagues saw him as an engineer: a civil servant who coolly calculated each step, working out in great detail what was required before committing himself.

John Bromley provides a wonderful example to illustrate how Birt's mind worked. 'Now if you or I had a tape to send to Norwich we would say to the courier: you have to catch the 1.30 from Liverpool Street, here is the tape, make sure you make the train. John would say, "Hang on a minute, how does he get to Liverpool Street? There are six different ways of getting to Liverpool Street. You could go by cab, by tube, by bus, by cycle, walk or take the car. Now let us find out what is the most economical way of getting there." This is all very well but the problem with Birt's approach is that by the time you have done all that, the 1.30 train has gone and the tape does not get on the air. Grady would not bother with such intricacies but would make sure that the tape got on to the train and on the air.'

Birt would never have even entertained the idea of coming on as a warm-up man in the way Grade had done, and whereas Grade encouraged everyone to believe that his door was always open, Birt, recalls Bromley, 'would get into the lift and would not talk to anybody. He found it difficult to communicate. He would only communicate with senior executives in any department. If the senior executive was on holiday he wouldn't want to talk to junior executives. He would prefer to wait until the senior executive was back from holiday. Grady, in contrast, was very accessible, anybody could talk to him. They were like chalk and cheese, but it worked well when Grady was boss. Grady worked instinctively. Grady would say, "Love that idea, develop it, kill that." He would see the potential of a show immediately: if we can change that, bring that character there, rejig that, and in another ten minutes he has decided. He had this gut feel, flair. Birt wouldn't make a move unless he had everything researched.' To be fair, Birt wasn't all austere scholasticism. He loved football, and the Liverpool football team in particular, almost to distraction. One of his programme innovations was *Blind Date*, fronted by the Liverpudlian Cilla Black, a programme that Lew Grade would have had no quarrel with nor Leslie any problem in placing. But his approach to television was a world removed from Grade's. This became clear as Grade started explaining his television philosophy.

Birt had spoken of the bias against understanding. Now Grade, clearly borrowing that phrase, began to speak about the bias against entertainment at ITV. At the Network Controllers meeting he would often look round the table and realise that he was the only person with a background in entertainment. He hankered for the days of the old ITV which had been built on light entertainment. ITV, he felt, had tried too hard to lose its candy-floss image and had become rather too serious. In a lunchtime talk to the Broadcasting Press Guild in October 1977, he recalled how 'ITV was a pioneer in light entertainment, with programmes like *Dave King*, *The Army Game*, *Please Sir* and *Sunday Night at the London Palladium*. But having achieved such heights it tried to match the success with cerebral television. We've gone from *Spot the Time* and *Beat the Clock* to *Weekend World* and *The Naked Civil Servant* and have neglected entertainment.'

Birt was moved by a mission to explain and a desire to change television. Grade was nourished by nostalgia, the desire to see the re-creation, at least in Light Entertainment, of the old ITV, the ITV that his Uncle Lew had helped create and whose sources in variety had enthralled him ever since he had sat in Row C of the Palladium watching Leslie's shows. Grade did not seem to realise that this ITV had been discredited by the Pilkington Report on Broadcasting which, in turn, had helped launch LWT and prompted some of Birt's thinking. Pilkington had suggested that by pandering to public taste, television can underestimate and debauch it, but then Grade had not really moved away from the ideas expressed six months after becoming Bennett's deputy, when he had spoken of his mission to fulfil public taste, not seek to transform it.

Grade's frustration was all the greater because, while Birt, with his carefully researched programmes and his thesis, provided much of the success in the field that Grade was supposed to know best, Light Entertainment, LWT still seemed to be lacking any truly brilliant ideas. Tony Wharmby's Drama Department did provide Grade with some winners: *Lillie*, the story of Edward VII's mistress Lillie Langtry, *The Gentle Touch*, *The Professionals* and the Agatha Christie mystery *The Seven Dials Mystery*. But none of them was of high artistic merit and there were several major failures such as *Thomas and Sarah*, the follow-up to *Upstairs Downstairs*, and *People Like Us*; all the while the BBC continued to win the Light Entertainment war.

Even when Grade did get a winning formula for a situation comedy it soon ran into trouble. Tesler had suggested that *The Education of Hyman Kaplan*, dealing with America in the thirties and the immigrants adjusting to the new land, might be transferred to the London of the seventies. The result was *Mind Your Language*, which was set in a classroom where immigrants from various countries came to brush up their English. The idea was to use the situation to explore the problems of immigrants settling in this new land. The series proved immensely popular, watched by 18.2 million on 10 February 1978, a LWT record which was not broken until some years later, by *It'll be All Right on the Night*, and then only by a few thousand viewers. It showed you could pander and pander very well to public taste; this was exactly how the public saw immigrants. But even before *Mind Your Language* reached such heights Tesler was getting worried.

The premise, he said in a memo to Grade, 'is no longer credible'. The characters all talked in perfect colloquial English until the lessons started, then they spoke in awful accents; the misuse of the English language, far from being part of the gag, had become the gag. At the Edinburgh Television Festival that autumn Grade was attacked for putting on a series which seemed to stereotype minorities and encourage racism. He decided to discontinue it.

Not being a programme maker, Grade could not devise programmes that might enable ITV to get back its lead. He was particularly unhappy that ITV's structure placed LWT in an impossible situation. Every Monday morning at 10.30 a.m. the Network Controllers of the five major networks, Thames, ATV, Granada, Yorkshire and LWT, met to hammer out the schedule. Grade both loved it and hated it, and hated the effects it had on his scheduling. He would later describe it as 'a wonderful floating poker game where each plays host in turn. We meet at 10.30 a.m. and go on till it's finished. Lots of paper, lots of coffee, lots of smoke. It's like putting a giant jigsaw together. If Granada has a great show I have to convince Granada that the best place to put it is the weekend and Thames have convinced them that the best place is midweek.'

But often this could be a kind of commercial television Buggin's Turn whereby each of the major stations was allocated time on the national network in ratio to its individual advertising income. In contrast, the BBC placed all of its ratings' winners on Saturday night, something the ITV system could not accommodate. Grade had long argued that LWT should, as specialists in weekend programming, be allowed to provide the Saturday night schedule but it was rationed by the demands of other commercial stations. Grade also resented the fact that the BBC had two channels, therefore it could offer more choice to light-entertainment artists and use the second channel as an experimental one to feed to its first, mass-audience channel. But while his calls for ITV 2 were duly reported, he was merely joining a chorus of ITV voices saying the same thing. This still left the problem of how to combat the BBC over the weekend. ITV just could not attract entertainers or at least the stars to put their trust in the commercial channel. So what could Grade do to break the stranglehold the BBC had over the weekend?

The option he came up with would have delighted Leslie or Lew; it was an agent's solution to a television nightmare. If he could not beat the opposition he could pinch their best stars. The BBC at that time started its Saturday night schedule with Bruce Forsyth presenting *The Generation Game*, a game show in which a family – father and daughter, son and mother – competed against a similar family for a host of prizes. Forsyth had presented the show for seven years and created both an extremely popular programme, one that regularly topped the charts, and a phrase that echoed around the country, 'Didn't he do well?', which was the cue for the audience to break into loud applause.

But after seven years presenting the show Forsyth was tired. He saw himself as an all-round entertainer, not just a presenter of a game show, and felt he could not give any more to the show. Like most British artists, he wanted to make it in America and feared that British television was 'eating' him up. Grade was well aware of Forsyth's frustration. Forsyth was one of Bill Marsh's main clients and almost from the moment Grade had jointed LWT he had been talking to Marsh and Forsyth about devising a format that would be quite unique to this country. Finally, on 27 July 1978, he wrote to Marsh about *Bruce's Big Night*: a two-hour programme that, Grade felt, was 'a vehicle, the like of which has never been seen on British television'. He proposed twelve programmes between October and Christmas 1978 and Forsyth was to get £15,000 a programme.

That very week Forsyth had had to close *The Travelling Music Show*, an attempt to transfer *The Generation Game* to the stage, and had lamented, 'I didn't do very well, did I?' Now as the announcement was made he was pictured pouring out champagne and although the press did not know that Forsyth was to get £15,000 per show (the *Daily Mail* speculated that it was £5,000 a show), it could still say 'Didn't he do well after all?'

This bubble of optimism prevailed until the second show was broadcast on 14 October 1978. The first show had attracted 14.5 million viewers: top spot in London, number six in the national charts. But the second week saw the viewers fall to twelve million while Larry Grayson, who had now taken over *The Generation Game* on BBC1, hit the Top Twenty. The bubble had burst. The show, which was meant to be unique, was shown to be a remarkable pot-pourri of game shows, quiz shows, stand-up comics in the shape of Cannon and Ball (then being introduced to television), sitcoms like *Workers* and *The Glums*, topped up by the presence of American stars such as Sammy Davis Jnr and Bette Midler.

The mix was proving too much for the viewers. Grade and David Bell, whose *Stanley Baxter Moving Picture Show* had proved so popular and who had finalised the programme, had worked on the assumpion that if the audience liked one part of the programme they would stay for the entire two hours. This, in the days when remote control was not all that familiar, was sensible. But it proved false.

As the consultants Tape, who had advised on the programme in its early stages and who were called in to do a damage-assessment exercise, pointed out, its choppy style was the main problem. 'There is very little inter-relationship between each section. By darting from one feature to the other in this way, the show lacks any climax, which is the vital ingredient to sustain audience interest, and which is the key to the success of both *The Generation Game* and *3–2–1*.'

What made the BBC success so piquant was that it was led by Grade's mentor, Bill Cotton, who tried to soften the blow for his protégé by pointing out that *Bruce's Big Night* was attacting 10–12 million viewers against the top opposition that he had to offer. 'That is a very good performance – I don't see it as a reason for moving the show.' Curiously, that autumn both BBC and ITV were getting higher viewing figures because more people were watching television. In October 1978 an average of 28.1 million viewers had watched television, surpassing the 26.9 million of October 1977, which was already an historically high total.

The tabloid press, however, which had been so eager to build up the programme, were now only too eager to knock it. 'Hasn't he done badly' was a common theme and, with the *Sun* leading the tabloid press, the show was denounced as a disaster. The alleged libel of Patience Strong did not help. Worse, Bruce Forsyth's private life, his marriage to Anthea Redfern, who was also his co-worker, were raked over in the style the tabloids had begun to specialise in. The *Sun*, in the middle of telling the world all that it never knew about Forsyth and probably never wanted to – Bruce had wooed Anthea with 'jam doughnuts . . . it all started at a leg show' – spoke of 'The rise and fall of Brucie'. The *Daily Star* dug up old photographs of an old flame of Anthea's.

Grade was now, for the first time in his life, subject to mockery. Will nothing, asked the *Daily Mail*, make this man lose his cool? 'While Brucie's programme slides into oblivion watched finally, one suspects, only by Anthea's aunt in Torquay ... merry-hearted, intrepid Mr Grade is still to be seen skipping through the holly chanting "We're completely happy, we're very, very happy, we're more than happy".' The writer stated that if the world was ruled by NUPE and he was caught at Crewe station on a wet November Sunday with the trains on strike and his savings pinched, 'I only pray Lew's dear nephew is at my side to cheer me up!'

Grade had to act and act quickly. He decided that 7.25 p.m. was a bad time for the show to go out. The BBC were soon to show *The Two Ronnies* and Bruce was quickly rescheduled for 6 p.m. which meant starting against not *The Generation Game* and *All Creatures Great and Small*, but *Basil Brush* and *Doctor Who*.

Grade confessed, 'This is the toughest decision I have had to make. Given time we might have just scraped through to get back much of the audience that watched us the first week. I would have been able to do that, had we not taken such a merciless pounding from the tabloids – and not just about the programe but about everything in Bruce and Anthea's private life they could rake up or invent by digging up old photographs, ringing our production secretary at home, the lot. The viewers have been told categorically by the mass press the show is a disaster and they have started to believe it.'

What was more damaging for Grade, the networks also believed the show was a disaster and while Grade denied he was under pressure from the networks (he told Peter Fiddick, 'The network is very happy') in reality they were getting very nervous and began to lean on LWT, which forced Grade to switch. But publicly both Grade and the IBA, in its Annual Review, found it convenient to blame the press.

Bill Grundy in the *Evening Standard* sounded a warning to Grade. Grundy was baffled 'how LWT ever came to put this farrago on'. Surely Grade, with show-biz bred 'into his blood, bone and brain' and Tesler, 'one of the best-polished of television's top brains', should have known better. Probably, Grundy concluded, they were the victims of the BBC curse. If a light entertainer moved channel from BBC to ITV, then he must fail.

Grade had touted the capture of Forsyth as his big idea. Publicly Grade never accepted it had failed and for months afterwards, as late as March 1979, he kept repeating that he was pleased with the show and it all formed part of his aim in television to surprise viewers. But by

December it was clear that the big idea had failed and Grade wrote to Marsh outlining a new contract, which meant returning to a much more conventional format. By then Grade had other things on his mind, including, as we have seen, the fight with the BBC over football, and his personal life was the subject of open newspaper speculation and comment.

The rift with Penny had never healed. Grade had found a new companion, a researcher called Victoria Pushkin, who worked for Dennis Norden's *It'll be All Right on the Night* programme. She was soon to be promoted to producer of the children's programme *Our Show*.

Penny had taken Alison and Jonathan from their Dulwich home back to St John's Wood. She could not quite go back to the BBC as a librarian, so she decided to work for an estate agent. But determined as she was not to feel sorry for herself, she felt deeply about Michael's decision to leave the family home for another woman.

It would be tempting to say that Grade emerged from the traumas of the autumn of 1978 as a stronger man. He certainly was a marked man, at least as far as the BBC was concerned after the *Match of the Day* fiasco. Anger there about Grade's behaviour took a long time to cool and even a year later, at a dinner given by George Howard, then BBC Chairman, in front of several senior figures of ITV, Howard denounced Grade's 'disgraceful conduct' and blamed it for fouling up the usually cosy relationship between ITV and the BBC. Freeman tried to defend Grade but noticed that few ITV executives joined him in defending Grade.

In February 1979 Grade opened the Tenth Manchester Broadcasting Symposium, an occasion for academics who make a study of television to pontificate about its effects and for broadcasters to meet other broadcasters, gossip in the bars and occasionally to say something profound about their programmes, although the profundity rarely lasts longer than the next drink. On this occasion Grade had been asked to open the proceedings, the invitation having come long before the fuss about 'Snatch of the Day', but the BBC were so upset with him that many boycotted the occasion, certainly the London establishment of the BBC. Many ITV figures were also absent from the conference and even Granada, which was only four miles down the road, extended hospitality but sent no programme makers.

Grade was a natural for the conference since its theme was 'Broadcast Entertainment', but he seemed to be stung by the criticism he had generated. Richard Last, in the *Daily Telegraph*, felt he struck 'an embarrassingly defensive posture on behalf of his comedy makers.' 'It's all so much easier for drama,' he quoted Grade as saying. His paper used surveys showing the gulf that separated the 'followers' who watched television, as opposed to the 'opinion leaders': academics, professional classes, communicators. Two-thirds of the 'followers' watched television, only half of the 'leaders', and the 'followers' preferred ITV, while the 'leaders' did not. For Grade this illustrated the major problems faced by makers of light entertainment programmes, particularly comedy shows: it was a 'monumental task' to make programmes that catered to both groups. 'Light entertainment programmes, being the most ageless and sexless of programme categories, once again have an extraordinary job to do in satisfying all components of the total audience', a problem that was made worse by the 'utter inconsistency and unevenness' in the quality of the enormous press coverage devoted to television and to entertainment in particular.

But although Grade felt that the public was ready for a change in light entertainment and it was necessary to avoid 'the lowest common denominator', the problems were the same as he had identified when he had first come to television: 'not enough writing talent to go round'. He was no nearer a solution now, though there was a suggestion that greater choice might come if people had greater prosperity. His loudest lament was that only twelve per cent of British homes had a second television set and this figure was unlikely to change as the second television set would have to be in a bedroom that, in the majority of homes, had no heating.

By the spring of 1979 Grade had turned what might have been disastrous defeats for others into propaganda victories. The Bruce Forsyth disaster was forgotten and the 'Snatch of the Day', or what Grade now referred to as 'The Football Saga', far from being a coup that never was, was now a 'saucy football bid', all part of the 'popular, amusing and cunning' Michael Grade. Or at least that is how Maureen Cleave saw him in the prestigious interview slot in the *Evening Standard*. Although the *Standard* is strictly speaking only an evening paper for Londoners, because it operates in the capital city its articles have as much, if not greater clout than those of some of the national papers.

The interview, accompanied by a picture of Grade holding a football marked LWT, was headlined, 'Fourth Grade: he tried even harder', and revealed between the lines the skilful use Grade could make of the press. He had been describing to Cleave the meetings where the Network Controllers met every Monday to hammer out the schedules. The meetings were dominated by ITV politics and, said Grade, 'for network politics you have to be devious, persuasive and cunning and you just hope the honours even out at the end of the day.' Cleave suggested Mondays sounded a nightmare. No, no, said Grade: Mondays were great, wonderful, he loved Mondays.

Grade mixed charm and shock in good measure to enthral Cleave. When she asked about marriage he shocked her by saying 'Marriage gets in the way of business'; then charmed her by saying he had a strong sense of family and a strong sense of religion; he would not go anywhere but a synagogue on the Jewish Day of Atonement. While like all Grades he was keen on business, he assured her that it was not because of the rewards but for the game itself; he strove not because he lusted after riches but because he liked the chase.

But behind such a confident public façade there was a troubled man, or at least one who was weary – weary of the trouble with the BBC over the football saga. As we have seen, he had requested John Bromley to arrange for them to get away from it all by going to Augusta to see the golf. He had told Cleave how his father used to start work at 6.30 and felt guilty if he enjoyed a round of golf. Now Michael had decided that a week watching golf was the cure he needed.

V

COFFEE WITHOUT CREAM

*It does relate to something quite central, very attractive
and quite dangerous in a sense with the kind of
impresario figure Michael is. You could have meetings,
whether it was lunch or something else, when everything
seemed possible . . . Then you discover it ain't like that*
KENNETH TRODD, drama producer

GRADE'S RETURN FROM AUGUSTA also marked the formal end of his marriage to Penny. On 22 May 1979 she was granted a quickie decree nisi because of his adultery with Victoria Pushkin. This, however, was a relationship that was never likely to last, although it produced a curious moment. One of Victoria's friends used the same hairdresser as Lynda. One day she came up to Lynda and said, 'I know we don't know each other, but would you like to have lunch with me?' Lynda agreed. During the lunch, unaware of Lynda's true relationship with Michael, the friend kept asking questions about him. 'Is he happily married? Is he really close to Penny?' Puzzled, Lynda coped with them as best she could. Weeks later she learned that this woman was a friend of Victoria.

Grade settled into a flat at the Barbican and to those who enquired about his future marriage plans he said, 'I'm obsessed by my work. I always put it first. I can't, therefore, expect anyone to come to terms with that.'

He was much taken by the idea of having the first history of the family written – starting with Olga and ending with himself. He had felt the need for such a history for some time, and he believed it should be done while Olga was still alive. He had mentioned this to John Birt who had suggested Hunter Davis as a writer. Already well known as the biographer of the Beatles, Davies had just the sort of Northern credentials that Birt liked. But Davies was not sure he should do it. He knew nothing of television, show business or the East End – essential elements in the Grades' story – nor was he Jewish. But in the end he was persuaded. Davies saw his book as one that Michael Grade could give his grandchildren and made sure there were no constraints on him.

Clearly, the story of Lew and Bernard would dominate – they had now been ennobled and taken their places in the House of Lords, as Lord Grade of Elstree and Lord Delfont of Stepney. But one of Michael's motives in having the book written was that it would highlight the neglected Grade: Leslie. If, during the first twenty years of his life, his moments with Leslie had been strictly rationed, now he spoke to him five or six times a day; nothing exciting but the sort of trivia – 'What did you think of the Spurs result?' – that indicated the growing intimacy and warmth between them. Leslie had made an attempt to come back into business but he was clearly not fit – some of his business decisions were dubious and lost money – and increasingly he spent time in his villa near St Tropez. Davies did not get to meet him. In the summer of 1979, as Davies was still researching, Leslie was taken so ill that he had to be admitted to hospital in France. For months he lay there, his speech gone, able to communicate only with Scrabble letters. His Jewish faith still meant a lot to him and although in the last few weeks he was barely conscious, the day before Yom Kippur he spelt out the words on his Scrabble board. Just over a week later, on 15 October 1979, he died.

Leslie was buried at the Jewish cemetery in Willesden and his will revealed that he had left just £445 net in Britain. It was said that his main capital, having been left in a family trust, was safe from the penal taxation of the UK but Lynda got nothing and doubts if he left much. The deals he made after his stroke were not always judicious and lost a lot of money. On the evening of Sunday 2 December 1979, Michael returned to where he had been married to Penny, the Liberal Synagogue at St John's Wood, for a memorial service to Leslie.

Leslie may have been the quiet Grade but the service showed how his life had touched the world of variety: Bill Cotton Jnr, Mireille Mathieu, Cliff Richard, David Jacobs, Robert Morley, Frankie Vaughan, Bob Monkhouse, Leslie Crowther and even Ralph Coates and the entire Leyton Orient football team where Leslie had been a director attended the service. In an evening of laughter, Leslie's football days produced the best joke. Once Leyton Orient were losing 6–0 at half-time to Fulham. Leslie insisted they could still win. The final result was a 7–1 defeat. Leslie, the eternal optimist, said, 'There you are, we drew the second half.'

Only one Grade was not there: Lynda. She was in Rome at a

Christie's auction when Anita's brother rang to tell her about Leslie's death. Later she regretted not making it to the memorial. But now Lynda goes to the cemetery 'every high day and holy day. In our custom when you go to visit a grave you leave a stone on the grave, the largest stone you can find. I have never seen another stone, so I don't think Michael or any other member of the family goes. Arthur came with me last year and dug out all the weeds.'

Michael was devastated by his father's death – the more so as theirs had been such a late-blossoming relationship. Now it was nipped in the bud. This probably contributed to Leslie becoming in Michael's mind an even greater hero figure than he might have been if the two had had a more conventional father–son relationship. Michael had never resented his father for not being there when he was a child and has always been faithful to his memory. Whenever he speaks about his father he refers to him in the most flowing terms. More than fifteen years after Leslie's death, he said, 'When I was growing up he was busy building an empire. I never resented that. He was a brilliant man, a great judge of people, and he made his own luck by working hard.'

Davies tried his best to capture all this but despite the loving chronicle of the Grades, particularly that of Olga and her bond with Michael, he gained the impression that Michael did not like the book. Although Michael raised no objections when he read the copy of the manuscript Davies sent him before publication, Davies just had a feeling that he did not like it. 'Perhaps I had not made Leslie as prominent as he should have been. Michael was very close to his dad. He worshipped him and I have this feeling in my head that he wanted me to make him the hero of the story.' But despite massive research Davies could find few people who could make Leslie come alive and he remained in the book, as in life, overshadowed by Lew and Bernie.

If this period was a fallow one personally for Michael, professionally it marked a new departure. So far he had been associated with sports or light entertainment. Now Grade the promoter of arts and drama suddenly emerged. He had coveted BBC's light entertainment and sport; now his designs were on its reputation for being the home of British television drama.

Television has provided a very accessible medium for many British writers and in the sixties and seventies the BBC's *Play for Today* had been a shop window for dramatists like David Mercer to display their works. These writers saw the drama department of the BBC on the fifth floor of Television Centre – anarchic, flowing with ideas that were often impractical, but always receptive to new influences – as their natural home. They rarely looked at commercial television. This was particularly true of the two outstanding dramatists whose television plays were always a major event: Alan Bennett and Dennis Potter.

But in early 1978 Alan Bennett had 'defected' to commercial television by contributing a series of plays to LWT. Not only had LWT attracted Bennett away from the BBC, but it had also got Lindsay Anderson, who had achieved a sort of cult status with his film *If*, to direct Bennett's plays. Anderson was so enchanted by his experience of LWT that on 23 February 1978 he wrote to Grade thanking him 'for the opportunity of working – and it doesn't happen very often – in such a friendly, supportive and stimulating atmosphere as I've found at LWT . . . an extraordinary contrast to the atmosphere I've generally felt in British film studios'. This generated a collective pleasure within the company which Grade was keen to build on. His target now was the other great British television dramatist: Dennis Potter.

Potter was ready to be lured. His major triumph on BBC, *Pennies from Heaven*, had turned sour and both he and his producer, Kenneth Trodd, were upset by the BBC – Trodd has such spasms of doubt every ten years – and were keen to escape what they felt were the artistic and other shackles of the corporation.

Both men had worked for commercial television before, in particular for LWT, and both had their doubts about it. Potter had worked with Humphrey Burton in the early days of LWT and recalled a famous exchange when Burton had said to him, 'I really must draw the line at "bollocks". May I suggest "knackers"?'

Trodd's experience had been just as dispiriting. Kestrel Productions, the directors' collective he formed – an early version of the independent companies that are now such an important feature of television – had worked for LWT in its early chaotic days and Trodd's abiding memory was of being asked by Cyril Bennett to remove the word 'wank' from one of Dennis Potter's scripts. Bennett suggested, 'I would prefer if you say "play with yourself" ', which Trodd found even more obscene.

Nearly a decade had passed since those events, however, and now Trodd's *bête noire* was Alasdair Milne, Controller of BBC 1. He had banned Potter's *Brimstone and Treacle* because, as he would explain in a letter to Trodd, 'I have looked at it again and I can only say it always was diabolical.' Given that the play was about the devil this was, albeit unconsciously, a very revealing remark. Trodd increasingly saw Milne as a 'tragic figure, a man with little imagination who went to the theatre no more willingly than did the Queen'. Milne's time as Controller had seen the BBC embark on the Shakespeare project, but Trodd felt that 'as far as dealing with the culture in the contemporary world was concerned, I don't think he was at home with it, quite out of his depth, which is why he could make that remark about a play dealing with the devil as being diabolic.'

Trodd and Potter had set up their own company, Pennies from Heaven Ltd, and, with early memories of LWT overriden by recent experiences of the BBC, they were once again ready to be courted by the commercial boys. Grade did this expertly. In the spring of 1979 he had lunch with Potter, followed by several meetings with Trodd. This period was, in Trodd's memory, 'really one long honeymoon. He was wooing us, he wanted us. The overtures came from him rather than from us.' Those early meetings were quite euphoric. Trodd recalls: 'It does relate to something quite central, very attractive and quite dangerous in a sense with the kind of impresario figure Michael is. You could have meetings, whether it was lunch or something else, when everything seemed possible. It started off that we would do six films with Dennis Potter. But Michael would say, "Is six enough? You wouldn't like more?" Then I would say, "Of course, Dennis is not the only writer we want to work with," and he would say, "How about nine, ten, twelve?" It is the atmosphere Grade managed to create in that honeymoon period: really giving us all a sense of euphoria, of coming together, a feeling that everything was possible, everything would be wonderful. Probably whenever you create an enterprise it has to be like that. What compounded it in this case was that there was something in Potter which corresponded to Grade.'

Not that Potter has the hospitable, extrovert personality that Grade has – quite the opposite. But, as with Grade, there is, says Trodd, 'an element in Dennis by which he can create an atmosphere, a situation, a feeling of euphoria when everything seems possible. When it comes to reality, and the reality fell to me, things were, inevitably, different.'

Years later Trodd was in Rome when Grade, by then at the BBC, flew in to see the screening of *Mussolini* in which Bob Hoskins played the dictator. 'Michael came for the day and I was told a story that he came to Rome specifically to see the screening. He promised to buy it, went back on the plane and never followed it up. It chimed in very much with what happened with us at LWT.'

What had started with champagne and lunch was to end in tears. Within a year of the lunch with Potter, the Association of Independent Producers was branding Grade a coward and David Docherty has since dubbed the company's partnership with Pennies From Heaven Ltd as the small screen's version of the fiasco that United Artists suffered with Michael Cimino's *Heaven's Gate*. As Trodd said, 'That is when you get to the downside. These deals are done when the feet are off the ground. At some point the feet have to come back to the ground. Then you discover it ain't like that. Not because anybody is trying to mislead you or be a spider on the fly, but that is the effect of it.'

Trodd is hardly an unprejudiced witness and Grade's 'impresario qualities' (promises made over lunch which didn't last beyond the champagne) may not have been the only culprit. But he is right in saying that one of the problems with the deal was that in many ways Grade was doing with Trodd and Potter what he had tried to do with Forsyth and *Match of the Day*, just buying a product that the BBC had produced. 'What he wanted,' says Trodd, 'was to buy what we had been doing at the BBC. He wanted that commodity transported to the ITV screen. Ours was very much a BBC commodity. *Play forToday* was a product of the BBC culture. My view is that, with the partial exception of Granada, ITV companies never do that kind of work naturally; it is never part of their natural habitat. They do it out of the stimulus of rivalry, as when Granada made *The Jewel in the Crown*, or they do it because they are worried about their franchises.'

Indeed, Trodd believes that Grade had a deeper reason for trying to woo them. 'The underlying cynical motive was that LWT had to do the franchise shoring-up and he needed a posh shop-window display. He needed bespoke drama. Bennett had done some, but not much. It was never expressed as boldly as that, but I don't think anyone was under any illusion.'

Perhaps the cynicism was not quite as obvious as that. But the franchise application must have entered Grade's calculation; it did cast its shadow. Franchise applications force commercial companies to search their souls and put on shows which suggest that television is not a licence to print money, as Lord Thomson had suggested. Both Freeman and Tesler were aware of how Michael Peacock and David Frost had created LWT almost from nothing and were just as painfully aware of LWT's tortured history and its past problems with the IBA. Officials there had often made it clear they thought LWT was obsessed with the programmes that were always financially rewarding. Had the franchise renewal taken place in 1973, which had been the original idea, or 1976, when LWT's contract was renewed, LWT might well have lost. Now it was due to be examined in the summer of 1980 and it would have made sense in the year leading up to the application to screen prestigious drama.

A few months after Trodd and Potter had been wooed by Grade, Freeman appointed Jeremy Potter, whom he had known from his own days as editor of the *New Statesman*, as director to co-ordinate the franchise application. Drama was a particular worry. In the spring of 1980 the top management of LWT gathered in Brighton in a skull session similar to that at Selsdon and Tesler fairly laid into the various series produced by Tony Wharmby's drama department: Wharmby never allowed the characters to develop a rhythm and the series never established a long run. Tesler's criticism was so devastating that after the session Wharmby rushed back to his hotel room and threatened to resign. Against such a background Grade was well aware that a shop window of Potter plays would go some way to convincing the IBA that LWT was not all about making money.

The deal Grade secured with Potter and Trodd was that Pennies From Heaven Ltd was not expected to find any money, would retain its independent status, providing directors and producers and following LWT's accountancy and production procedures. The deal seemed ideal for Grade. He was buying Potter, Trodd and their collective dramatic experience and ability, while LWT controlled the money. But this left open the question of what money and how was it to be allocated and accounted, a question that would make this relationship quite the most difficult Grade experienced during his time as Director of Programmes.

This was the moment, as Trodd saw it, when reality came in: 'Lunch is over, Michael Grade has gone back to the twelfth-floor office and is controlling programmes, Dennis is writing plays and I, the whining self-pitying figure, am having to deal with the difference between appearance and reality. That was very much the substance of it.'

Costs are always a difficult thing for a film or television company to determine; control of costs with two organisations involved was something new for British television and in this case the very structure of the deal made it almost impossible. LWT paid the money, it provided the crews who answered to LWT over whom Trodd had no control; also, he did not know how LWT calculated costs and how much their money could buy. Or very simply, he knew what a BBC pound was worth but he did not know what a LWT pound would buy him in terms of drama.

Common sense may suggest this is absurd – a pound is a pound is a pound. But television companies follow their own weird accounting rules and the BBC has such absurd rules that few inside the organisation understand them. For instance, it might seem that if Trodd wanted to make a film with a London BBC crew in Northern Ireland it would be more expensive to film than, say, in Ealing, which is next door to BBC's Television Centre. But in his budget for the film Trodd would have to account for only six of his crew. The rest of the crew would come under what Trodd calls 'the irrationality known as the daily rate. The cameraman and those who don't immediately belong to the drama department are charged at the daily rate and the cost of feeding and watering them is not supposed to be any different than if he were filming in Ealing and they were getting home every night, instead of staying in an expensive hotel in Belfast. The cost of their hotels is met by some other BBC department and would not affect my budget.'

If, however, Trodd wanted to cross the border to film in southern Ireland, everything would change. This entire crew would have to be met from his own film budget, which is what makes filming in southern Ireland almost as expensive as filming in Italy – one of the delicious ironies of BBC accounting. This is the sort of irrationality that grows up over the years and Trodd had learnt to live with it. Just before he left the BBC for LWT he had made a film with Peggy Ashcroft called *Caught on a Train* which, by these weird rules, had cost between £400,000 and £500,000, although it had included going to Germany. Grade looked at these costs and thought Trodd could deliver similar drama for the same money.

Trodd believes that before he got to LWT, 'Michael Grade had done a deal with his financial people. He had said, we are going to make these deals with PFH Ltd and it will cost X. I was never told what the figure was and I didn't encourage them to do that. But it was very clear from the beginning that they had underestimated X.'

Perhaps Trodd should have asked what the X was – it might have avoided a lot of problems. But by the time he moved to LWT the first three Dennis Potter scripts were already completed and his attitude was, 'Let us talk in terms of kind. You want me to make those films on the kind of scale with the kind of values that I had at the BBC. We understand that. You tell me what it will cost you, or don't even tell me, give it to me. We promise we are not going to be extravagant and insist that because we are at LWT we've got to make everything in North Carolina or take twice as long to do it.' Such *laissez faire* in a tight commercial set-up was never going to work out and the very first play, *Rain on the Roof*, signalled the problems.

Like all Potter plays it was supposed to be made on film. But as soon as Trodd got to LWT he was asked would he mind shooting it on tape in a studio? It would cost less, but this suggestion was like a red rag to a bull. Ever since the mid-sixties shooting plays in the studio has been frowned upon by the major playwrights, directors and producers. Plays shot on film on outside locations were considered the only way a proper film-maker could operate. This had been Trodd's ideology for four or five years and 'the whole artistic and creative pressure was to make plays on film. There was no prestige in working in the studio; nobody got any buzz out of it. It was a kind of Cinderella way. You paid your dues that way while graduating to real film-making. There was a kudos from working on films that didn't exist in the studio.'

Trodd has a reputation in the industry for being an aggressive character who speaks his mind, and to be confronted by the question of studio versus film made him doubt the whole enterprise. 'Clearly what had happened was that they had miscalculated about the money required.' Potter had mixed feelings about going on to film. Indeed, some of his early scripts for the BBC had been written with the studio in mind, before Trodd converted him to the virtues of film by saying that otherwise he wouldn't get a quality director. Potter was inclined to compromise, recalls Trodd, 'Why not go quietly and accommodate? I feared that if we compromised it would damage our credibility. There was a lot of excitement about us going to LWT and I feared that if we gave in, we would never make a play on film. If you start that way, that's how it would go on. So I kept them to the deal.'

To be fair to Grade and LWT, they had never met an animal like Trodd before and their drama department was very unlike the BBC's. Its expertise in producing serials like *The Professionals* just could not cope with Trodd. Although *Rain on the Roof*, the first Potter play, was made on budget, *Blade on the Feather* forced wide open the agreement Grade had reached with Potter and Trodd, ending hopes of artistic cooperation.

As luck would have it, wider events had made this a very topical play. Just as Potter was delivering the script, Sir (as he then was) Anthony Blunt was revealed as having spied for the Russians, the fourth man in the infamous spy ring of Philby, Burgess and Maclean. *Blade* was about British spies, with Tom Conti playing a journalist researching a book about the Philby-style figures played by Donald Pleasence and Denholm Elliott. But the making of the drama itself became a story of rumour and intrigue with LWT officials acting as spies as they reported back to Grade on what was happening.

Once Grade had negotiated the deal with PFH Ltd, he was no longer directly involved on a day-to-day basis with the production, busy as he was in his job as Director of Programmes. As the problems escalated he was seen, at least by David Docherty, as caught between the demands of Trodd and the feedback he was getting from his own people – yet keen not to jeopardise the investment he had made. Trodd increasingly saw him as the master puppeteer, sitting in his twelfth-floor office in Kent House, but pulling all the strings.

The actual report that Grade received, however, suggested Trodd was pulling the strings and some bizarre ones at that. It began with the choice of director.

Trodd had wanted Joseph Losey to direct and David Niven and James Mason to be the principal actors in *Blade on the Feather*. It turned out that Niven and Mason had an old feud which meant they would not set foot on the same set; Losey went off to direct something in Austria and Trodd settled on another director, Richard Loncraine.

Loncraine was an odd choice. He had made money patenting a certain kind of toy which had made him a rich man. And his experience of directing films was in advertising. But he was very keen to be a director of feature films and Trodd saw him 'as a person with a lot of talent – not a conventional choice at all, but Dennis and I liked him. London Weekend, as is evident, saw him as a really diabolical villain. They saw me as having brought the villain in. I certainly gave him licence, but by my memory not an enormous amount of licence.' The licence, however, extended to Trodd accepting Loncraine's decision to shoot on the Isle of Wight instead of in Sussex.

On 23 June 1980, a little over a month after the filming had begun, Vic Gardner, who was keeping an eye on the production for LWT, wrote a memo to Grade which spoke of 'the complete absence of producer control over a director acting like a spoilt child'. LWT had never experienced anything like this and Trodd replied by asking whether they wanted a good film or one under budget? 'To a considerable degree the producer chose not to control him. The fact is that we got a very good film. My philosophy is, does anybody say, "You know that film at the Haymarket? I must go and see it, it came in under budget." Nobody ever said it. What they go and see are good films. So if ever I was in a position that Richard wanted something he felt was crucial to the film, I backed him.'

One such item, small as it was, caused the explosion. Loncraine wanted a bridge in a crucial scene where Conti more or less captures Donald Pleasence and is leading him through pouring rain into a summer house in the garden. Loncraine wanted to construct a bridge, a little wooden bridge, but this fell right in the middle of an inter-union dispute at LWT. On the sets there were carpenters who could have made the bridge, but LWT's union agreements meant additional men from London would have to go to the Isle of Wight to build the bridge. Trodd felt, 'If London Weekend had arrangements with those unions, then that was their problem. I wanted a bridge, my director wanted the bridge; it was a simple thing to ask for, they should have solved it. But it became, if you like, a bridge too far. Now if Richard had said, "I want to have an elephant", of course, I would have said "Bugger off."'

The bridge was eventually provided, but by now problems with *Blade on the Feather* were, as Grade said in a letter to Trodd on 24 June, the source of a wave of rumour circulating LWT's headquarters. 'There are all kinds of horror stories about the profligacy and lack of control on the production.' Grade had already asked an independent panel to report to him on how far these stories were true and he stressed to Gardner that it was very important not to generalise. If there was a problem he needed 'a decent case'. Then if there was one 'I can go to bat'. But whatever happened, 'I am very anxious nobody loses sight of the importance of these plays to LWT.' What angered LWT's executives was Loncraine's 'slightly patronising deprecation of LWT's management and procedures sadly characteristic of the unproductive aspect of PFH's attitude.'

Grade finally stepped in when Loncraine asked for a flashback scene which had not been provided for in the budget. Loncraine had originally proposed a flashback sequence that would have required one day and one night's filming in London. This became two nights in Cheshire, a sequence with a train and a day's filming at Dudley Zoo. It would have cost an extra £65,000 but Grade did allow one day's shooting for a flashback at a cost of £30,850. *Blade on the Feather* was eventually completed but to a budget that had gone way over its initial estimate of £309,000.

Cream in My Coffee, the Potter play starring Peggy Ashcroft, also exceeded its budget by £45,000. The plays were at least completed. However, they were but a prelude for the battle over *The Commune*. This was a Jim Allen play set in an Oldham school with a cast of 400 schoolchildren. Trodd had got Roland Joffe, a formidable director and also a man who would not stand any nonsense, to direct the film. It was to be very different from the Potter films that LWT had made. 'Our ambitions for *The Commune*', says Trodd, 'put it in a different league from the costs of the other three.' But as the budget negotiations went on, Trodd gained the impression that London Weekend did not want to do *The Commune*. This revived memories of his earlier experience with Granada when he and Colin Welland had become interested in a play about a textile factory in Leeds, but Granada 'would do anything but produce this play – renew our contracts, get us to do other plays, but not the one we wanted to do.' Trodd actually concluded that, 'This type of work, this working-class epic, would only be done by the BBC.'

The proposed budget for *The Commune* was £780,000, which was clearly going to be too much for Grade. He was getting increasingly strapped for cash. As we shall see, at about this time he had tried to tempt a top BBC executive to LWT but had failed because he did not have enough money. He had also had to announce the end of *Saturday Night People*, LWT's controversial late-night gossip show, with Janet Street-Porter, Russell Harty and Clive James, which had never really worked as the three presenters each tried to elbow the others out. Harty eventually left for the BBC. Grade had denied the programme was cut because of lack of money, but the projections that landed on his desk suggested that, with the recession deepening, advertising revenue might fall. (In the event the recession had little effect on advertising.)

On Monday 30 June, Grade met with Trodd and others from PFH who suggested that it might be possible for LWT to 'loan' to PFH the money for production to begin in the summer of 1980. It was not an idea that appealed to Grade but he told Trodd he would sleep on it. The next day Grade, joined by Potter, met in Grade's office at 11 a.m. Grade quickly said that after a night's thought he had come to the conclusion that he couldn't accept the loan idea. It would not work.

Trodd was outraged and made it clear he considered Grade the villain of the piece. Potter had to intervene, more than once, to try to calm Trodd. 'Keep cool,' he kept saying to Trodd. But Potter, too, threatened Grade about exposing everything to the press and going to the IBA. Eventually it was agreed that the film would be made for £675,000; LWT putting up £500,000 in 1980 and the balance of £175,000 the following year on agreed dates. Grade could live with that as it would ease his cash-flow problem. But by that afternoon the deal was off as PFH found that it could not manage with £675,000.

By Wednesday the deal had been revived. PFH's problem was the additional fees to be paid to artists over a split period of time and, after much discussion, by 3 p.m. that Wednesday, LWT had looked again at the budget and produced £712,000 plus cast additions plus inflation on the £175,000 earmarked for 1981. However, Grade could not budge from £675,000 plus inflation plus cast excess and there seemed no way the difference could be narrowed. Grade met Roland Joffe who offered to reduce salaries – his own and others – but this meant a saving of only £25,000.

Thursday was the crucial day, with Trodd – according to LWT's version of the story – by now making threats. That morning Potter was due to hold a press conference and Trodd told John Howard, who was overseeing the budget for LWT, 'Dennis has a press conference later today about another project. If we are not spending money on the production by that time, this will be the story. He'll spill the beans.'

Everything depended on Grade. That morning he was at a screening. While they waited for him to emerge, Trodd, Joffe, Howard and other LWT executives met. It was agreed that a final budget figure of £692,000 plus inflation plus cast excess could not be reduced. It was clear a decision had to be arrived at by 11.30 a.m. Trodd had told the meeting, 'If this film isn't on by 11.30 this morning, we're out.'

Grade called from his screening and Howard told him what the situation was and that an answer was necessary by 11.30 a.m., otherwise 'we would risk losing a major artist'. 'Michael thought about it a moment, I explained the figurework once more, then he told me to tell Trodd that, on these figures, it's off. I then mentioned, as an aside, that Trodd was making threats. Michael simply repeated, "Tell them it's off."'

When, five minutes later, Howard told Trodd this, he was bewildered and surprised. The next day he returned to Howard's office, denied he had made threats, accused him of being a liar and threatened to sue him for slander if he repeated the accusation.

That afternoon Grade, back in his office, gathered his staff and got them to repeat Trodd's threats. Then he began dictating a letter which condemned Trodd's behaviour and indicated that LWT would find it difficult to work with him again. Grade then set about organising the press release. It was masterly. Even now, many years later, Trodd winces as he recalls the press announcement.

'The press release managed to outsmart PFH and put all the blame on us and our organisation. We tried to make our case, but it was so shrewdly done that anything we said was as if answering the question, "When did you stop beating your wife?" You always had to defend yourself. LWT's press statement was extremely elegant but basically it said we were unprofessional and it was, well, this side of libel. Very, very clever. That had the hand of Michael Grade. It illustrated to me the impresario, cosmetic effect of Michael Grade. I remember that in the process there emerged from London Weekend a department that was so much better at its job than most of the others I dealt with. What was that department? The press department.'

But while such a masterly press campaign worked wonders in London things were different in Oldham. There Joffe, who is a bit like Ken Loach in that he prefers to work with amateurs rather than professional actors, had become part of the school in Oldham. When the schoolchildren heard that *The Commune* was to be cancelled they, encouraged by Joffe, quickly painted Grade as the Scrooge. The children were threatening to march on London egged on, Trodd believes, by Joffe who had described Grade's action as 'graceless and shabby' and was probably organising the coaches for the march at the expense of London Weekend Television!

If the march had taken place it would have undone all that Grade had achieved with his press campaign and he decided to go to Oldham to use his charm and skill to defuse the situation.

A month after the break with PFH Ltd Grade drove to Oldham, spoke to the schoolchildren and did manage to calm things down. But he was lectured by a mother on the virtues of thrift, and had to promise to pay £1,500 to the Oldham Theatre Workshop. The visit to Oldham was initially kept a secret, but when it was revealed, Grade skilfully laid the blame on PFH Ltd and insisted that LWT's budget had not been cut, pointing out that only that week the company had signed up the Goodies.

However, no amount of press releases could repair his relationship with producers and the Association of Independent Producers which was at a very low ebb. AIP roundly condemned his withdrawal from the film as a 'cowardly volte-face'. They also suggested that there might have been a more cynical motive. Potter's three plays had been done; they had given LWT the image it sought before the IBA, so why should it bother with a more complex venture in association with a producer it found very difficult?

Trodd not surprisingly tends to support this allegation. 'By this time I think two things were beginning to happen. For all the mayhem

London Weekend had got three Dennis Potter films which were certainly going to do quite a lot of the window-dressing they needed to do
for their franchise application. And they had by this time, I think,
learnt that their only rival for that particular franchise was one fronted
by Hughie Green. [This became known on 1 May 1980, much to
LWT's delight.] Grade had got what he wanted from our deal.'

But despite the venom and bitterness, Grade did not allow his personal relationship with Trodd to be affected. Indeed, later that year,
when Trodd arranged for a joint preview of the Potter films – one made
at the BBC, the other at LWT – at the Bijou, a small theatre in Wardour
Street, Grade accepted the invitation to attend with alacrity, although
he arrived so late that the theatre was packed and he ended up sitting
on someone's lap.

Also, while this may have confirmed some people's impression that
Grade was good at negotiating projects but not at completing them, it
did have an effect on him. Through it he had become more aware of
drama. When he had started out with Trodd in 1979 he was looking
for quantity, now he had developed a genuine feel for quality.

In November 1980, the two Potter films, *Caught on a Train* and
Cream in My Coffee, both starring Peggy Ashcroft, were shown on
television. The LWT one, *Cream in My Coffee*, was shown on a Sunday
evening and Trodd swung it with the BBC, where he was now back
working, so that the BBC Ashcroft, *Caught on a Train*, was shown on a
Friday. As it happened, that Friday night Grade and Trodd were
supposed to be in Southampton at a conference arranged by the Royal
Television Society at the Polygon Hotel.

'Both Michael and I were supposed to be speaking and this was
billed as a gladiatorial contest. But Michael didn't appear at the conference on the Friday night. I later learnt he had stayed at home and
watched the BBC Ashcroft film on television. This was in the days
before video when if you wanted to watch something you had to stay
in and watch. That impressed me. It showed our experience of working
together had affected him. He had learnt something about quality
drama.'

The following March, the BAFTA Awards were held, as usual, at
the Grosvenor House Hotel. Three of the four films nominated for the
awards were by Trodd; two of the Potter films made for LWT and the
BBC *Caught on a Train*. Trodd was worried by the possibility that the
fourth play, not made by him, might win. A former girlfriend was on
the jury and Trodd 'bribed' her to reveal whether one of his films would

win. She assured him that one of them had and he went to the ceremony sitting at the BBC table; Grade sat at the LWT table. As Trodd collected the award for *Caught on a Train*, Grade, as debonair as ever, came up to him to congratulate him. There was some compensation for Grade as Denholm Elliott got the best actor for *Blade on the Feather*, and *Cream in My Coffee* went on to win Europe's greatest television award, the Prix Italia.

Although his involvement with Trodd grabbed the headlines, it was not the only major project Grade was concerned about. Just five days before the crucial meeting with Trodd, Grade had received a call from Desmond Wilcox. It was as unexpected as it was welcome. Wilcox was head of the BBC's general features department based in Kensington House, whose most successful programme was *That's Life*, presented by his wife Esther Rantzen. Wilcox was skilful and much admired for his work on the screen, but his style of operation – he ran the department as if it were his own personal fiefdom – and his romance with Esther Rantzen made him a constant visitor to the pages of *Private Eye*. Rantzen had started as a secretary in his department, but through diligence and not a little skill had evolved the *That's Life* programme. Wilcox and Rantzen began an affair that led to Wilcox leaving his wife and marrying this much younger woman. Although there was a BBC rule that husband and wife should not be working together, Wilcox and Rantzen did and created what became known in the BBC as 'the Desmond and Esther problem'. BBC insiders joked that the features department was in reality Wilcox Rantzen Enterprises.

The problem had been simmering for some years, with Rantzen's producers unhappy that if they disagreed with her she always had a higher court of appeal in Wilcox. In the summer of 1980, Adam Clapham and Tim Slessor, two senior producers in Wilcox's department, decided that things could not continue as they were. In June 1980, with Wilcox on holiday, these two men went to see Milne, the managing director of BBC television, to discuss the problem. On 25 June, Wilcox returned from holiday and was summoned by Milne to be told that he had mutineers in his ranks who were upset about the way the features department was being run. Wilcox, unhappy about this betrayal, sought a way out; if necessary, out of the BBC.

That very day, soon after he had returned to his office from visiting Milne, Wilcox put through a call to Grade to find out if he would be interested in screening a version of *That's Life*. This, like Bruce Forsyth or *Match of the Day*, was one of the BBC programmes Grade had long coveted. It made his Sunday scheduling all the more difficult and when he had met Wilcox once he had told him that if he ever thought of leaving the BBC, he should give him a ring. Now Grade suggested they have tea at the Grosvenor House (he assured Wilcox that he could speak for the team) and this was later followed by a lunch at the Howard Hotel to which Grade took along his accountant. There was a third meeting to which Wilcox brought his agent, Richard Armitage. The talks proceeded so well that by the time Grade had to journey to Oldham to placate the schoolchildren, Wilcox was planning his department at LWT, personnel for which he would have to recruit from the BBC.

On Monday 21 July, a final clinching meeting was set for the LWT deal. Grade, along with his accountant, journeyed to Wilcox's home in Kew. Wilcox poured out the wine, but no sooner had they started sipping than it became clear that Grade did not have the money to buy the *That's Life* team. A similar series would cost three times as much at LWT as it did for the BBC: Wilcox's salary would go up from his BBC £22,000 to £30,000. Rantzen would get more as well, and so would the rest of the team Wilcox was hoping to tempt. Also, the studio facilities at LWT would be tied up for quite long periods and this would affect other programmes.

Wilcox quietly sensed what Grade was getting at and said it for him. 'I can see you haven't the heart for it now. Shall I let you off the hook? Shall we call it a day?' Grade agreed. However, news of their talks leaked within the BBC. It is not clear how. Michael Leapman's *Last Days of the Beeb* records that Wilcox himself told Milne, although the gossip in Kensington House was that Grade had tipped off his old friend Cotton. Both explanations may be true. In the end it did not matter. Wilcox was, as Leapman says, too dynamic, too charismatic for the BBC of the eighties to be able to accommodate him and on 8 August he was given a Hobson's choice by Milne: 'If you want to stay with the BBC, go to New York. Otherwise, leave.' That night they had dinner at the elegant Belvedere in Holland Park, near Milne's home, and on the back of a menu card Wilcox drafted his resignation.

Grade was also deeply involved in what he would later describe as a 'government-sponsored nervous breakdown' – the commercial television franchise application which comes every decade or so. In 1991, advising a different generation going through a similar experience, Grade would dub it as a 'time for caffeine and Valium, wet towels and word processors'. The word processors were not there but otherwise in that winter of 1980 Grade felt the heat and the pressure just as much, as he helped Freeman, Tesler and the others secure the LWT franchise.

Why Grade and LWT in general should have felt so apprehensive is difficult to say. Hughie Green's challenge was hardly formidable. Probably the tension was caused by the arbitrary nature of the process. In the previous round in 1968, which had led to the creation of LWT, ABC had applied for the north-west franchise and come away with a part of London. D. C. Thomson was sacked as Southern TV contractor but asked to take a stake in what has become Central.

The arbitrariness was heightened by the interview with the IBA at their offices on Brompton Road when Grade and his colleagues faced Lady Plowden, chairman of the IBA. They were meant to supplement the written applications but television folklore maintains that franchises were decided at this stage. A year's work could be undone by a few moments of *viva*. Grade should have been expected to shine at such face-to-face encounters but he was terrified that his top teeth and gums might dry up as they tend to do in situations of extreme nervousness. Tesler's stories of how such interviews worked did little to reassure him.

In 1968 Tesler had been part of the ABC team when they made their pitch. Things were going badly when a Scottish band started playing bagpipes down Brompton Road. The mood lifted and ABC came away with a controlling interest in Thames TV – something it had not even asked for.

John Freeman sought to prepare them by arranging mock interviews where Jeremy Potter played Lady Plowden. As Potter (Lady Plowden) asked Grade a question about Saturday night light entertainment Freeman interposed, 'Before I ask Michael Grade to answer that, may I say that this question really goes to the heart of the issue as far as we are concerned and it is something which has given us much pause for thought. Michael, perhaps you could respond?' At the real interview, when the real life Lady Plowden asked, Freeman intervened again and Grade was, obviously, relieved. 'My goodness, it gave me pause to think – a few precious seconds to remember or make up an answer. More important, it gave me time to lick my top teeth and gums . . . Who knows, if my top lip had stuck to my teeth, Hughie Green TV might have been born.'

There was never any danger of that even if Grade's mouth had run dry. On Sunday 28 December, Tesler and Freeman went back to Brompton Road to receive the sealed envelope which contained the news: they were safe for another eight years beginning on 1 January 1982.

The franchise application had been accompanied by renewed specu-lation about Grade's private life. Contrary to most such gossip, it had a new angle – a possible remarriage. Ever since his divorce from Penny there had been intermittent stories that they might be reconciled, inspiring the odd diary item, particularly in a thin week. In November 1980 there was something more substantial when Michael was observed escorting Penny, his stepmother Audrey and a family friend, Douglas Woolf, to the greyhound races at White City. When photo-graphers moved in to record the scene, Grade, uncharacteristically camera-shy, moved away and left Penny to be photographed between Audrey and Woolf.

By the beginning of December, Dempster in the *Daily Mail* had a picture of them lunching one weekend at the Savoy. Grade had done his share of baby-sitting for Penny and told the *Mail* he was seeing her three times a week.

'Will you remarry?' asked Dempster.

'Anything is possible,' replied Grade. 'We have to take it as it comes.'

How much of this was wishful thinking on Grade's part is difficult to say. What was significant was that the initial comments, which gave legs to the story, came from Michael. Penny was busy trying to become an independent woman, had taken up tennis and had even won a minor tournament. In March 1981, just as Hunter Davies' book on the Grades was about to be published, the *Evening Standard* carried a long piece on Penny and Michael.

Penny revealed herself as a woman who was very different from the one Michael had left. The new Penny Grade was someone Michael Grade had to 'reckon' with. And as for remarriage, Penny said, 'Who knows? In a year, five years, ten – we might.' As it happens, within days of the article appearing Michael Grade met a woman who completely stopped all talk of a possible remarriage – and introduced him to a very different world.

I once asked Michael: what motivates you? He said:
Power, money and success
SARAH LAWSON, second wife

IN MARCH 1981 MICHAEL GRADE gave the *Guardian* Film Lecture at the National Film Theatre. In the audience was Sarah Lawson, a twenty-six-year-old lawyer who had just joined the Curtis Brown agency as a first step in what she hoped would be a career in films and television. She had heard of Grade, knew a little of his activities as Director of Programmes at LWT and had quite looked forward to his lecture.

She came back to the agency somewhat disappointed. She had found him good fun, very entertaining but 'there was an awful lot of words and not much content. An awful lot of waffle, in fact. But it was good waffle.' At the agency she shared an office with Anita Land. Sarah knew Anita was Michael's sister and, as much out of a sense of fun as anything, she told Anita her reaction to her brother's lecture.

Anita, a bubbly extrovert woman with whom Sarah got on well, laughed and replied, 'That sounds like the start of a good relationship. I might get the two of you together. He is looking for a wife but I warn you, you will have to change your religion.'

'Hang on, hang on a minute,' protested Sarah, 'I am not looking for a husband at all. But I would quite like to meet Michael.'

So the first and last blind date that Sarah has ever been on 'was a blind date with Michael', except it wasn't quite blind. Anita and her husband Brook came along and the pair met at the Villa Bianca, a small but highly regarded Italian restaurant in a cobbled pathway just off Hampstead High Street. As Sarah drove up to Hampstead she felt nervous, not sure what she had let herself in for. Michael, in contrast, looked and acted in grand style as if he did this sort of thing every evening.

Some time during the dinner they were joined by an uninvited guest, a friend of Michael's and Anita's. In his hand was a copy of the *Evening Standard* that featured the article discussing Michael and Penny's relationship. In it was a photograph of them taken just as they were leaving the Savoy following their much-discussed lunch and the headline asked: 'What does it take to mend a marriage?' Sarah did not know Michael had been married, let alone that he had two children. The similarity with Leslie's life is almost uncanny. Forty years before, when Leslie was wooing Audrey, she did not know he had been married and had two children until well into their courtship.

If this caused a tiny frisson of anxiety it soon passed. The evening was turning out wonderfully. Not only was he 'lots of fun, attractive, and a good guy', but with effortless command of the social scene, Michael capitivated Sarah through his wonderful sense of humour and above all his ability to generate an almost instantaneous warmth. She laughed at all his jokes and wondered how he managed to be so good at telling them, always getting the punchlines right. Sarah left the Villa Bianca thinking it would be very nice if Michael called. She thought he probably would, although she wasn't sure how much Michael had liked her.

He had liked her a great deal indeed, which was proved the following day when he rang. Michael invited Sarah to two dates, one of which was the premiere of *Chariots of Fire*. Sarah 'did the usual bit of playing relatively hard to get' but the *Chariots* invitation was a very clever thing to use. Although he was not to know that, part of it had been filmed at Sarah's parents' home in Beaconsfield, Hall Barn. Sarah could hardly resist and, having played the obligatory coy woman for a short while, she quickly accepted.

The first visit to the pictures was almost as successful as the first dinner. Soon they started going out together. It seemed the most natural thing in the world. 'There was no doubt, we got on wonderfully well. Love at first sight? I think it probably was.'

Little tokens of affection quickly followed. Sarah introduced Michael to the colour red: red socks and red braces. 'As in any relationship, you buy things for each other. I thought they suited him.' What Sarah did not know was that by introducing Michael to red she was bringing him closer to his uncle Bernie who never left home without having something red, a pullover, handkerchief, anything, near him for luck. He had already picked up the cigar habit from Lew; now the red braces completed the Grade/Delfont circle. They also joined the cigars as the hallmarks of Michael Grade's persona. Sarah's final touch to the new Michael Grade was to get rid of his glasses. He had worn glasses ever since his Stowe days and although they had changed over the years, wide-rimmed in his early LWT days followed for a period of tinted, even dark, glasses, he had never discarded them. Sarah thought they did not do justice to his prominent blue eyes which could seem to be boring into you and which were so captivating. She persuaded him to try contact lenses.

The Michael Grade image was now assuming its contemporary shape.

If Michael Grade was a man in need of a wife, at least according to Anita, then Michael had also come into Sarah's life at just the right time. She may have protested to Anita that she did not need a husband but she was at that most vulnerable stage: getting over a fraught relationship. She had just come out of an affair with Jeff Beck, an investment banker on Wall Street.

Wall Street in the eighties was to produce some remarkable characters, enough to populate a film of that name starring Michael Douglas. Beck, who had a cameo role in the film, was the most remarkable of them all – a cross between Walter Mitty and Jay Gatsby. He told many people, including Anthony Bianco who knew him for several years and eventually wrote his biography, that he had played big-time college football, served in Vietnam with the US Special Forces and was a billionaire several times over with a holding company called Rosebud. None of this was true. Beck had met Sarah in 1980 at a dinner party on a trip to London. The next day Sarah rang him at his hotel. Beck invited her for dinner, and they talked long into the night. Despite their very different backgrounds, they got on well together, and Sarah instinctively liked him. He was invited to spend the weekend at Hall Barn where, alternately fascinated and repelled by the English aristocracy, Beck felt he was being patronised by Lord and Lady Burnham, Sarah's parents. According to his biographer, Bianco, on the Sunday evening he told Sarah, 'Well, Sarah, it was so nice to meet your family and be treated like a fucking moron for a whole weekend. I really don't see any point in seeing each other again. In fact, I think I'll go now. So have a nice life.'

Despite this, and the fact that Sarah found Beck's New York home 'terribly poky', their transatlantic romance began to blossom over time.

How close they came to getting married is debatable. Sarah's memory is that Beck proposed marriage, then things started going wrong. Although Beck claims that marriage never crossed his mind, Sarah's recollections are clear and very much to the contrary. At any rate, he indicated to Sarah the vast gulf between their worlds and was finally put off by the adverse reaction of Sarah's parents, Lord and Lady Burnham. When their critical scrutiny became too intense, Beck hastened back to New York and the relationship withered, although Sarah and he continued to be friends. Sarah was ready for a new adventure, even if Michael was not only totally unlike Jeff but unlike anyone else she had ever met.

'I think I was awed by Michael because he was very important in the profession I was in anyway . . . But as a person I was not in awe of him. I just thought he was lovely.' While Beck may have been put off by her parents, Sarah was not worried that this would be a problem with Michael. True, she could not have been more different from Penny. She was the Hon. Sarah Lawson, the youngest daughter of Lord Burnham, the family that had owned the *Daily Telegraph* and whose barony had been created in 1903 with a family crest depicting Clio (the Muse of history) and Hermes, carrying the motto 'Of Old I Hold'. The Lawsons had originally been Levys, Jewish immigrants just like the Winogradskys, but this was a long time before the Winogradskys had thought of leaving Russia and they had long since been converted to the Church of England. If at the beginning of the relationship Sarah was aware that her background made her very much a part of the traditional English establishment, as it developed she came to realise that Michael could also claim to be part of the establishment, the entertainment establishment, and as a Grade had much to live up to.

It is interesting to note that Michael met Sarah just two months after Olga's death in January 1981, but although Sarah was far from a north London Jewish girl of the type Olga would have approved of, she did not have quite the classic upper-class upbringing. This was partly due to her own temperament, partly because she had been treated by her parents as the son they never had.

Sarah, the youngest of six, had arrived after her mother had already lost three children – two of these were stillborn and one lived for only a week. Her parents had wanted a son and before she was born there was considerable hope that she would be a boy. And despite her actual sex, Sarah was brought up in some ways almost as if she had been a boy after all. 'I dropped out, I rebelled badly against Heathfield, where, when I was there, if anybody got into Oxbridge we had a school holiday. I did thirteen O levels which I suppose is quite a lot but I did not really get beyond O levels. After Heathfield I went to a tutorial college in Oxford to do my A levels and got four. I thought life was an experience, didn't think it was a very interesting thing to get A levels. At nineteen I wanted to read English at Oxford, couldn't, so qualified as a lawyer instead. Then after qualifying I could see where I would be aged fifty.'

That vision frightened Sarah and she set about trying to change her career. Sarah had always produced shows and acted in school plays but she knew little about the world of showbiz. With the thoroughness that has always been her forte, she took herself to the City library to find out, looked up what the director did, what the producer did, what the agent did. 'I decided that the producer was the part for me.' Through lawyer contacts she found Curtis Brown but 'the guy who ran the agency said you don't want to be a producer, you want to be an agent; what's more I am going to offer you a job. You could take over from where I leave off and I am going to train you.' Sometime in 1980, just a few months before she attended the lecture at the National Film Theatre, Sarah began work at Curtis Brown, negotiating contracts for screen writers.

By the time Michael came on the scene she was ready to cope with his very different world. 'When you come from the sort of background I was brought up in you are pretty well trained to be comfortable in a whole load of different situations. In any case because I had dropped out and because I rebelled I did not have the sort of prejudices that people of my background can have. I was lucky to shed them a long time ago.'

Sarah was also intrigued by how different and yet how similar their personalities were. She was quickly aware of Michael's impulsive, instinctive nature. Yet more often than not they would come to the same conclusion to a problem but 'Michael would come to it by a much shorter route. He would arrive very instinctively and then work out how he got there. I'd still be working on how to get there, but we would meet up in the end.'

The courtship started off where the dinner had left off. When Michael took Sarah back to his Barbican flat, she was not much impressed. But then he brought all his talents as an entertainer to play and Sarah let Michael do the wooing. 'Michael fell in love with me far quicker than I fell in love with him. I was probably at the beginning infinitely more reserved with Michael than Michael was with me. I look reserved, I don't think I am wild but I am a very open person. I think I have quite a reserved and sometimes quite stern façade but it is a jolly effective front and that is what it is. In my background you learn all sorts of unwritten rules; you learn to behave and perform in public so you give nothing away. But that is just a front.'

Sarah, in turn, opened Michael's eyes to the modern, independent woman, helping him make the journey from Olga in nineteenth-century Russia to the contemporary woman of the 1980s. Sarah was very different to Penny. She was not a north London Jewish woman, nor was she a wife and mother like Penny. 'That was something I was not good at.' Michael came across to Sarah as the medieval horseman who rides into town and covets the best place, the best castle, the best woman. 'I think it plays a central part in his thinking. That is at the heart. I was the prized conquest. Yes, I think I was. Penny had been the traditional woman, she had not enlarged his circle. I definitely provided Michael with a key to another world, another world in terms of women. Michael told me I was different to most women he had met. That had a lot to do with his upbringing where women have a certain place within society.' She was probably the first independent woman Michael had met.

As a Grade Michael may have been part of the entertainment old guard but Sarah sensed in him a desire to be part of the real English establishment of power, money and influence.

'He wanted to understand and conquer, push out the boundaries, become a comfortable part of an area he felt excluded from. Michael is not the only one to feel that; this desire is part of the family.'

Sarah was made very aware of this when one day she asked him, 'What motivates you?'

'Power, money and success,' replied Michael.

Sarah, in contrast, is motivated more by a desire to express some sort of creativity. His relationship with Sarah meant that he now 'felt completely comfortable in another world. So that he wasn't outside it any longer.'

If Sarah provided the key to something Michael had always coveted, then Michael too opened doors for Sarah. To that extent the relationship had echoes of *Pygmalion*. 'One of Michael's great abilities,' says Sarah, 'is spotting raw talent in others. He was a brilliant agent. He knew that with a bit of moulding he could turn me into something that I wanted to become anyway. He loved the chance to do that. It benefited him in all sorts of gratifying ways. In his world he was Professor Higgins and I was the flower girl.'

Thus matched by their twin needs they started what seemed 'a perfectly good relationship'. And soon enough they were engaged. This showed the Michael Grade style at its most flamboyant, show-business best. One weekend he just turned up at Hall Barn and took Sarah off in his BMW, refusing to tell her where they were heading or what he had planned. It was only when she saw the lights of Elstree airport that she realised what might be in store. Michael had chartered a plane and after they were airborne he revealed that they were going to Bordeaux for dinner: the Hotel Atlantique, a great favourite with both Michael and Sarah. Although it looked like nothing on earth, it had one of the very best restaurants, highly recommended by Michelin, where the seafood was wonderful. Both of them had happy memories of dining there. As the coastline of France approached, Michael, with a flourish, brought out a ring and proposed to Sarah. The scene might have come straight out of a movie produced by Lew.

Unfortunately, at this stage Sarah did not follow the script. 'No,' she said. 'Not with that ring. Could you change the ring?' While Michael looked bewildered, Sarah explained that he had proposed with a ring which was the double of an engagement ring she had been given by Jeff. Despite this slight hiccough and the nerves Sarah experienced as she saw the ring, there was never any doubt that Michael and Sarah were going to get married.

The coincidence of the ring was not the only similarity to Sarah's relationship with Jeff. Quite amazingly, about this time Michael's romance with Sarah turned into a transatlantic one, for the simple reason that Michael now sought his fortunes in America.

One of the problems with British television is that the executives who run it can rarely become really wealthy. Lord Thomson may have seen commercial television as a chance to print money but it provides no scope for a Ted Turner or Bill Paley, a man who can both influence events and make money, to rise. Grade did see himself as the entrepreneur in the middle of the LWT programme makers and his salary of around £30,000 was a very comfortable one in the London of the early eighties, but for a man of his tastes it was nowhere near enough. His was a case of nice job, pity about the money. The salary, says Sarah, 'was the same as his overdraft. He was heavily in debt and there was no way he was going to be out of debt with the sort of job and the sort of salary he could attract in this country.'

It has always surprised Grade's friends to learn he is short of money. The scion of the first family of British entertainment is not meant to go short. But Leslie had left little or nothing for him and, as Sarah says, his tastes always ran ahead of his means. Partly this was due to his generosity but also because 'he knows how to enjoy himself, which means there is a constant flow. He doesn't like things to stand in his way. If he has a good idea he wants to carry it out.' In the past Michael Grade had seen no reason why his desires should be constrained by his bank manager, and now the overdraft was becoming a pressing issue.

While the desire to keep the bank manager happy was a strong motivation, there was also in Grade a deep psychological need. Freeman, who had grown very fond of Grade, sensed in him a desire to go and make his fortune.

'If you are a Grade you have very strong feelings that you have to make good in your own right, and I think that Michael had a very great psychological need to go out into the world and make his fortune or make his name.'

So, in theory, while Grade was at the top of his tree, considered by many, as Sarah puts it, the 'sexiest programme controller' in television, he was strapped for cash and really quite desperate to leave LWT. But where could he go to make more money? LWT could hardly provide much more. True, it held out the prospect of becoming managing director, Tesler having pencilled him in as his successor. That was a few years down the road, however, and Grade did not much relish the idea as it would mean, as Sarah saw it, 'losing that creative edge' that he so valued. He may never have made programmes but as Director of Programmes he was close to them; being managing director would push him further away. Nor could he go to the BBC because, as he told Sarah, 'they have never recruited from ITV at that level, certainly not somebody who was Jewish.' The only alternative was America.

For some time now Grade had been friendly with Jerry Perenchio and Norman Lear. Perenchio, who was known as the smart money man of American entertainment, was an old friend of Lew Grade. They would always meet at the Cannes Film Festival, and Michael had known him since his days as an agent.

A buying mission for LWT to Los Angeles – Grade bought the series idea *Good Times* which got converted into *The Fosters* – had brought him into contact with Norman Lear. Lear was a man who had done much to change the face of American television, often successfully adapting British shows such as *Till Death Us Do Part* and *Steptoe and Son* for American audiences. He had now teamed up with Perenchio to start a television company, Tandem Productions. The company had established a reputation for producing good comedy shows in the US and Lear offered Grade the job of president of the company. Based in Los Angeles it would mean he would have 'creative control' of Tandem – his role was to expand it beyond comedy and into drama, mini-series and movies for television. What is more, he could at last earn real money: a million dollars (then about £550,000) over a two-year contract period. It was an offer he could not refuse: it would wipe out his overdraft, keep his bank manager happy and fulfil that deep psychological need that Freeman had sensed.

Grade was not unique in the desire to go and make money and a name in America. This is something that almost everybody in the British entertainment industry experiences. The tradition of the British entertainer journeying to America has been long established. Generally, says Sarah, 'there are three reasons for going to America. In the entertainment business, if you have made it in the States you have made it; it is much harder in the States, the competition, the backstabbing, the risk-reward. Los Angeles is the entertainment capital of the world and to prove that you could make it in the biggest, most demanding field in the world means a lot.' But usually it is actors or actresses who travel to America; executives crossing the Atlantic are a more recent phenomenon.

Before Grade, the biggest executive name to make the journey to America had been David Puttnam. Puttnam was not sure how long Grade would last. When Grade's appointment became known Puttnam took Sarah out to lunch – he knew her through her work at Curtis Brown, Sarah having sold various things to him – and he warned her, 'He won't last that long but you have got to go and help him out.'

Puttnam, who had made two such journeys to America and in a few years was to take another job at Columbia, was keen that Michael should fully understand what going to America meant. 'You have got to understand, Sarah, you have got to explain this to Michael. In this country it is like fortune's wheel. The press will love you when you are at the bottom and will take you up to the top but as soon as you are at the top they pull you back. It is going to happen to Michael. You have to go away in order to come back.'

Of course, Puttnam going to America was the great British talent providing culture to America. Grade was different. He was the entertainer going to the entertainment capital of the world. But, says Sarah, common to both Puttnam's and Grade's overseas sabbaticals was the fact that 'they were both English, both very big fishes in small ponds here, but very small fishes in quite big ponds over there. When you come back from a big pond you tend to have become a bigger fish over here. You have that extra something that no one else has. David was right, you have to go to America in order to come back.'

Initially, Grade played his offer from America close to his chest. He told Tesler, Freeman and a select few close to him but Tesler, who knew he could not match the American offer, wanted to time the announcement right and it was decided to delay any public disclosure. Amazingly, even in such a gossipy world the secret was well kept. Grade, normally an inveterate gossiper, proved rather good at keeping his own secrets and carried on as if nothing had happened.

Not that he kept away from the press. Indeed, as ever, he courted them. And with television preparing for the start of the autumn season, probably the most important in the television calendar when goodies to attract viewers are unveiled, Grade gave a series of interviews, apparently talking very freely about his plans. The autumn of 1981 promised to be particularly important, with ITV gearing itself for the arrival of Channel 4 (it was to start in November 1982) and coping with the fall-out from the franchise changes made by the IBA.

Grade, in extensive interviews with *Media World* and *Marketing Week*, important trade papers, sketched out his vision of the televisual future. He said little that was startling: he was still fascinated by the 'Saturday night chess game' of trying to match the BBC schedules and still unhappy that as a weekend contractor he had to battle against the best of the BBC programmes without any help, forced to plough a lonely furrow on a Saturday night.

What was more revealing was that both magazines, more than four years after he had succeeded Bennett, were still intrigued by him. He was still the only man in British television to hold such a high position without ever having made a programme and while *Media World* saw this as an enigma, *Marketing Week* concluded he had 'some of the making of a great eccentric.' Richard Addis, the writer, suspected that this may have been 'his secret ambition anyway – it would, after all, fit in well with the eccentricities of his peripatetic youth.' Yet Addis sensed a danger. Grade's eccentricity might have a restricting influence on programmes. He was already exercising 'his own personality quite heavily on the programme makers at LWT. If he becomes a great eccentric, it's going to be difficult for the rest of the team, inside and outside LWT, to keep up.'

Although the press did not divine Grade's American intentions, there was speculation about his future with rumours linking him with Lew. Lew Grade's ATV had very nearly lost its franchise. IBA were upset that ATV had breached parts of its franchise agreement which required it to operate from Birmingham. ATV had never properly followed this proviso, preferring to be based in London, and it required all the charm of managing director Jack Gill and director Lord Windlesham to keep the franchise. However, they had kept only half the franchise, as it were. ACC, the parent company, was ordered to sell forty-nine per cent of its shares to local interests and the ATV name went, being replaced by Central. ACC was already in trouble with the City which, perturbed by the company's profit decline, was calling for Lew Grade's blood. Instead, on 26 August 1981, Grade forced the removal of Gill in a theatrical boardroom coup and there was talk of Grade calling in City headhunters to find a replacement. This, in turn, fed speculation that Michael might be drafted in as managing director. There was never much substance to such rumours and, in any case, Lew Grade was soon to lose his company.

All this kept the press from prying into the real story, which suited Tesler well. Tesler had wanted to keep Grade's move a secret because this was the year for the Royal Television Society convention held every other September at King's College, Cambridge. It always developed into a bash for the television folk, a time to gossip, drink and throw a few ideas around. Tesler was keen to avoid announcing Grade's move until after the convention as he feared that otherwise the talk would be of nothing else. However, during that weekend's television retreat, Tesler went for a walk across King's hallowed turf with Sir Brian Young, head of the IBA, and told him of Grade's move.

He also wanted to make sure the announcement was made after he had the succession sorted. This time there was no need for the prolonged auditions that had preceded Grade's appointment. Tesler's choice was simple: John Birt. What is more, Tesler knew that this would take Birt's mind off a recent disappointment. Birt was then co-ordinating programmes that LWT would offer Channel 4 but he did this with a heavy heart. The previous year he had worked long and hard to apply for the job of chief executive of this new channel, only to find Jeremy Isaccs being preferred. The failure had quite devastated him.

Grade had told Tesler about his decision to go to America just as Birt was going on holiday. So now Tesler and Grade waited for him to return. The day he did so, Grade dropped into his office and asked him to meet him, Tesler and Freeman at six o'clock that evening. Grade could see Birt was taken aback. He met Tesler and Freeman only when he had to make a major financial deal, like hiring Brian Walden, but Grade quickly assured him, 'Don't worry, there's no problem.' Birt took the capacious LWT lifts up to the thirteenth floor where Tesler offered him the job, 'if you think you are up to it'.

On 21 September 1981 Tesler was finally ready to reveal what was quickly dubbed as television's 'best-kept secret', with journalists impressed that he and Grade had kept it for so long. At the press con-ference Grade made all the right noises: 'There's a whole new world of television opening up in America and it is a chance to go and find out for myself what's happening over there. It's a once-in-a-lifetime oppor-tunity. It is, if you like, a gamble and I want to take it.' Asked how much he would earn, he wittily deflected the question by saying it would provide him with 'a living wage'.

Tesler couldn't help commenting that it was 'a living wage for someone who wants to live well'. He confessed that he had not tried to stop Grade: 'To try and keep Michael would have been to match the offer and it's not the sort of match British TV can attempt to make.'

Television pundits may not have been sure of Grade's worth but it is a measure of the rapport Grade had established at LWT that, contrary to Tesler's hopes, his departure and the choice of Birt as his replacement caused anguish and alarm in the organisation. The memory of Grade coming on as a warm-up comedian wearing a revolv-ing bow tie was still bright. In contrast, Birt had established few per-sonal links. He was distrusted and his department actively disliked, being seen, as Tesler had confessed to LWT's Brighton conference, as a 'cross between a cuckoo in the nest and the Incredible Hulk'. Birt, when agreeing to succeed Grade, had told Tesler that his style would be very different. 'As you are well aware, I am a very different person. I don't have Michael's instinct or gut feeling for Saturday night's schedule, but what I don't have by nature, I can acquire by analysis and applied intelligence.' The men and women on the studio floors feared that the replacement of the man of instinct by the man with the calculator would mean the loss of the fun that had characterised LWT.

Clearly, for a man who evoked such feelings, the farewell would have to be special and Bromley, after recovering from his shock at the news of Grade's departure, was determined that he should have a send-off the like of which had never been seen. But he wondered, 'How do you say goodbye to a mate? The Savoy, the Dorchester seemed *passé*. Then the idea came: how about flying to Paris?' But it would not do just to invite him to Paris, it had to come as a surprise and be suddenly sprung on him, just as he had sprung Bruce Forsyth and 'Snatch of the Day' on the BBC.

In a plan that bore some of the hallmarks of Grade's own style, Bromley recruited Sarah and Grade's driver to the cause to help get Michael to Paris almost without his knowing, a sort of friendly kidnap. 'We stuck his dinner jacket, passport and overnight gear in a case and arranged for the chauffeur to drive to the heliport at Battersea but without Grady getting wind of the idea.' On the appointed day Grade was to go to a meeting. The chauffeur was told that on the way back to Kent House he would divert Grade to the heliport. The chauffeur did as he was told but as he drove to Battersea, Grade realised that this was an unfamiliar route and asked, 'Where are you going? Why are we going this way? This is not the way to Kent House.'

'I have got to go this way,' replied the chauffeur.

'Why?' asked Grade, irritated by what he saw as time-wasting. He had better things to do than drive through unfamiliar parts of London. 'Get me back to the office.'

'I have got to go this way, it is nothing to do with me,' the chauffeur insisted. Grade reluctantly gave in and it was only when the car drove up to the heliport and Grade saw Bromley, Birt and Wharmby standing there that he realised something was afoot.

Grade feigned surprise but was delighted and the four got into the helicopter and flew to Heathrow where they boarded the British Airways flight to Paris. On arrival they headed for the Hotel Bristol where Bromley had booked the accommodation. Bromley had planned meticulously but: 'On the way to the Bristol we go past the famous strip show. Birty says he has never seen it. We stop the car and we all troop in, have a drink. Then we go to the Bristol, put on our DJs, and go to a very smart restaurant in the Champs Elyseés. Grady is overcome with emotion: he cannot believe we are in Paris, that we would go to such lengths to bid him goodbye. By eleven o'clock he is pissed. Grady has never been a great drinker and he is emotionally overcome. So we have to put him in the car, drive back to the hotel and put him to bed. But the night is still young and we go back to town to continue with our party while the guest of honour is in a bed in the Hotel Bristol snoring.'

Grade himself was also keen to bid goodbye to the journalists. The industry may not have always agreed that Grade was 'the sexiest controller in TV' but their appreciation of him ranged from Peter Fiddick in the *Guardian*, who had spoken of Grade putting 'a spark into the ITV attitude' to those who just enjoyed his company and his willingness always to talk to them. No other television executive had developed quite such a rapport with the media and Grade held a lunch at the Howard Hotel to thank them for 'their understanding'. The journalists responded by presenting him with a container for his contact lenses.

Maggie Forwood, the TV editor of the *Sun*, and the LWT press office had thought this was too good an occasion to miss and organised a little surprise. This consisted of a certain Sue Scadding, working for the Songbird Kissogram Company and wearing not a lot, to come prancing into the room and plant half a dozen kisses on Grade. Unfortunately, the negative recording the event got ruined and the next day's *Sun*, which had hoped to print the photograph, had to be content with featuring a more familiar picture of Sue on page 3.

The only person, apart from the journalists, who saw Grade with the lipstick marks was John Freeman. Grade had a meeting with him after lunch and Sue had done her kissing with such perfection that it took some time for Grade to remove the lipstick marks; even then traces of it were still on his cheeks when he walked into Freeman's office for his four o'clock appointment.

VII

THE KILLING FIELDS OF LA

We thought Michael would love America and Sarah
would hate it. It turned out the reverse
PAUL FOX

DAVID PUTTNAM HAD TOLD SARAH that Michael had to go to America in order to come back. But in the beginning he had, of course, to come back because of Sarah. She had continued with her job at Curtis Brown, not at all sure she wanted to follow him to America, and this meant an even more exotic transatlantic romance than the one with Jeff Beck, all the way between London and Los Angeles. Occasionally Sarah went halfway to meet Michael and in his early months at Los Angeles they would often meet in New York, in John Heyman's apartment. Heyman, already legendary as Richard Burton and Liz Taylor's agent, had set up a £350m film company in New York, which saw him shuttling between Japan, Los Angeles and London. Both Sarah and Michael found him an incredibly impressive figure, much appreciated his hospitality in New York and decided that, when they married, Heyman should be the best man. Michael had chosen Trevor Chinn as his best man when he married Penny, grateful that Chinn had given him a home; Heyman was now doing something very similar.

Although Grade's move to Los Angeles did nothing to reduce his ardour, Sarah still could not imagine getting married. 'I was very hesitant. It was, I suppose, sixty per cent on his side and forty per cent on mine. But I knew it would change and it would be the right thing to do. It was just that I needed to do a bit more growing up. I was twenty-six at that time and not at all sure about going to Los Angeles.' But then, she reasoned with herself, timing can't always be perfect. In any event, for the first few months of Grade's stay in Los Angeles a decision was postponed because his decree absolute hadn't come through. When this did, in March 1982, Sarah knew 'there was no way I could hedge any longer.'

In his own circle Michael had already established Sarah as his partner and although she didn't really get to know Penny, she and Michael would take the children out. Sarah was much taken by the fact that Jonathan and Alison spent such a lot of time with Anita. 'I thought that was great.' Anita, in effect, was Michael's family, for although he spoke to Lew often he rarely saw him. As the marriage bells began to ring, Michael took Sarah to meet the wider family, introducing her gently to the Grade clan, well aware that this could overwhelm her. It did.

'It did blow me away was when I realised how important the family is in the Jewish sense. That I wasn't prepared for and that, I thought, was wonderful.'

Not that the Jewishness came in the way of the marriage. Anita's forecast that Sarah would have to convert had long been forgotten. Michael had hardly ever mentioned it and both of them knew they were never going to get round to it. But that still left the question of where should they get married. Michael had long conversations with Sarah about reconciling the Jewish and the Christian religions; they analysed their feelings endlessly and debated if they should get married in a church. They both felt they shared the same god, so it didn't matter what the surroundings were, and they both wanted some form of relig-ious ceremony. They could not, of course, marry in a synagogue but, much to Sarah's surprise, Michael felt very comfortable in a church. At Stowe he had sung in the choir, which was about the only happy memory he had of the place, and was quite happy about the idea of getting married in a church.

But which church? The logical choice was Beaconsfield Church, near Sarah's parents' home. That is where the reception was to be held and it made perfect sense. When Sarah and Michael went to see the local vicar they hit a snag they had not even imagined existed. They had thought there might be problems about Michael being Jewish but during the conversation with the vicar it became clear that there was another problem. The vicar said he would give the blessing but he couldn't marry the couple. They would have to marry in the registry office and come along afterwards. The reason? Michael Grade was a divorced man.

Sarah recalls getting 'very cross. I was absolutely furious, very angry, incredibly angry. It didn't make any sense. I went and asked several bishops but none of them could help me. They are prepared to marry murderers but if you have been married before you are lower than murderers.'

Finally, Sarah's father helped out and through his army connections found a church which was broad-minded enough to marry the couple. This was the Guards Chapel, a church which viewed such things as divorce as more the natural order of things, and the wedding was fixed for 11 September 1982.

There was, however, a religious fall-out which nearly caused another rift in the Grade family. Anita wasn't very comfortable about a church wedding and Rita announced that much as she loved her nephew she could not bring herself to go to a church to see him getting married. Michael was aware of the Jewish sensibilities of his family and as they sharpened he took Sarah to see Bernie. They met in Bernie's office and, sitting across the desk from his uncle, he said, 'I'm marrying Sarah. Do you mind that she wants to get married in the Guards Chapel which is truly a church ceremony?' Bernie, who was not religious in that sense and didn't know if Michael was, replied, 'It makes no difference to me.' However, he could not help feeling strange; in his experience, Jewish people who marry out of their faith marry at a registry office or quietly somewhere, as he had done with Carole. But he had always thought Michael was a romantic and his decision to marry in a church seemed to confirm that.

No one appreciated the strangeness of the occasion more than Sir Paul Fox (then plain Mr Fox), who has never been shy about his Jewishness. When he got to the Guards Chapel he could see 'the Jews all to the left and the Gentiles all to the right, very funny.' Later at the reception in Beaconsfield he saw Lew Grade sitting on a sofa next to Sarah's father. 'There they were, my Lords Grade and Burnham; Lew, the Russian Jewish immigrant who had become such a success and next to him Lord Burnham, also descended from Jewish immigrants but so long ago that he was now considered part of the establishment. Both of them sitting side by side and Lew's little legs didn't even reach the floor. It was a very striking scene.'

The wedding itself was just as memorable. Having to shift the ceremony to the Guards Chapel meant that the guests had a long drive to Beaconsfield for the reception. But this was the cue for Michael Grade to demonstrate his showman's style. He arranged for a helicopter to bring him and Sarah back from Beaconsfield to London where they were to spend the night at the Savoy.

'The helicopter,' recalls Sarah, 'landed on the opposite bank. The car did not come to pick us up. Michael had a friend in hospital, so, clutching a couple of champagne bottles, we decided on the spur of the moment to go and see him, then we walked across the bridge to the Savoy.'

Next morning, the newlyweds went to Victoria Station to board the Orent Express to Venice – the perfect honeymoon after what was seen as the perfect wedding.

Sarah had by now overcome her reservations about going to America. After all, she reasoned, she had married Michael, he lived in Los Angeles, how could she get out of that? Yet she had no desire to be a housewife in Los Angeles and neither did Michael want that for her. Luckily, there was no shortage of job offers in America for Sarah, the most enticing being the one from David Puttnam. He wanted Sarah to start a Los Angeles office for Goldcrest so they could have a base in Hollywood.

'It was,' recalls Sarah, 'a crazy idea because I knew nothing about what it takes to open up such an office.'

But Puttnam said the board would decide in 'ten days/two weeks time/ten days/two weeks maximum'. Later, after several such 'ten days maximums' had come and gone, she finally telexed Puttnam and he accepted defeat, telling her to accept another job.

While this mini saga with Puttnam was going on, Spielberg offered Sarah a job on *Indiana Jones and the Temple of Doom*, as production co-ordinator. She turned it down as it was for only one film and was an administrative job, a decision that was to cause her anguish later, particularly over the way in which she made it. She thought she was overqualified for it and when Frank Marshall, who was interviewing her, said, 'You can have the job, it will be a great learning experience,' Sarah had replied, 'I am an agent and a lawyer. The job is for co-ordinating bits of paper; I think I would be over-qualified for it.'

Marshall nodded his head. 'I see your point. For example, I am a producer. At one point in my life I worked behind a bar, and when we went into a set-up where the location was a bar, I knew everything. I was overqualified for that set-up.'

At that moment Sarah wanted the floor to swallow her up. She says now, 'In many ways, it would have been wonderful if I had taken that job.'

Don Taffner, an agent connected with Thames Television, offered Sarah a job running their West Coast office. It was an executive job which held the prospect of her becoming a packager: a producer of drama and comedy, just the thing she wanted, and she accepted with alacrity.

Sarah's job seemed to settle all the problems for the Grades. The conventional London wisdom had been that while Michael would love LA, Sarah might not enjoy it. Now she had a job, the main problem appeared to have been solved: the Grades, all their friends agreed, had made the transition. Certainly the outward signs of success were many and obvious.

They lived in a Spanish-style house, complete with patio and the obligatory swimming pool, in Sierra Alta Way, one of many pretty lanes that climb up the foothills of the Santa Monica mountains from Sunset Boulevard. Not quite Beverley Hills but only a rung or so below it. Grade bought a car appropriate to their new lifestyle, a 1865 Bentley S3 which he and Sarah called Bartholomew – Bartholomew Bentley, becaue it was such a stately old gentleman.

After Sarah joined him, towards the end of 1982, Michael bought himself a huge red Cadillac convertible with a white top which made him seem highly unusual to conservative California and helped him establish a reputation for English eccentricity. The fashion then in LA, certainly among the rich and well known, was to buy BMWs, Mercedes, Jaguars or some other European car. It was considered odd to go about in an American car, but this endeared him all the more to Sarah who thought it was infinitely to Michael's credit. Due to its look and size (it was a huge great boat), the Cadillac was dubbed 'the Mafia staff car' and Michael simply loved driving it to work. Sarah had a Pontiac, making them they only couple in Sierra Alta Way, or possibly the whole of LA, to have two American cars. If this set them apart from the rest, Sarah and Michael did not mind. 'We liked it and that was what counted.'

The couple soon acquired a dog, called Henry, and this seemed to complete the picture of Californian happiness.

Grade also appeared to have settled well into a work routine, starting at Metromedia, a large studio complex where they had so many productions on the go that the stages were used all the time, then moving to the Universal lot with his corporate offices in Century City.

The work Grade was doing was, of course, very different from anything he had done in the UK. Networks in the US cannot do their own programmes. They have to buy them from independent producers. So ABC's drama department, as opposed to ATV's drama department in Birmingham, would be staffed by executives rather than producers, a bit like the commissioning editors for Channel 4. The US networks have only a certain number of hours for their own produced programmes, most of which tend to be news and current affairs. Prime-time drama, television drama and comedy that is net-worked between 8 and 11 p.m. is all bought from studios like the ones Grade was now in charge of. In theory this put Grade in a very heady position and Embassy had, thanks to Lear, a good track record with comedy series such as *Archie Bunker's Place*, *One Day at a Time*, *Square Pegs* and *Gloria*.

Grade had left London with the expectation that if any Englishman could be said to be made for America, then it was Michael Grade. Was he not aggressive, competitive, outgoing, great with the publicity, just the qualities the British associate with Americans? Paul Fox had worried about how well Sarah might cope with America, she was so English.

'We all thought Sarah would not like it, but about Michael we had no doubts. He would love it, we said.' The press echoed such optimism. In December 1981, just as Grade was preparing to leave London, *Broadcast* had predicted that he 'should fit into the Hollywood scene like a pea in a pod. There you need to be competitive, aggressive, and be able to keep your head while others are losing theirs.' No other Englishman matched this supposed American profile and initially he lived up to it: in his first year five of the series he did went on the air.

But this success proved very illusory. Many of the series were cancelled after one season and one of them, *Square Pegs*, left a trail of drugs, chaos and brusied egos. During the shooting a crew member died of heroin addiction and although Grade passed it off as 'a tragic incident to do with his private life' the allegations of drug-taking on the sets could not be brushed aside. Another crew member told the press that cocaine had been regularly snorted, and Merritt Burke, one of the stars of the show, readily agreed that there were drugs on the set but added that drugs were now routine on every Hollywood show.

'On *Square Pegs*,' he said, 'it was certainly no worse – about average.'

Drugs in any case were much more part of the wider social scene than in London and Grade soon learnt to watch for parties where drug-taking was the norm. There were also reports about a fight between Grade and the show's originator, Ann Beatts, and suggestions that the money was being badly managed. The series was cancelled in mid-run.

The writer Bruce Robinson has said, 'There are only two types of animal who roam the Hollywood jungle. Those who do the fucking and those who get fucked. You just try to ensure you're one of the former for they'll shaft you in every orifice they can find, then they'll cut you open and fuck the wound.'

Sarah makes the same point with a more delicate and arresting comparison between London and Los Angeles. 'Michael found he had left the grey television fields of London to arrive in the killing television fields of Los Angeles.'

In London Grade could appear polished, ruthless, a man able to handle anything, but in America a different kind of ruthlessness was required and he couldn't quite cope.

The British may have thought Grade very American but in America the fickleness of the media left him breathless. Later he would joke about the series that was cancelled almost before it was aired. It had been shown on prime time on the East Coast, the instant ratings were poor and by the time prime time came on the West Coast the series had been cancelled. Perhaps the most unsettling thing was that while he was president of Embassy Television, a division of Tandem, he was really once again back to his pre-television days as an agent: more of a seller rather than a buyer.

Many years later, after it was all over, he would confess to the Edinburgh Television Festival that 'basically my job was selling crap to arseholes.'

He particularly resented the 'pitching season' when he was required to sell shows to the networks. It meant doing the rounds of LA: visiting Du Paris Coffee Shop next to CBS studios, Harry's Bar next to ABC and the Commissary near NBC's studios in Burbank, where 'frantic studio executives whose jobs are on the line, neurotic writers who have several mortgages and alimony to pay and agents with huge taxes due, rehearse, rehearse and rehearse.'

The craziness of this American system was summed up for him when he and Alex Haley pitched for a twelve-part series on the rise of modern China.

'We pitched our hearts out, with passion, with all the storyteller's art. Super, colossal, kids' appeal, URST, rooting factors up the kazoo, jeopardy, lust, suspense, action, sex, American heroes, Commie villians, dot, dot, fucking dot. It went like clockwork – we knew we'd done well. The moment of truth. I looked at the web honcho [network boss]. 'Well?' I said, breathless.

'"One question," he replied. "If we're gonna do history, why should we do Chinese history and not American?"'

Grade knew there was no answer to that.

He should have been warned when, even before he had really got down to his job, he had been summoned by Jerry Perenchio and Norman Lear. They both called him into their offices for separate meetings on the same day. Lear, living up to his image as the great guru of American comedy shows, had a simple message: 'I don't care what you do with this company, I don't care how much you spend, as long as we are really proud of the product that we produce. You don't have to do anything, but whatever you do make sure it is good.'

Later the same day, Jerry Perenchio, living up to his reputation as the very smart money man, said, 'I don't care what you do but we need quantity.'

Grade had already accepted the job and he realised there was a totally divided leadership.

To an extent this is the classic conflict in the American film and television industries, between the 'creative men' of the West Coast and the 'money men' of the East. Sunset Boulevard versus Wall Street. There is only one outcome: Wall Street always wins.

Sarah knew once this happened it meant defeat. 'That is not Michael. That is not the way he likes to operate. So when the bottom-line thinkers started to come in there was a very sharp lack of understanding between the way Michael saw the nurturing of talent and how much it cost, and the way the money men in New York saw it. Their thinking was, if you are going to pay $X million to a writer under an overall deal, why aren't they coming up with the goods now? This led to huge ideological differences developing over a period of time and basically it led to Michael's downfall. Michael is no good at protecting his back.'

As the money men made their move, the strategy began to come apart and the company started to have cutbacks which Grade found very distressing. So far he had enjoyed the sunshine, the more open American ways and had revelled in the Californian lifestyle. Now he was exposed to the other side, the much harsher American business world where the high rewards were offset by a ruthless ability suddenly, dramatically, to put people on the streets. And he couldn't quite handle that.

The shattering, disillusioning experience came on Christmas Eve in 1982. About a hundred people were 'pinkslipped', an Americanism for getting the sack. Grade, recalls Sarah, took it very badly. 'He found that very depressing; when they fire somebody in LA they don't do it kindly.'

If the human misery affected him, the sackings also revealed he was powerless. 'He found', says Sarah, 'he couldn't control it, even though he was president of the television company.' It made him realise that in corporate terms the Americans could be killers.

So what had happened to the famous Grade ruthlessness that his London friends and enemies had confidently predicted would make him a natural for Hollywood? It was still there, but it was no match for the Americans.

'Yes,' says Sarah, 'I think he can be ruthless, completely ruthless, but not as ruthless as the Americans. Theirs is a different kind of ruthlessness.'

Perhaps, as Sarah believes, he might have matched their ruthlessness if he had tried, but he 'did not want to take them on at their own game'.

By the summer of 1983 it was clear that Grade did not have much of a future at Embassy. On 23 June 1983 the *Daily Mirror* reported: 'Hollywood Sacks TV Boss Grade: Michael Grade, the former ITV boss who landed a top job in Hollywood, has been sacked. The American firm Embassy Communications fired him because three of his shows were axed by the US networks and he had no replacements to offer.'

The next day the *Mirror* was forced to publish a retraction. It quoted Norman Lear as saying that Grade had not been sacked and that 'we are about to begin negotiations with regard to his long-term future at Embassy. We have no intention of losing him.' As if on cue, other papers picked up this refrain, glad to rubbish the *Mirror*, although in the end the press comments just left everybody confused. It was all neatly summed up in the *Screen International* headline: GRADE: COMING OR GOING?

The fact was, Grade was going and the *Mirror* was nearer the truth than it could have imagined. Very simply, Embassy gave him the option of becoming an independent producer.

Skilful publicity had presented a defeat as a victory, but this still left a dilemma: What should he do? Buoyed by confident London predictions that he would succeed in America, Michael had not anticipated dismissal and was totally unprepared for it.

Here the contrast with David Puttnam is very illuminating. In 1986 Puttnam was lured by Columbia to go to Hollywood for three years with the hope that he would stay longer. Puttnam hated it, describing Hollywood as a despicable place, a place of fear. When after two years he found he could leave, he saw it as a moment of release, the end of a nightmare. But Puttnam had gone into Hollywood without any illusions. He had never liked the American way, decided he wasn't going to play the game the way the Americans did and had constructed his golden parachute to make sure he landed safely. A brilliant marketing man, brilliant at creating an image, he had got the money and the publicity right. He went in with all guns blazing and left in a blaze of press releases and statements, knowing that whatever happened in America he could always come back to England.

Grade had gone to America with no such strategic plan. 'Michael', says Sarah, 'went there with an idea that maybe he would be there for five or six years. He want because he desperately needed the money. There was no alternative for him.' Unlike Puttnam he had no parachute, nowhere where he could safely fall. His instincts, which had worked so well for him in British television, had now got him into a cul-de-sac.

For long hours into the night Sarah and he discussed 'Michael's option', trying to sort out whether he wanted to become an independent producer or what else he wanted to do. It was clear Los Angeles was proving a chastening experience but Grade refused to let this dim his natural optimism. He kept telling Sarah that he could do it and convinced himself and the world that this sacking was a new, glorious opportunity.

Despite this, he could not always hide a certain unease about his very situation in America and friends who visited him were struck by how Grade, who was supposed to take to Hollywood like a pea to a pod, was increasingly looking like an Englishman in exile.

'It was,' says Adrian Metcalfe, who had a meal with him on a visit to Los Angeles, 'like he was serving in an outpost of the Empire. Anyone who came through and spoke English, he wanted to see them. He gave the impression nobody in Hollywood was normal. He was greedy for new, gossip, as if to say, what's going on in the real world? I am stuck in Beverley Hills, what's really going on?'

Grade's pleasure at seeing Metcalfe had been increased by the fact that he presented him with a box of fifty Havana cigars. As the US does not trade with Cuba, it is difficult to get Havanas in the States and Metcalfe had smuggled them into the country. But the present of the cigars was a temporary release. What struck Metcalfe was how unhappy Michael was.

Metcalfe had been surprised when he had heard Grade was going to Los Angeles to make money, because he had always thought he wasn't short of it. Now he found his old friend 'didn't like the way Americans did business. He had had a lot of fun at LWT. He wasn't getting the same buzz in America and the Americans had a very different sense of humour. Michael was not on their wavelength.'

In September 1983 Grade returned to England for a visit and an alternative presented itself. In January of that year, Lord Delfont had carried out a management buy-out to form First Leisure, which comprised the old leisure interests of EMI such as arenas, theatres and the Blackpool pier. Delfont was now seventy-four and the board at First Leisure was getting increasingly worried about his age and the fact that he had no designated successor.

'I was concerned as I wanted a successor. I thought Michael would be a good choice. Quite frankly, I would have liked him to join this company. So when he came to England and saw me I spoke to him. Then I wrote to him in America saying I would like him to join First Leisure with the prospect of taking over from me. He wrote me a very nice letter saying his heart was in television, he wanted to come back to England, but he didn't want to come back to anything other than television.'

Although Michael turned down Bernie it was on that visit to England that a way out of Sunset Boulevard presented itself. And in the best traditions of television soap opera, such a prospect opened up in the bar at King's College, Cambridge where the Royal Television Society was organising its biennial conference. The previous conference had seen Tesler take Sir Brian Young for a walk to inform him that Grade was leaving for America. Now Grade had a long chat with Brian Wenham, BBC's Director of Programmes and seen as a future Director General. This chat would mark the first step towards Michael's return to Britain.

The BBC seemed in a trough of despair. The advent of Channel 4 had removed much of the gloss from BBC 2. Channel 4 was now being seen as the new frontier of British television. Also, BBC 1's ratings had slipped and Granada, with *Brideshead Revisited* and *The Jewel in the Crown*, which was just about to be screened, suggested that the BBC no longer held the monopoly on quality television drama, let alone occupied the intellectual high ground. Wenham bemoaned the state of television and Grade came away with the impression that he was sounding him out for a job.

Wenham, who has the reputation for being an intellectual and a cool, detached man, rather like John Biffen in Mrs Thatcher's Cabinet, does not remember it exactly that way. 'It was like one of the many discussions you have in the bar, moaning about the world in general.' However, he had heard from Melvyn Bragg that Grade was unhappy in Los Angeles and was keen to come home and he thought there might be a job the BBC could offer: perhaps as Head of Entertainment.

Wenham returned to Television Centre and told Cotton, who had alway been keen to get Grade to join the BBC, 'I think Michael would come back. What do you think?'

Cotton was instantly enthusiastic: 'Very good idea.'

So in a very BBC way negotiations were opened up. Over Christmas Wenham wrote to Grade but nothing concrete emerged.

In January Wenham himself came to California, staying, as BBC executives do, at the Bel Air, a picturesque colonial-style hotel whose bar has the reputation for having hatched most of the deals in LA. Wenham, who had come on a mission to buy US series and films, took time off one day to drive out to 1300 Sierra Alta Way and spend a day with Grade. The two men watched a lot of television, sat by the pool – it was not quite warm enough to swim – and discussed the BBC.

But Wenham, with his reputation for delicately fencing with people, gave so little away that at the end of the day Grade was none the wiser. If September and Cambridge had suggested to Grade that Wenham might come up with an offer, then that day by the poolside in LA dimmed the prospect.

However, Wenham had come back from America with the conclusion, recalls Cotton, 'that Michael would like to be here, he had children here, he was always going to be British in America. Wenham was quick enough to realise that he was available if you could pulled the right lever.'

In February Grade was in London and had drinks with Aubrey Singer, managing director of BBC Television, and then dinner with Milne, who was just completing his second year as Director General, Grade arrived for dinner thinking that any offer of a BBC job must have evaporated with Wenham's LA visit. In any event Milne could be expected to be a barrier; the two men had little in common and Milne had expressed himself very strongly about Grade's 'Snatch of the Day'.

But the dinner passed smoothly and both Singer and Milne, much to Grade's surprise, once again raised the question of his joining the BBC. Clearly this was still very much a live issue and had, perhaps, been discussed by the board.

What Grade did not know was that a few weeks before the dinner with Milne an event had taken place which would considerably smooth his path to the BBC. This was when Milne had effectively sacked Singer, showing how ruthless he could be.

The two men are both great enthusiasts of shooting. On Saturday, 7 January 1984, Milne drove Singer to a pheasant shoot near Hungerford in Berkshire. They shot a hundred pheasants, had a good lunch, then on the way back Milne plunged the knife in. He made it clear to Singer that he wanted him to take 'early retirement'. Singer, at fifty-seven, was three years away from the BBC retirement age, and had thought of going early, perhaps a year before he reached sixty. But, as they drove back, Milne, to Singer's utter surprise, said he wanted him to go in a couple of months' time. It was only after he returned to Los Angeles that Grade learnt about Singer's departure, which meant, of course, that Cotton would become managing director of BBC Television. The mentor was now in a very influential position and the stage was being prepared for Grade's entry.

Cotton had the reputation in the BBC for being garrulous and always full of plans for change. Now he made a bold proposal for restructuring the BBC.

'What I wanted to do was have controllers of output rather than controllers of channels. Cut the power of the channel-controller so that controllers of drama, light entertainment, sports would have more access to airtime. What you get in the BBC is two very strong channel-controllers confronted by strong output-controllers. You then get a Mexican stand-off situation where one has the money and the airtime and the other has the talent with which to make the programmes. In the end, if you are not careful, channel-controllers who control money and airtime can play fast and loose over output-controllers' heads and start commissioning on their own accounts. That can be very damaging. Also, while it may work internally, it is confusing to people outside the BBC. I don't think the BBC has the right to confuse people.'

Milne, who had always wanted Cotton as managing director, supported him in his plans. Cotton rang Grade in Los Angeles and offered him the job of Controller of Drama and Entertainment, an important position in the proposed set-up. Grade sensibly replied that he could not quite grasp the intricacies over the phone and the two agreed to discuss it when Cotton visited Los Angeles in March.

Cotton could sense that in America Grade was back as a seller and not enjoying it. He had not been a seller since he had left London Management to join LWT. And much as his family had made selling its own special niche, the failure rate in America was high: one successful show for every thousand ideas.

It meant, as Sarah realised, that 'You have go to be able to cope with rejection. Michael knew himself well enough to know he wasn't going to be happy doing that. So when the BBC opportunity came he saw a way out.'

At their first meeting on 9 March, Grade seemed to grasp the opportunity but hedged an acceptance: he wanted to talk about it with Sarah. He and Cotton agreed to meet again on 13 March, just before Cotton flew back.

During those five days Michael and Sarah thought long and hard about the offer. To an extent, Cotton's plans were similar to the restructuring of drama and current affairs undergone by LWT under John Birt. Grade could see little merit in coming back to a position similar to the one he had held in his early days at LWT. Michael, as Sarah well knew, 'was much more ambitious but it started the discussions.'

When Grade met Cotton on 13 March he told him he 'had thought about it but by and large he wanted to run the channel.' He either wanted the job of being the joint controller of BBC 1 and BBC 2, the new post proposed by Cotton in his plans, or controller of BBC 1 if the system remained unchanged.

Cotton did not see this as a rebuff and left Los Angeles determined to try to secure the job for Grade. If he as an older brother figure could not rescue Michael from Hollywood, who else could?

Cotton's description of how he did it is very simple: 'I managed to convince the Director General who in turn convinced the board and then he came.'

In fact, it was not quite as easy as that. It would take further meetings in London and Los Angeles and almost three months of negotiations.

Cotton was helped in his mission by the state of the BBC. It was losing both popular appeal and intellectual credibility. By early 1984 Granada's *The Jewel in the Crown* had proved a great success. It had engaged the middle and upper classes in anguished nostalgia about India. Against this all the BBC could offer was *The Thorn Birds*, a tawdry Australian series. *The Thorn Birds*, while watched by almost three times as many people as *Jewel*, was condemned as the sort of imported pap the BBC should never show, let alone offer against high-quality home-produced drama. It revived the old debate about cheap American import versus quality home-grown British drama. What gal-vanised the critics was that the cheap imported rubbish was on the public service channel funded by the licence fee while the commercial channel, which could be forgiven for serving pap, was providing the upmarket drama.

On the face of it, this was hardly an argument for recruiting Grade. His expertise was certainly not in producing upmarket drama. But the BBC was also losing the ratings war. Its combined ratings had dropped at times to forty per cent. Anything below forty-five per cent was con-sidered critical. Wenham thought too much fuss was being made about this but, along with the argument about *The Thorn Birds*, it posed a serious problem for the BBC management. Not only were there not enough people watching, but those viewers who did were being forced to watch rubbish. So why should the public pay their licence fee, let alone see it increase as the BBC wanted? Grade might not bring quality but he could improve the ratings and boost morale.

After some thought Milne and Cotton decided that a reorganisation was too difficult; it would open up the question of what to do with Wenham, though they were adamant Grade should come in as Con-troller of BBC 1 in the existing set-up. There was only one problem. BBC 1 already had a controller, Alan Hart, the same Alan Hart who had been Head of Sport when Grade had done his 'Snatch of the Day'. History for poor Hart repeated itself. Grade had outsmarted him then; now he ousted him. Hart learnt about Grade's arrival while on holiday in Greece, as Cotton presented Grade's appointment as the only solu-tion to a crisis. Hart was expendable; Grade was a saviour.

'Here was a man who, as far as I was concerned, had sympathy for and knowledge of the world of popular entertainment and also had a decent understanding of news, current affairs and the arts, yet also an ability to communicate with the producers and understand the audience.'

With the BBC under attack on such a wide front the governors accepted that something drastic was necessary and agreed to suspend the usual process, which would have meant advertising the job, in order to get Grade. William Rees-Mogg (now Lord Rees-Mogg) was then deputy chairman of the governors and while, philosophically, he could not have been more removed from Cotton or Grade he accepted that bringing Grade in would introduce the sort of professionalism that BBC Television needed. Cotton and Milne spoke about Grade's ability as a scheduler and Rees-Mogg agreed that his scheduling skills made this a very good appointment. Cotton rang to tell him the news and in May Grade flew to London to meet Cotton and finalise the details.

There had already been rumours of such an offer and it had to be done with the sort of secrecy that Grade himself had displayed in his television dealings. So, on Thursday, 17 May, Grade and Cotton met in a London hotel room and discussed the fine points of the contract.

Grade still had some doubts. He wanted to be sure he would have freedom of action and control over the budget. And then there was his salary. The best the BBC could offer was £50,000 which meant a cut of nearly £100,000 from what he had been earning in Los Angeles. Later Grade had dinner with Milne and Cotton where, to Grade's surprise, much of the conversation was taken up with the past and the 'Snatch of the Day'. Grade was amused to hear Milne, who had been furious about Grade's competitiveness then, now talk about how it would help the BBC. Grade, however, made it clear to Milne that his coming to London was not cut and dried. Although he was interested he could give a final answer only after he had spoken to Sarah.

Unlike in his marriage to Penny, Michael saw Sarah as a partner. He would get upset if people called her Mrs Grade; she was Sarah Lawson, he would remind them, and he could hardly take such a major decision without her involvement. Grade was aware of the dislocation it would cause. Contrary to what friends in London had predicted, as he increasingly felt an outsider in Hollywood, Sarah had found her feet there, loved it and had truly taken to it. Sarah, as television vice-president of planning and development at Don Taffner, was making ten times what she had in England and moving back to London would affect her career.

Money as ever was important to Grade. He was supporting his two children, which was expensive, and although America had helped him wipe out his debts he was very far from the pot of gold with which he had hoped to return from Los Angeles.

Phone calls with Cotton had established that D-day was 24 May. That was a Thursday and the day the governors were due to meet in London. Cotton would have to know by that morning so that if Grade declined he could present an alternative plan to the governors. That meant, taking the time difference between London and Los Angeles, decision time for the Grades was midnight on 23 May. Grade promised to ring Cotton by then to let him know.

That night Michael and Sarah had dinner with friends, then, still feeling unsettled, took Henry the dog for a walk. Sarah had never seen Michael like this. He was proud of his instincts and ability to decide what he wanted but now he just couldn't make up his mind. As they walked up and down Sierra Alta Way, up the slope away from Sunset Boulevard, then a turn by the semicircle of three houses which ended the lane, the arguments went back and forth: should he go back, or shouldn't he? Just as they turned in to 1300 Sierra Alta Way, a few minutes before midnight, he finally made up his mind. He was going to stay in America and turn down the BBC.

Sarah recalls: 'We had been going to and fro, to and fro, to and fro. This had been going on for three months and he was really in two minds. I wasn't pushing him one way or the other but he could see I was happy in LA. It was also in the very early days of the independent producer. He knew in his heart of hearts he could make a very big success of it but he didn't know for sure. It was very nerve-wracking but in the end he had decided he was going to say no to Bill.'

Michael dialled London and Sarah went next door.

'Somehow for some reason I picked up the book *The Prophet* by Kalil Gibran which I had given to Michael as a present. There was a little marker in it and the page opened up on that wonderful passage: "what profits a man who loves his work", and I realised that we were making a terrible mistake. I knew the best thing for Michael was to love his work but not have the stress of being out here in the cold. He needed to be back in the warmth and the BBC would give him that.'

Sarah rushed back next door and almost shouted, 'Michael, you've got to go back! You've got to go back.'

Michael had already got through to Bill but Sarah snatched the phone away from him and said, 'Bill, I am terribly sorry but we have got to talk for a second.' She put the phone down and they talked. As Sarah urged him to accept the BBC, a huge sense of relief swept over Michael and in the end he offered little resistance as Sarah presented the argument for changing his mind. A few minutes ago he had seemed quite settled in LA; now he agreed he would go back.

'I think Michael was enormously relieved, hugely relieved. It was absolutely the right decision for him. In times of stress he is a nail-biter. I think he would have bitten his nails down to the quick if he had stayed there.'

A few minutes later Grade called Cotton again and told him he would accept. Cotton said, in a line overused but appropriate, 'I knew that it was an offer you couldn't refuse.'

As he put the phone down Michael told Sarah, 'It is the first time the BBC have taken in somebody from outside at this level, and never before has he been Jewish.' It made Sarah realise how much the appointment meant to Michael and why it was the right one for him.

Michael was free from the nightmare America was becoming. The one Englishman who was seen by almost everyone in England as the most American had now found a way out of America.

But if Michael was freed, there was a price for that and Sarah now feels she has paid it. The decision marked the turning point of their marriage. 'No, it wasn't the right decision for me. But then in a marriage there is give and take. I knew I was sacrificing myself. If Michael had stayed on as independent producer he could have conquered the world. He is incredibly creative. And yes, we would have stayed together. It was a turning point.'

However, all this came much later. In keeping with the Grade story, his arrival at the BBC, instead of being seen as a release from the coldness of Hollywood into the comforting warmth of the BBC, was presented as a triumphal return: a long line of unbroken success which had seen him go from the *Daily Mirror* to being an agent, then on to LWT and now, via Hollywood, to Television Centre.

Cotton presented Grade as having learnt new things in America and done very well there; the BBC trumpeted its capture of Grade and it was only much later that Grade confessed how much he had loathed Hollywood. This is when he told the Edinburgh Film Festival that he was 'glad I trucked off'.

But by then he was Director of Programmes at the BBC, billed in some quarters as a future Director General, and the confession could be seen as part of the Grade charm, rather than as an admission of failure.

VIII

THE AUTUMN BELONGS TO ME

Michael Grade has a complete understanding of the
publicity potential of both television in general and
himself in particular
MICHAEL BUNCE, Controller of Information Services, BBC

As GRADE WAS WRESTLING with the offer Cotton had made, Paul Fox visited Los Angeles. Since he was no longer with the BBC he stayed not at Bel Air, the normal haunt of BBC executives, but at the Beverley Wilshire. The Saturday before he was due to return to London Grade came to see him. They repaired to the coffee shop for coffee and bagels and discussed whether he should accept the BBC's offer. Fox sensed the intense struggle that was going on but assured him that the trick at the BBC was not to worry about which buttons to press; what was more important was to know which buttons not to press. 'There are some pompous, boring people in the BBC. Steer well clear of them.'

The button Grade found easiest to press was the publicity button. America may have been a professional disaster but it had further sharpened his considerable awareness of how to handle the media machine and long before he left LA he was showing a mastery in this field that was quite amazing. News of the appointment made British journalists ring him in Los Angeles. The Grade they knew was the ruthless commercial television man plotting the downfall of BBC programmes, certainly not the sort of person who would or could be a BBC man. Yet, within minutes of being appointed, Grade, with uncanny ability, had begun to sound like a man who had been honed on 'BBC-speak' all his life. He had not yet set foot in Television Centre but already he had begun to reflect its colour and taste.

Earlier in the year he had criticised the BBC's reliance on the American mini series to win audiences but now he quickly deflected the question by saying, 'You have to judge a television network on the basis of its output over the year. The fact that the BBC continues to dominate the British awards must say something.' The job was 'an enormous responsibility. It is going to be a battle to surpass standards of excellence for which the BBC stands and to try and provide the best programmes across an extraordinary wide range of interests.'

Grade's appointment had touched off a great deal of speculation that it meant a ratings war and ITV executives, including Fox, had expressed some alarm that the way the BBC had done the deed showed a ruthless streak more usually associated with commercial television or indeed America. But Grade gave answers which could not have been better scripted by Television Centre's press officer. 'Ratings are important but they are not the most important thing. It would be very, very easy to go and push the ratings up virtually overnight by going downmarket but you just would not do that. I hope people will understand that I am not too populist.'

Grade was aware that his British image as a brash commercial television man meant that there was a public relations job to be done and he shrewdly used the months until he was due to take over demonstrating how well he understood the popular medium of newspapers by generating a succession of stories about himself. He wittily spoke of the sacrifice he was making in leaving America (when journalists had questioned him about the drop in salary he said, 'I might have to give up eating') and built up a wonderful sense of expectancy about his arrival.

In June he was back in London to finalise a deal on a house in Beaconsfield, next to Sarah's parents, and while this hardly seemed ideal for a photo opportunity, Grade milked the occasion for all it was worth. Peter Fiddick of the *Guardian* 'spied' him back in London 'driving down Portland Place in an excessively modest little brown saloon, presumably in the hope that the governors of the BBC might see him.' A far cry from the limos of LA. Fiddick saw this as Grade trying hard to rehearse for the style the BBC would accustom him to.

The car Grade was driving was a hired Vauxhall Nova and it provided Richard Last in the *Daily Telegraph* with some riveting colour in another piece speculating about the coming Grade reign; he described Grade driving to Television Centre and struggling to park in the 'minuscule space' given by the stern uniformed BBC attendant there. Grade assured Last that 'what matters is making programmes we're proud of'.

The BBC did make good programmes; its problem was its inability to publicise itself. Grade wanted the Corporation to shout 'a bit louder' about the virtues of working for the BBC.

By the time he was ready to take over he was doing the shouting, at least on his own behalf, so well that the publicity machine was running into overdrive. Eleven days before he was due to start his job, on 1 September, there was an 'exclusive' interview with David Lewin of the *Mail*. The headline, HOW I PLAN TO SHAKE YOUR TV VIEWING, caught the flavour of the piece perfectly. Lewin told his readers the time Grade would start work, eight o'clock, assured them that the precious BBC heritage was safe in his hands and that the first results would be felt by Christmas when ITV would realise they were in for a 'long hot winter'.

The Sunday before he joined, Grade himself wrote an article in the *Observer* attacking American television – 'I am glad I went. I'm glad to be coming home' – and in the morning he moved into his cream and beige office on the sixth floor of Television Centre with its bank of five TV sets, and Cotton, Wenham and the others in offices next to him on that circular floor, there was yet another article speculating on what he might do. Even the fact that on his first day he got to the office before the cleaners had time to clean up his office made the papers.

No British television executive had ever had such a publicity platform and all this even before he had begun his job. In his first few months Grade lived up to this billing – at least in terms of generating news stories. The range of his public utterances was truly extraordinary. Within two months of taking over he had attacked his former colleagues at ITV, the IBA and even taken the BBC weathermen to task for not washing their hair.

In November he travelled to Cardiff to address the Royal Television Society where ITV was under the Grade hammer for a whole raft of things: scheduling the *A Team*, a show that gloried in violence, at 6 p.m., an hour normally seen as part of children's viewing; trebling the game shows from three to nine every week (in his day at LWT, he said, the IBA restricted it to only three a week), and ditching an edition of *TV Eye* in favour of *Miss World*. He even criticised the IBA for bending its own rules and allowing TV-AM's Sunday show, which went out at a time when a good many children watched, to be crammed with adverts for toys and Christmas goodies.

While the attack on IBA was good grist for the quality press, the aside on weathermen's hair was clearly aimed at the tabloids.

'I have been away three years,' he said, 'and the BBC weathermen still don't look as if they wash their hair.' The weathermen, not used to such close attention, at least not from the Controller of BBC 1, reacted with incredulity. Ian McCaskill, one of those castigated, retorted that he washed his hair every day with a mild baby shampoo. Bill Giles, who had had letters from viewers saying he had nice hair, said he washed his three times a week. It was very trivial but it showed up the Grade style well and, as the controversy raged, Grade brushed it aside as an affectionate remark that had been misunderstood.

Grade as controller seemed to be everywhere. He replaced a *Question Time* programme with one about the miners' strike – a very topical move as this was one of the great political battles of the Thatcher era – and then told Robin Day, presenter of *Question Time*, not to close the programme with his usual advice to viewers of 'sleep well'. That, he admonished, was a disincentive for them to stay up for the programmes that followed.

He won brownie points from the women's lobby by cancelling beauty contests. 'They are anachronistic in this day and age of equality and verge on the offensive.' This showed that Sarah had tutored him well on the virtues of the modern woman, although it did make Grade the target of a *Sun* editorial (they had also advised Robin Day to ignore Grade's advice about *Question Time*). But Grade knew that with ITV having the prized *Miss World*, the BBC was restricted to screening the second-division beauty contests and these did not get much of a rating in any case.

Inevitably in this welter of publicity there was the odd anti-Grade story. He had been at the BBC less than two months when he was reported to be furious with the opposition he was getting from BBC executives fearful of 'Grade's swinging axe'. In the Byzantine ways the BBC works, Cotton's old plan to have a joint controller for BBC 1 and BBC 2 was now leaked to the press. Grade was supposed to assume this role and was pictured as a hatchet man ready to bring in his own people and 'shake up' the BBC bureaucracy. This was as unreal as the publicity which suggested he controlled everything that moved in the BBC, but it hardly mattered; as far as Grade was concerned, it was no news that was truly bad news.

The press had built up the Christmas schedules, always the most fiercely contested period between the BBC and ITV, as Grade's big test. In truth Grade could have done little about the programmes; they had been commissioned and even made long before he was offered the job. He had to play the hand he was given but he could affect the presentation and this he proceeded to do in masterly style.

Michael Bunce, as Controller of Information BBC Services, oversees all press and publicity of the BBC and he watched with fascination as Grade set about organising the launch of the Christmas schedules:

'That Christmas of 1984 was his first launch and all the people who worked with him were immediately made aware of this innate skill he had for publicity. Before Michael arrived the launches were held in a large sixth-floor entertainment room by a person sitting and talking to a group of journalists. It was a case of a person delivering a text and talking, without any razzamataz. Michael applied the medium to the launch and used all the skill at his disposal within the organisation to market it to the press as effectively as he could. In effect Michael stage-managed the launches, producing them in the way a producer might produce a programme. He was amazingly entrepreneurial.'

Grade decided to move the launches to a television studio and they now took the form of tapes containing extracts which were very skilfully put together and linked with a narrative script. There were also a couple of artistes at the presentation ready and willing to be questioned by the press, which helped introduce just the right degree of colour and humour guaranteed to engage the media.

Grade, recalls Bunce, 'had a flair for publicity and for using the right descriptive language which was simple language but designed to promote the channel and the programmes.'

This flowed naturally from Grade's belief that the BBC was not using the resources available. As he would declare later, 'I think the BBC still knows how to make great programmes, but it has been taken for granted far too long. It's too shy and conservative to bang its own drum and to promote its programmes properly on the air.' In contrast to his predecessors, Bunce found Grade always ready to listen to ideas about marketing, make funds available for them and encourage them to 'do things that other people might have considered unnecessary. Michael saw promotion as very important and the budget for the promotion as an integral part of what the television service should be doing to aid its own perspective in the outside world. He was always supportive in giving money for promotion and was much more supportive in that respect than had been the case in the past.'

All this was helped by Grade's natural affinity with journalists. Some of his predecessors had not been so relaxed. Cotton, although from the world of showbiz, was never very comfortable with the press. As he himself admits, 'Michael Grade is much better at publicity. I am dreadful. Michael will ride bad publicity or people who twist stories, then afterwards tell me, "That guy is a shit, what are we going to do now?" '

Wenham was more relaxed with the press than Cotton but a bit too intellectual, while Michael, says Bunce, 'wasn't frightened of journalists, he enjoyed their company and he could see what the journalists could do for him. Whether it came from being a journalist himself or whether he would have had it in any case is quite difficult to say, but there is no doubt he has always had a skill in understanding what newspaper people wanted. He rarely let them down.'

The press reactions to the Christmas schedules showed how well Grade could exploit his media advantage. The Christmas schedules that year featured film-length versions of such popular programmes as *Last of the Summer Wine* and *All Creatures Great and Small*. Alan Hart, Grade's now forgotten predecessor, had pioneered this trend the previous year but the journalists concentrated on Grade's declaration that this was 'the best Christmas I have ever scheduled' and made much of his statement that there was a good deal of home-grown programming in the schedule.

Scheduling, of course, was his great forte; that was why he had been brought to the BBC and this, of course, meant he had to get audiences away from ITV.

A television audience is a very conventional animal. Seventy-five per cent of all viewing takes place in peak time between 6.30 p.m. and 10.30 p.m. and research has shown that during this peak time the total audience is always the same: measure the audience every half hour from 6.30 to 10.30 and it is always twenty-four million people. It is this that makes scheduling so important; a good scheduler can so arrange programmes that more people will be enticed away from the opposition to his own channel.

Grade had displayed signs of his very individual technique even before leaving for America. This was when he decided to move *Tenko*, a series about British women held as prisoners of war by the Japanese in the Second World War, from Thursday evening to Sunday evening. The change meant it came on after *Just Good Friends*, already an established popular comedy show. The benefits of this move were immediately felt. *Tenko*, which had done nothing very much on Thursday evenings, now acquired a minor cult status and ended its run with 16.5 million viewers. Grade, revelling in the success, attributed it to his famous gut feeling. 'It smelt like a Sunday show to me. It was just instinct.'

Instinct did not, however, play as great a part in Grade's scheduling as he made out or the press fondly believed. He did not shun research and statistics and as at LWT used it to back his hunches. If *Tenko* was moved because of Grade's extraordinary sense of smell for successful shows, then there had been BBC research to show that audiences liked drama on Sunday night. Surveys were as important to him as instinct. What set Grade apart from other schedulers was the use he made of research to back his instinct, and one woman now came to play a vital part in this.

Pamela Reiss was a bright young blonde who worked as a statistician in the BBC's Woodlands office, up the road from Television Centre, acting as a sort of link between controllers and audience research. She helped with the schedules, measuring audiences and surveying what people thought about programmes.

'I had always worked closely with the controllers, interpreting the data, helping a bit on the planning of the schedules. When Michael arrived he wanted to use me more, so he gave me an office on the sixth floor as well, next to Bill Cotton's office. I was there as often as I was at Woodlands, which caused problems for me in my department because I was still in broadcasting research. But Michael and I were just on the same wavelength.'

Reiss was quickly captivated by Grade's charm, particularly his habit of fixing his large blue eyes on the person he was talking to. 'I don't like people who don't look at you. He looks at you. I always divide people into those who are warm and those who are cold and he is a warm person. He has charm oozing out of every pore. He is a fun person; he made it all such fun.'

In an organisation which can be so bureaucratic, almost outdoing the civil service in that respect, Grade tore through the forest of rules and petty regulations.

Once Reiss and Grade were doing the schedules in his office. There was a big drum in a corner. Reiss asked, 'What's that?'

Grade replied, 'A friend of mine in LA has sent me this big drum of popcorn because I like popcorn when going to the movies.'

So they opened this drum and as they did the schedules kept eating popcorn, as if they were kids at the movies. Within days of assuming his job as Controller Grade had given Reiss his home number and she could 'always pop in to his office'. It wasn't a case as with the others of 'come along at three o'clock on Thursday'.

The previous bosses Reiss had worked for wanted everything down on paper. Grade, refreshingly, didn't. 'If he trusted you to give him information and you told him what he needed to know then he trusted you and it didn't matter what your title was or how much you earned or whether you were senior or not. I found this liberating. My boss,

Head of Broadcasting Research, Peter Menneer, was a man you worked for and not with. He was formal. Michael would say, "I don't want anything in writing." ' Reiss still did put things in writing just to keep Menneer happy but would then, 'stick a little note to Michael saying "Throw this away but had to put it in writing to cover myself." '

Not surprisingly, Reiss became an unabashed Grade fan. 'The thing about working with Michael is that if you did something he always said thank you. Very often he gave handwritten notes. If there was a programme he really liked he would send the producer a little note. Consequently you ended up doing anything for him.'

Every Wednesday morning at 9 a.m. Reiss would go across to Television Centre and take the lift up to the sixth floor to meet Grade and provide him with the facts and figures from BARB, which measures television audiences. Half an hour later they would both take the lift down to the basement to Room B209 for the weekly programme review. This weekly meeting has an historic status within the BBC, often an occasion for settling scores but one never to be missed.

When Wilcox's future was in debate within the BBC one thing he was very keen on was to retain his right to attend the weekly programme review.

Chaired by the managing director of television it brought together the heads and their assistants of what the BBC calls output: drama, documentary, sport, current affairs, some sixty people in all. It was in the BBC style; quite formal with everyone having an assigned place round a big oblong table. At the top of the table sat the bosses: controllers, director of programmes, managing director of television. In this predominantly male, grey-suited audience there were only two women: the notetaker and Reiss.

Before Grade arrived Reiss used to sit at the far corner of the room, largely disregarded and considered by some as the funny, strange woman who had something to do with audience research.

'Michael said, "I want you to sit at the top table, up near me." Before that I did exactly the same thing but there was never any allusion to the fact that I had done it. It was as if they had thought through all the figures. Michael used to refer to me. "Pamela has told me this." He has the confidence of referring to his subordinates. That is what I mean by a confident manager, a man who is not worried about good people working for him and recognising that. That is why he gained respect. You know he is not going to plagiarise. Wenham pretended to ignore research but he used it without acknowledging. Michael used it and acknowledged it.'

While the press were billing Christmas 1984 as the big test for Grade, his eyes were fixed on the autumn of 1985. This he saw as his chance to stamp his personality on the schedules and, recalls Reiss, 'everything was geared towards that.' But before he would do anything he wanted to know more about his audience.

It was decided to carry out a survey to find out what people knew about BBC schedules and in the autumn of 1984 some 1500 people were questioned in one of the most far-reaching surveys of its kind undertaken by the BBC. The results were astonishing.

'We asked people first of all do you know what's on? Most of them said yes. But when we asked them to write out last night's and tomorrow's night schedule on the two main channels we found people could name only two programmes and one of them was the news. So the knowledge was not there, even though people thought they knew.'

From this survey evolved one of Grade's first ideas that 'people need fixed points' in the schedule that they could identify with.

Television is now dotted with fixed points. The BBC had *Wogan* three nights on Monday, Wednesday, Friday; *EastEnders* on Tuesday and Thursday. ITV has similar fixed points: *Coronation Street* on Monday, Wednesday, Friday; *The Bill* at eight p.m. on Tuesday and Thursday. Grade hoped these fixed points would anchor the audience, give them programmes they could hook on to, mixed with a few surprises to whet their appetites.

The other thing to come out of this research was just as interesting. The survey showed that people thought in terms of hours and half hours, yet the BBC never made a half-hour or an hour-long programme and their programmes never coincided with the hour hand or the half hour.

'People', says Reiss, 'thought *Tomorrow's World* was on at seven when it was actually on at five to seven. The majority of the people knew *Top of the Pops* was on Thursday night, but thought it was on at seven-thirty. But before Michael arrived it was never on at seven-thirty. It was either on at seven-twenty-five or seven-thirty-five. They were sure *Panorama* was on at eight when it was ten past eight and had been for years.'

This may seem trivial but in television terms it was crucial. For years the BBC had been showing 25-minute or 55-minute programmes which, as Fox has explained, were 'unhappily, the internationally

recognised time periods'. They arose from the fact that such standards were set by the Americans where the programmes were shown
along with ads so a 25-minute or a 55-minute BBC programme
when shown in America became a half-hour or an hour-long show.
But for the BBC, showing them without ads, it meant an evening full
of programmes beginning at odd times, such as the main evening
news at ten to nine and *Panorama* at ten past eight. The news had
been shifted to nine before Grade arrived but now he used this
research to demand, recalls Reiss, that, 'as people think in terms of
hours and half-hours, I need thirty-minute pieces. I cannot schedule
a 25-minute programme.'

Grade's scheduling philosophy was based on what he called the
marketing approach.

'What used to happen before he arrived was Head of Light Entertainment would come in to see the Controller and say, "Well, I have a
Paul Daniels, a Russ Abbott and a this and a that." The Controller
would say, "Right, I'll take the Paul Daniels and put it on a Saturday
and take this other one and put it on a Thursday." Michael's approach
was, "You start with what you want from the schedules, not with what
you've got. So you say, I want a thirty-minute light entertainment programme that I can show on a Wednesday evening at eight o'clock. Or I
want a fifty-minute drama that I can play early evening." He would
then tell the Head of Drama, Head of Light Entertainment to "Go
away and make me the programme." It is a completely different attitude. It was in strong contrast to Alan Hart who was taking what the
heads of output offered and putting them in the schedules instead of
saying, as Michael did, "I want this and give it to me so I can schedule
it."'

As it can take two years to get a drama or a comedy series on the
screen, for the moment he could not practise such revolutionary tactics
and while he planned the 1985 autumn schedule he had, as Reiss
admits, to deal with the 'programmes that had already been commissioned. It was a question of putting what we could where.'

The hand he had been dealt was not all bad, containing as it did two
new important programmes: *Wogan* and *EastEnders*. *Wogan* had not
been intended as a chat show – the ideal slot for that would have been
about 10.30 p.m. What Terry Wogan was supposed to do was transfer to television what he had done so well on radio, providing a marvellous blend of chat and Irish humour that had so captivated Radio 2
listeners for years. Wogan found this impossible but despite this, in the

winter of 1984–85, the show did serve to refresh BBC schedules in that difficult period between 7 p.m. and 9 p.m. when, according to television wisdom, the viewers are not only adults but children as well.

EastEnders was BBC's long-awaited attempt to resurrect what was called 'the bi-weekly drama series'. (Officially the BBC never use the word soap.) Back in the sixties the BBC had run a soap called *Compact* but this had not been sustained and since then the field had been left to ITV, which dominated this genre, led, of course, by *Coronation Street*. While Grade was in America the BBC had, at last, begun to plan an attack on this ITV monopoly and developed the idea of the East End folk to match the Manchester folk immortalised by *Coronation Street*, complete with a pub that more than matched the Street's legendary Rover's Return. *EastEnders* was launched in February 1985, six months after Grade arrived.

The crucial question was, when should it be scheduled? *Coronation Street* then went out at 7.30 p.m. on Monday and Wednesday and Friday and always attracted fifteen million viewers. That left only nine million of the maximum 24-million audience to play around with. Soon after he arrived, Grade had joked about putting *EastEnders* on against *Coronation Street* but he knew that would have doomed the programme even before it had started. At that hour victory just had to be conceded to ITV. However, he felt *EastEnders* could take on another ITV soap, *Emmerdale Farm*, and it was decided to put *East-Enders* against that at 7 p.m. on Tuesday and Thursday. *Emmerdale* has a geriatric profile, sixty per cent of the audience are aged over fifty-five, it does not do well in London but does brilliantly in Yorkshire, Granada and Central. *EastEnders* with its London appeal was expected to score. It did not quite work out that way. *EastEnders* began by getting about seven million which, as Reiss admits, 'is what *Angels* had got or any other BBC soap opera.'

It was the summer of 1985 before things started looking up and that due to the fact that ITV switched to the traditional summer policy of showing repeats. Bored by *Emmerdale Farm* repeats, the audience began to switch to *EastEnders*. Grade fine-tuned the schedule and, realising 7 p.m. had not worked, shifted *EastEnders* to 7.30 p.m. But the key decision was still to come, and came, as the best decisions do, quite by accident.

Some time during that summer Reiss was in Grade's office and as ever they were looking at the ratings and how various programmes had fared. Suddenly Grade said, 'How come *Brookside* [a Channel 4 soap] in the BARB book gets about three million, and in the Top Ten it gets about six million?'

'That's because there is a narrative repeat on Sunday and under the BARB rules for the Top Ten purposes you add the two transmissions together,' replies Reiss.

'Can we do that?' Grade asked.

'Yes, we can,' said Reiss.

'Right,' said Grade. And one of the greatest ratings victories had been conceived. It was decided to have an omnibus repeat of *EastEnders* on Sunday afternoons.

The BBC had repeated programmes before – the omnibus *Archers* edition on Radio 4 on Sunday mornings was the most famous example – and even on television, programmes such as *The Borgias* and *Horizon* had successful re-runs. But those programmes had originally been on BBC 2 and the intention had not been to get into the Top Ten. The repeats were considered a good idea, giving people who had missed the programmes the first time round another chance to watch them.

Grade's repeats were meant to hype the show and create what is known in the trade as 'the *Dallas* effect'.

This is how Reiss describes it: 'When *Dallas* was in its heyday, if you were working in an office or a shop and you came in on a Thursday and you hadn't seen *Dallas* the previous evening, you couldn't join in the conversation because everybody was talking about it. So the idea was to get an audience, a big audience and get that printed in the papers: twelve million are watching this programme and then people who have not seen it feel, "I've never seen it. I am going to be out of it." If you can get a programme into the Top Ten, you create the *Dallas* effect and then it feeds on itself.'

The idea worked brilliantly. Due to the Sunday omnibus edition *EastEnders* got into the top ten, first at twelve million, and once there it began to feed on its success, rising to thirteen, fourteen and finally twenty million and topping the national ratings. Soon people were talking not so much of the *Dallas* effect as the *EastEnders* effect.

Grade faced a trickier task when dealing with *Panorama*. This was shown at 8.10 p.m. every Monday and cut right across his schedules. Before Grade, the BBC and ITV had always scheduled current affairs head to head. *Panorama* was on at 8.10, *World In Action* at 8.30 p.m. The schedules were done in the days when there were only two channels and represented the broadcasters' idea of making the public, which generally shuns such programmes, watch current affairs, rather like forcing a child to have some necessary but bitter medicine. When BBC 2 and Channel 4 came along, the equation changed, with the result that on Monday nights between eight and nine these channels just gained viewers. This was reason enough to move *Panorama*, to exploit the 8.30 p.m. slot opposite *World in Action* and clear the mid part of the evening to win against the commercial channel.

Panorama was then being viewed by about three million and by occupying a vital Monday evening slot it was like a road block on Grade's attempt to give a lift to the start of the week's viewing.

Grade reasoned that ITV gave the BBC two soft slots in the schedules: 8.30 p.m. on Monday and 8.30 p.m. on Thursday, when it screened another current affairs programme called *This Week*. He wanted to exploit both these and felt the slots would be particularly useful for developing comedy programmes.

All the research showed that television audiences took time to get used to new comedy. Most people preferred what they already knew. Grade reckoned if he put his new comedy – and he was about to screen one called *Bread* – at 8.30 p.m. on Thursdays, then faced with *This Week* on ITV, it would be guaranteed an audience of ten million, since a current affairs programme rarely got more than five million. Re-scheduling *Panorama* would remove the blight that was ruining his Monday evenings and create a similar window of opportunity in this crucial early evening slot.

Grade quickly realised that he faced his first great scheduling test with *Panorama*. This is the flagship BBC current affairs programme which has an ethos and a style all of its own. It was then housed in a row of Edwardian houses in Lime Grove just off Uxbridge Road, an empire on its own and one that was jealously guarded by those who worked there. They were some of the big names of BBC current affairs, such as Tom Bower, Michael Cockerill, John Penycate, Fred Emery, Chris Oxley, Lorraine Heggasy. Andrew Clayton was deputy editor of *Panorama* and he was well aware of the supreme arrogance of the men and women of *Panorama*. 'They were people with a tremendous opinion of their own ability and used to living in a way that was as close to the ITV people's lifestyle as you could get in the BBC. It was a devil of a job to stop some of them flying first class round the world. Even if they were booked second class they would on the spot use their IATA cards to upgrade to first class. It was like working in a piranha fish bowl. Their great desire was to produce a programme which extended either side of the nine o'clock news. It got to the stage where they felt they only achieved anything if the programme straddled the news.'

Grade's plans to move *Panorama* and cut it from fifty minutes to forty minutes outraged Lime Grove.

'The piranha fish there,' recalls Clayton, 'just thought it was scandalous. There had always been grumbles that the programme was underfunded, which I doubt. Now there were lots of grumbles that you cannot do serious journalism in forty minutes.' Grade could have over-ridden such grumbles and made the changes off his own bat but to his great credit he decided to meet them head-on. Controllers did not often do that. If they wanted to reschedule a programme they just went ahead and did it. But Grade visited Lime Grove and talked to the *Panorama* staff.

The meeting took place in an upstairs office room which had been created by knocking two rooms together. Grade and the *Panorama* staff crammed into the office and Clayton observed how Grade coped with the sheer arrogance with which *Panorama*'s stars treated him.

'He handled it very well. He was absolutely calm in the face of their arrogance. The unspoken agenda was how could a man with an entertainment background understand current affairs? He did not have to come. He could have perfectly easily done it off his own bat. It is very rare for controllers to seek the opinion of those on the programmes. But he came, he listened and explained his reasons.'

Panorama's stars asked: What guarantee is there you won't slip other things in after the news and before *Panorama*? Does this not mean a shift in priorities from current affairs to entertainment? Grade coolly met the grumbles, impressing Clayton with his skill in defusing situations. He did not totally satisfy *Panorama*'s big stars and had to return a second time, but he had drawn their sting.

His best argument was that he was, as Reiss says, 'prepared to ask the naïve question which we were all dying to ask. "Why at 8.10?" Just as he had asked, "Why do you make 25-minute or 35-minute sitcoms? Why can't you make them half a hour?" Then the answer was, "We've always made them that way." Now it was, "Well, it's always been there, you can't move it." He won them over and was prepared to say that if it didn't work he'd move it back.'

Grade was sure he could attract audiences to *Panorama* from the news who would then go on to watch a good adult movie. He 'felt it in his water, if you like', as Reiss says, that moving *Panorama* to 9.30 p.m. was not going to harm it. If anything, it would increase its audience. 'The sort of viewers you want to attract to current affairs are the more upmarket viewers, the male viewers. They are more available to view late in the evening rather than at eight o'clock.' Grade was to be proved right.

Clayton thought it was a jolly clever piece of scheduling and the figures backed him up. *Panorama*, which had been getting about three million, started getting 5.5–6 million when it was moved in August 1985.

The clearing of the schedules also helped Grade place his comedy programmes, particularly *Bread*. In its first season *Bread* was scheduled for 8.30 p.m. on Thursday and although it did well it was not brilliant and Grade recommissioned it not on the basis of audience size but on the basis of Appreciation Index ratings which measure how it is viewed. It was kept on Thursdays at 8.30 p.m. for another season. By episode six it had achieved quite high ratings and so Grade felt confident to move it to a more strategic slot: Sunday evening. It was now established and began to get a big audience. The whole thing showed what Reiss calls 'Grade's 'use of aggressive scheduling. Before Michael arrived the BBC scheduled defensively. Michael believed in aggressive scheduling.'

Grade was also a great believer in the need for long series. The research Reiss produced showed that audiences needed time to come to like anything. So instead of having a series of six parts he would ask programmers to make thirteen-part series. In a six-part series it took probably until the fourth part before people began talking about the series, but just as the *Dallas* effect might be taking hold, the series would finish. *Blankety Blank* was an example of a show which was given a long run so that it would make it.

Reiss saw Grade's success with *Bread* and his willingness to give a series a long run as the final clinching proof of his adventurous style, 'prepared to lose in order to win, unlike other television planners. They were happy if they did as well as they had done in the previous year. Michael just thought differently from them all, seeing *EastEnders*, for example, as a current affairs programme because it dealt with the social issues of the day in an acceptable format.'

Such an attitude did occasionally cause him some problems. In November 1985 Grade's decision to schedule a particular episode of *EastEnders* at 7.30 p.m. led to Mary Whitehouse, President of the National Viewers and Listeners Association, complaining that it offended guidelines about transmitting material unsuitable for children before 9 p.m. In the episode, Mary, the unmarried mother, becomes a stripper. When Whitehouse protested, Grade said, 'The whole point of Mary becoming a stripper is that it is a real solution for many unsupported mothers like her with no qualifications at all.'

Whitehouse retorted that this showed how far the thinking of Michael Grade as Controller of BBC 1 was far from the responsibility laid down on him by his job. She wrote to Stuart Young, then chairman of the BBC: 'I am more than tempted to say that if that is the level of thinking within the BBC, then heaven help us – not least those young girls who might get the message and find themselves involved in dangerous and demoralising situations.' Whitehouse pictured Grade as stopping 'nothing short of murder to increase his ratings'.

Grade was unmoved. He knew his scheduling was working and within days the Mary Whitehouse complaint was swamped by the chorus of praise the media now began to sing. On 5 December Grade received the ultimate Fleet Street accolade – at least from the tabloid end – when he was interviewed by Jean Rook, often described as the First Lady of Fleet Street. A whole page was devoted to him, complete with a picture of him with braces, cigar, and smile, over the heading BARNUM OF THE BEEB.

The *Express* sub-editors introduced Grade as 'How Young Michael is making the Grade in television's toughest job', and Rook could barely contain her enthusiasm: 'The day he walked (some sneer 'waltzed' thanks to his wickedly influential uncles) into the Beeb, it had one programme in the Top Fifty, *The Paul Daniels Show* at thirty-nine. Today it has the Top Two – *EastEnders* and *Open All Hours*. Michael has made the grade.'

Ten days later the *Guardian*'s Peter Fiddick announced, "It has been Michael Grade's autumn.'

Grade had united the two ends of Fleet Street in almost unanimous praise for his skill as a scheduler. Those two weeks in December 1985 marked the emergence of Grade as *the* great scheduler. All that had gone before him merely seemed to be a prelude to this moment and what made it all the more sweet and satisfying, the perfect end to this tale, was that it was also such an intensely romantic story: a case of a Brit, a famous showbiz name, returning from America and rescuing a great British institution fallen on hard times. At least this is how the press and Grade's admirers saw it.

There can be little doubt that in that autumn Grade turned BBC despair into joy with dramatic flair. Before he arrived the two BBC channels were getting a combined audience of, at times, less than forty per cent; now it was 47.5 per cent. His success may have been over-hyped, it was undeniable, but there was one element to the Grade hype that was disturbing. This was the myth that suggested that not only that he was a great scheduler but that he had made innovations to sche-duling technique that nobody had done before, almost as if before him there had been nobody who had given much thought at all to schedul-ing. In fact, television executives had spent years discussing how to get the best from positioning their programmes.

The basic art of scheduling – and there is dispute as to whether it is an art or a science – has not changed much over the years. This involves scheduling in what is known as the major and minor keys. In this country there has never been more than two channels on television in the major key: BBC 1 and ITV. There the object of the exercise has been to punch your full weight most of the time. The scheduler hopes he will drag people from one programme through to the other and if they do defect when there is an esoteric or an elitist programme then, hopefully, they will come back after having been away for a period of time.

When the third and fourth channels, BBC 2 and Channel 4, came along, schedulers began to take advantage of the gap in schedules, or the soft portions of the schedules of BBC 1 and ITV. The effect was that the whole tradition of scheduling, which had been to put on something very, very powerful at seven o'clock in the evening and then hold them through the evening, became a much more complicated process. The scheduling of BBC 2 and Channel 4 works on the counter-punching theory. The classic trick here is to place your most acceptable pro-gramme against the news of the major channels, not because the news is not popular but because there is a lot of news around. If you put a popular attraction against the news the chances are it will get watched by quite a large number of people. So the most popular programme of the evening on BBC 2 is nearly always put out against BBC 1's *Nine O'Clock News*.

Grade neither invented these theories nor made major innovations but he showed, as Wenham says, a nimble finesse in dealing with them, although even here not all his ideas always met with approval. Grade tried for complementary scheduling with BBC 2, particularly on Saturday nights when instead of BBC 2 showing esoteric opera he wanted it to show something like *Moonlighting*, entertaining but attracting an upmarket audience. But he never persuaded Graeme

McDonald, then controller of BBC 2, to do that. McDonald preferred to make a vivid contrast with BBC 1 with no concessions to popular taste.

So how great a triumph was it? Was the BBC success of 1985 all due to Grade?

Wenham, who had taken crucial decisions which provided Grade with *Wogan* and *EastEnders*, says, 'He inherited a situation which was turning up anyway. The decision had already been made to change the nature of the early evening by playing Terry Wogan three times a week and by playing *EastEnders* twice a week. He finessed the *EastEnders* by moving it from 7 to 7.30 p.m. He then dealt with the *Panorama* question. It has been at eight o'clock or 8.15 for so long that people got bored with it. By putting it after the news it quite refreshed Mondays. Generally speaking he was quite a nimble scheduler.'

The almost hysterical praise for Grade reflected what Wenham calls the peculiar rhythm of television. 'If you are lucky you get the benefit of deeds that have been done and seeds that have been sown many years before. When I running BBC 2 I had a very glorious autumn when we had *Life on Earth*, *The Voyage of Charles Darwin* and a whole raft of programmes, all of which had been commissioned by Aubrey Singer while he was Controller of BBC 2. So in a way giving any controller the full measure of credit for what happens in any given week or year is a bit inaccurate. After three or four years probably everything that is being shown is something that would have been commissioned by whoever the current controller is. But up to then you are playing a number of programmes which have been commissioned by your predecessor.'

It was Bill Cotton who had signed up Terry Wogan during the Los Angeles Olympics while Alan Hart, working with Jonathan Powell, Head of Series and Serials, and Julia Smith had conceived *EastEnders*. After much argument they had settled on a soap based in the London area (an alternative had been a caravan site in Newcastle), deciding to risk a southeastern bias to the schedule. When Cotton took over as managing director of BBC Television in March 1984 he had dinner at Brian Wenham's house in Weybridge. It was a fine evening and after dinner the two men sat in Wenham's back garden and discussed their plans for the BBC.

'I told Brian,' recalls Cotton, 'I want the news at six o'clock [at one time the news had been at twenty to six] going on to seven o'clock with a regional opt-out at six-thirty. Then at seven o'clock *EastEnders* two nights a week. Michael's move of *EastEnders* to seven-thirty took it away from toddlers' time a bit and he exploited it.'

Wenham recalls having arguments as to whether there should be *Wogan* five nights a week, 'but we settled on three. What you do as scheduler is quite a lot of choosing A rather than B. Filling of the time between seven and nine is more difficult than after nine because that is when anything that is adult, i.e. not juvenile, has to be put on. Between seven and nine often tends to be a waffly desert.'

Before Grade the most heavily competitive BBC 1 controller had been Bryan Cowgill whose view was that you should win every night of the week. He did once construct a schedule where the BBC was winning on six nights of the week. Wenham was then running current affairs and Cowgill came to him and said, 'I am winning six nights of the week. But we have this little problem on Monday called *Panorama*. Could you shift it to Sunday lunchtime?'

Wenham refused and says, 'The nature of the game is such that while it is fine if you win five or six nights of the week, if you won seven you would be fired tomorrow because you are not meant to do that. I think Michael was no more or no less an aggressive scheduler than Bryan Cowgill.'

Curiously, as the Grade scheduling success was taking shape he had a violent quarrel with Cowgill who was now at Thames. On 16 January 1985 Grade held a press conference to announce that the next series of *Dallas* would not be shown on the BBC. Cowgill had just bought it and this was Grade's turn to experience what the BBC had felt when he had tried to buy football. Grade was indignant that Cowgill had broken a gentleman's agreement for British television channels not to outbid each other for American series, thus pushing the price up for everybody. This meant once a channel bought a particular series it stayed with that channel all its natural life. However, Cowgill, paying £54,000 an episode as against the £29,000 the BBC were paying, had snatched away *Dallas*. Grade denounced the deal as 'shabby and underhand' and threatened to retaliate by holding back the remaining sixteen episodes of the series then being shown on BBC until the autumn. This would have meant viewers would have seen the next series on Thames before they had finished with the present one on BBC 1.

Cowgill refused to back down and the following week Grade cancelled the spring run of *Dallas*. The decision provoked a storm of protest and managed to unite the *Sun*, *The Sunday Times* and the *Mail* against him. The *Sun* ran three editorials on the subject; a letter-writer in the *Mail* said, 'Michael Grade should be sent back to kindergarten where his childish tantrums can be dealt with effectively.' A Sheffield councillor presented a petition containing 3,000 signatures to Mrs Thatcher, asking her to get the series back.

What is more, the cancellation became a useful stick with which to beat the BBC and *The Sunday Times* opined that 'if any private company acted with such disregard for its customers it would soon be out of business'. *Dallas* stayed with the BBC and the backlash was felt by Cowgill. Unlike Grade during 'Snatch of the Day' he had not lined up his ITV colleagues in support. His *Dallas* snatch led to such tensions within ITV and Thames that within six months he had resigned.

Was it not a Grade innovation, as his admirers such as Reiss claim, to schedule one's best programme against your opposition's weak points? 'Nonsense,' says Wenham. 'This is precisely what everyone else has been doing for years. I really don't believe there is anything unusual in the way he scheduled programmes.'

Even Cotton, Grade's great patron, accepts that the publicity building Grade up as the great scheduler was a bit overdone. 'Michael Grade's influence on the BBC was enormous. But he couldn't claim and wouldn't claim to have invented everything. It doesn't work that way. If he had wanted to do *EastEnders* when he arrived it would have taken two years to have got it off the ground. It takes an enormous amount to develop a thing like that in the BBC. I wasn't even in the television service when *EastEnders* was commissioned. *EastEnders* was started by Alan Hart and was placed by me before Grade arrived. I placed it in the schedules, he moved it to 7.30 in the evening. But Michael enjoyed the credit for being *in situ* when the success came in. This is life.'

This indeed was Grade's achievement: that although the early evening slot had been planned by Cotton and Wenham he was the one who exploited it. His forte, says Cotton, is to see the main chance often created by others and grab it. He also thought of the change of the time to 7.30 p.m., probably something Cotton would not have thought of. And, Cotton believes, 'He brought back, he reversed an atmosphere that was bleak, helped by the fact that he was obviously sympathetic and knowledgeable about production, he could empathise with the producers, the performers or the writers. He exploited that brilliantly.'

Does all this explain how the Grade myth of the great scheduler came to be born? Wenham has no answer. 'I don't know why he got this reputation as a great scheduler. I suppose people in the press wrote about it. I have no idea. He is very accomplished with the press, he was always pleased to talk to the press. To the extent he is a name and is keen to be in the papers, so much so that somebody rather more retiring like me [and here he smiles, a very Wenham smile] might never appear in the papers for years and nobody would worry. Nobody would say, what happened to Wenham? But if Michael did not appear in the papers for a fortnight there is a general sort of mutter going round town: what's gone wrong? He likes that. He likes giving inter-views, giving quotes. He was very conscious of that. What was unusual was that before Michael there was an unwritten assumption in the BBC that you didn't, by and large, get into the papers too often. I think it was a case of him packaging and representing himself.'

Cotton has probably the most persuasive explanation of why Grade received such publicity. It had, he believes, a lot to do with the state of the BBC at the time.

'The period 1985–86 was a pretty wretched time,' recalls Cotton. 'At my level it was terrible because you could see the man-traps coming but there was damn all you could do about it. The BBC had been created by Parliament and ITV had been created by Parliament and the thing worked very well. But we were subjected to tirades from a government and a self-interested press who couldn't wait to join in the BBC battle. Michael had an acceptable face as far as the public, and the press in particular, was concerned. He had the ability to meet the press head-on. He enjoyed his intimacy with them. By and large, as you know, when people have been criticised for so long it starts getting fashionable to praise them. He was the recipient of "Well, we might as well write him up. He is not a BBC man anyway".'

The fact was that Grade was at this time the only good news story coming out of the BBC. Everywhere else it was a disaster with a BBC scandal almost every day in the papers, and its enemies everywhere. There was John Perry of Saatchi's who wanted to get advertisements on BBC, people in right-wing think tanks who believed that the BBC as a large public enterprise was anachronistic in the world of Thatcherism, and Norman Tebbit, then a Cabinet minister, leading the Conservative charge of bias in BBC news. And this curious alliance came together just as the BBC became rather adept at shooting itself in the foot. A series of different and unrelated areas of criticisms linked up and form-ed a forest fire around the BBC, producing a very uncomfortable time for the organisation and the feeling among the staff that they were beleaguered. Grade's success was therefore all the greater because it was seen as such a release from the doom and gloom all around him. While the BBC seemed full of failures, Grade was the bright shining light of success.

I X

REAL AND MESSY LIVES

Michael Grade is in no way a party political man. But this often makes him blind to the political effect of a programme
IAN CURTEIS, playwright

GRADE'S AUTUMN OF JOY had been accompanied by the BBC's long spring, summer and winter of discontent. Milne's decision to appoint Grade as controller was about the only thing he had got right; on almost every other front his reign as Director General was proving a disaster. Every month, every week seemed to bring a fresh crisis. The BBC lost libel actions, incurred the wrath of the Conservative right, some of whose members felt they had been libelled, angered the Roman Catholic lobby by not broadcasting the Pope's Easter message – the first time such a thing had happened – and caused grave embarrassment by lifting an interview from TV-AM without permission.

Although these crises did not involve Grade, he would have been affected by the fall-out, initially benefiting from it but then, as the BBC was wracked by further crises and departures, he suddenly found himself in no-man's-land. In the autumn of 1985 Grade was being vaunted in some quarters, principally by Cotton, as the next but one Director General; by the time the Milne era was over, he was beginning to look at a very different future.

The various crises revolved around a very simple question – who managed the BBC? – and developed into a power struggle between Milne and William Rees-Mogg who was then the vice-chairman of the governors. As Rees-Mogg sees it, the battle with Milne went to the very heart of how the BBC ran itself and the whole direction of the organisation. Rees-Mogg took the view that 'the board of governors are the legal body. No money can be spent, no appointment can be made except under the authority of the board. They delegate their authority to the Director General and the board of management. You have got a two-tier board where the executive operation is conducted by the junior board. Milne took the view that the delegation of authority was total and the whole of the legal authority had been delegated to him; the governors were like trustees.' Rees-Mogg did not agree with that view.

He had come to the BBC as vice-chairman of the governors in 1981, with the idea that he would eventually succeed George Howard as chairman, but was quickly convinced that the BBC was in a very bad shape:

'My view centred around two points, firstly that when I came to the BBC it seemed, in commercial terms, grossly extravagant. They were employing 30,000 people for a job which I suspected could be done by some number in the low twenties. The executives flew Concorde across the Atlantic at the drop of a hat. The whole atmosphere was one of lax management. My view was that this was bound to raise great problems, because there was a sense that if the BBC was inefficiently managed the government was bound to be reluctant to give money to an organisation that was wasting the money it already had. So I thought there was a big commerical problem.

'The BBC was also in those days extremely slow to maximise its commercial revenues. There was an assumption that revenue was something you were given, not something you earned. So parts of the BBC that were earners rather than programme providers were, on the whole, underestimated and didn't work very effectively. George Howard was not interested in tackling that problem or indeed in the least bit clear about the problem. He thought the BBC was like running a large estate. He took a triumphalist view of his role in life. The business of reorganisation, which became in the end Mike Checkland's job, was something which did not interest him at all. Commercially he was actually opposed to it.'

Bill Cotton was fond of saying that he felt that the BBC as a public corporation existed to spend money. For Rees-Mogg this was 'exactly the damn fool remark that senior BBC executives would make. This is precisely the battle we had to fight.' But it was not merely costs that worried Rees-Mogg. He was also concerned that:

'The BBC was becoming very self-indulgent in programming. It was making a lot of programmes which were essentially editorial programmes rather than reporting. People could not rely on the BBC giving a fair taste of their case ad then giving a fair taste of the opposite case. Increasingly, programmes being made were from the producers' view of the world and the opinions of the people were slotted in in order to prove the producers' point of view.

'The concept of impartiality is an extremely difficult concept but we all know a programme which sets to allow people on both sides of the argument to state their case fairly and a programme which tries to prove a case. The proportion of judicial programmes to advocacy programmes had declined by the time I was made vice-chairman. I thought they ought to be increased. Milne always seemed to be uninterested in reversing this trend and indeed, as an ex-producer, sympathetic to it.

'I well understand the producer in his half-hour or hour sees it as a sort of blank canvas on which it is very attractive to paint a picture which is an expression of his personality and his views. An awful lot of producers do. I did not regard that as a satisfactory way to run a public body.'

Rees-Mogg's dismal view of the BBC had not been improved by having to work under George Howard. 'In my view he was totally incompetent, a very bad chairman, probably the worst chairman the BBC had since the war. A ludicrous figure. Part landlord grandee, part spoiled child, a thoroughly unsatisfactory man with whom it was very difficult to get on. Full of petty jealousies, a dreadful man, a sad, unhappy figure, he was utterly unsuited to the BBC.' When Rees-Mogg had first arrived Howard had refused his request to have an office in the BBC, on the grounds that a governor's job was part-time and it would encourage excessive meddling in the board of management's work. He had despised the donnish, intellectual world that Rees-Mogg represented and, as Milne has recorded in his memoirs, was 'at times almost brutally careless of William's position'.

It was at Howard's insistence that in December 1981 Milne had succeeded Ian Trethowan as Director General, Howard pushing for him hard over internal candidates such as Singer, Cotton, Dick Francis and an external one in Tony Smith, then director of the British Film Institute. Rees-Mogg approved of Milne's appointment 'with considerable reluctance. I thought Alasdair was a dangerous bet, although he might be very good. I liked him as a man. Our personal relationships were never difficult. But we represented very different points of view about the development of the BBC.'

Rees-Mogg's doubts centred on whether Milne 'had the understanding of the BBC or the understanding of the world outside the BBC to be a successful DG. In point of fact he failed. It was a time of transition. It was changing from the way it was seen by George Howard and Alasdair Milne and becoming the BBC as it is being seen by Duke Hussey [the present chairman of the governors] and – taking him as the symbolic figure – John Birt. I was significantly part of the transition because the sort of BBC I wanted is the sort of BBC we have got today.'

In the summer of 1982 George Howard retired. But by this time the plan that Rees-Mogg should succeed him had changed. While he was waiting for Howard to retire, 'two things happened. One was I was asked to become chairman of the Arts Council, which I decided to accept, and I obviously couldn't be chairman of both. The other was I became convinced that the commercial problems of the BBC were most urgent and in a sense the bigger of the two. If we could get the commercial problems right the editorial problems could come along. I regarded Stuart Young [another governor and brother of Lord Young] who was very experienced in accounts as much better qualified than I would have been myself to handle a commercial reform of the BBC. So I recommended that he should be appointed in order to undertake the commercial restructuring of the BBC, which both he and I thought to be necessary.'

Stuart Young was appointed Chairman in August 1983, just a month before Grade made his celebrated entry as Controller. In retrospect, this marked the start of Milne's problems. As long as Howard was there he was safe. Now Rees-Mogg began to exercise a decisive influence and Milne noticed the immediate change in the relationship between the chairman and the vice-chairman. Where Howard had been dismissive of Rees-Mogg, Young was deferential and seemed to feel a debt of gratitude to him. Rees-Mogg in turn began to play the role of king-maker with vigour. Within three months, however, Stuart Young was unfortunately diagnosed as having lung cancer. Although he gamely carried on for another three years, it had a tremendous impact on the BBC. Rees-Mogg is convinced this meant that 'the big reorganisation battle had to be put off'. And he is sure that if Young had not been taken ill, Milne would have fallen out with him much earlier and probably gone long before he did. While the personal relationship between Milne and Young remained good and Milne was very understanding about Young's cancer, Young, a dying man, could not summon up the energy to battle with Milne. But this could not disguise the fact, says Rees-Mogg, that 'there was a major division between the board of governors and the board of management, really from quite early on in Alasdair Milne's period as Director General.'

All this came to a head with the *Real Lives* crisis in August 1985. This was quite the most explosive of the many problems in Milne's troubled rule and proved that true stories are always more dramatic than any fiction.

It centred around a programme in the *Real Lives* series, *At the Edge of the Union*, which dealt with Northern Ireland, always a sensitive subject for British television. It included filmed interviews with Gregory Campbell, a Paisleyite Unionist, and Martin McGuinness of Provisional Sinn Fein, and was used by critics of the BBC to raise questions about what Mrs Thatcher had often denounced as providing terrorists with 'the oxygen of publicity'. In the usual fashion with such stories, news of the programme leaked, *The Sunday Times* skilfully used Mrs Thatcher to construct a story about the terrorists using television, Mrs Thatcher denounced it and Leon Brittan, then Home Secretary, requested the BBC not to show it. To complicate matters, just before the crisis broke, Milne had gone away on a fishing holiday in Scandinavia and it fell to Michael Checkland, who had just become his deputy, to hold the fort.

The whole matter revolved around whether the proper BBC procedures had been followed in the making of the programmes and whether the governors should see the programme before they decided on their reaction to Brittan's request. The convention in the BBC has been that the governors do not preview programmes. It is up to the DG and the board of management to take the editorial decisions so that the governors can act as a court of last resort. But the governors, led by Rees-Mogg, reacted furiously, feeling they had been put in an impossible position, and refused to follow conventional wisdom or to be mollified in any way. Much to Cotton's anger, who felt they should not interfere with management's responsibility, they not only insisted on seeing the programme but decided not to show it. BBC journalists, seeing it as a capitulation to the government, went on a one-day strike.

Cotton did feel some sympathy for the governors:

'Nice cushy job, made a fuss over, then suddenly drama in the papers, newspapers crucifying the programme, Prime Minister screaming like a fishwife across the Atlantic, Home Secretary emerging to say the programme should not be seen, nearly everyone from the camera man's girlfriend to the press had seen it but the governors couldn't. I had a great deal of sympathy for the governors.' On his return to Television Centre Cotton addressed the staff and finished up by asking them: 'I put it to you, would you take the job [of governor]?'

As the governors met to decide on *Real Lives*, Grade had been waiting in Cotton's office for his return from Broadcasting House, confident that Checkland, Cotton and Wenham, all of whom were on the board of management, would persuade the governors not to see the film or, even if they did, not to give in to Brittan. Then Cotton rang his secretary to give news of the disaster. By the time Cotton and Wenham returned to Television Centre to meet up with Grade, Graeme McDonald and Will Wyatt, whose documentary division had produced the programme, the mood on the sixth floor of Television Centre was sombre, touched with a great deal of anger.

As the drinks were poured out Cotton made no secret of how he saw this Rees-Mogg coup developing. 'When they had seen the programme they went way over the top and it was nearly a lynch mob, it wasn't a board of governors. It was the first sign they were trying to make a change in the management committee.' In other words, led by Rees-Mogg, the governors were out to get Milne and that evening – after drinks in his office Cotton and Grade went for a Chinese meal in neighbouring Shepherd's Bush – he and Grade discussed the implications of such a step, although neither was to know how dramatic it would prove to be.

The major fall-out from the *Real Lives* controversy was that Rees-Mogg became the demon as far as the board of management was concerned. Cotton felt this particularly strongly and while Rees-Mogg thinks Cotton's characterisation of the governors as a lynch mob is 'ludicrous', a year later, over a lunch with Wenham, he did confess that *Real Lives* was meant to end with the real sacking of Milne, it was just that the governors could not muster enough courage to do so.

Grade shared Cotton's feelings but some of his anger was also directed at *The Sunday Times*, which had cleverly whipped up the crisis. Two weeks later, at the Edinburgh International Festival, in a debate about the BBC, he would fairly snarl at Andrew Neil, editor of *The Sunday Times*. Neil had been talking of the delights of cable television in New York as compared to BBC programmes such as *Are You Being Served?*. This was quite the most dreadful of the BBC's sitcoms but Grade, incensed by the comparison, rose from the audience to say, 'A lot of us don't like what masquerades as journalism in *The Sunday Times*.' It was rare for Grade to drop his almost eternal bonhomie but it showed how much he had been irked by what he saw as *The Sunday Times*'s creation of the *Real Lives* controversy. It also showed how much he had moved away from any concept of American-style television in Britain, if indeed he had ever shared it. In the years to come, as Neil and his proprietor, Rupert Murdoch, argued for the Americanisation of British television and the opening up of the cosy cartel between the BBC and ITV with Murdoch's Sky Television attempting to muscle in, Grade came to perceive Neil and Murdoch and all that they represented as the great threat. The man who had been seen and is still seen as the most American of British broadcasters was turning his back on the concept of importing the American system into Britain. His years in America had cured him of any illusions about that country: more channels did not mean more choice; often it meant less choice.

But while Grade freely expressed his views on the crisis he was, of course, an interested bystander rather than an active participant in the *Real Lives* crisis, which largely swirled around him. Indeed, on the day Leon Brittan wrote to the BBC 'requesting' it not to show the *Real Lives* documentary, Grade was at this office meeting with representatives from four leading advertising agencies, Collett Dickinson Pearce, French Cruttenden Asborn, Lowe Howard Spink, Campbell Ewalds and Symington, briefing them on a million-pound campaign to improve the BBC's image. Grade was quick to deny any connection but the campaign was seen as crucial by the BBC. The government-appointed Peacock Committee was looking at the BBC's financing and there were familiar arguments about whether the licence fee, which had been increased in March that year to £58, was justified. (The BBC had asked for £65.)

The campaign was meant to focus attention on the quality of BBC programmes and resulted in press advertisements that autumn praising the BBC's output. A typical one featured BBC's comedy programmes under the heading: 'How much of the BBC's output would you describe as laughable?'

Grade was also free from the paranoia about the media that was now affecting the top management at the BBC. *The Times* had been a leading anti-BBC voice; its vociferous criticisms were to lead Milne to suggest it was an orchestrated campaign, and relations between that paper and the BBC were at a low ebb. Mark Lawson, then writing for the paper, decided it would be a good idea to praise the BBC rather than bury it as the rest of the paper was seeking to do. He requested an interview with Grade. Keith Samuels, Grade's PR officer at the BBC, doubted whether that would be at all possible. Suddenly one morning Lawson got a call at home. 'This is Michael Grade. I believe you want to talk to me. What do you want to know?' Grade was ringing from his carphone and the conversation was to result in one of the rare pieces in *The Times* in praise of the BBC. While this does confirm Grade's nose for publicity, it also made a deep impression on Lawson. He could not think of another BBC executive or for that matter television executive who would have been quite so direct.

Grade was not, however, completely immune from the Milne–Rees-Mogg war and once or twice his decisions fuelled the row further. One of these dated back almost to the time that Grade took over as controller in February 1985. Grade had decided that *Doctor Who*, the BBC's long-running science-fiction serial, needed a rest and postponed further showings until the autumn of 1986. But the postponement provoked a furious row from *Doctor Who* fans all over the world and the governors were suddenly in the middle of a classic row: fervent fans claiming a beloved British institution was being jeopardised, the governors dragged into a situation they never even knew existed and forced to defend a management whose duty, they felt, was to protect them from such events. It was seen as yet another case of management failure, one in a long chain. Grade defended his decision well and Milne had to admire the way Grade 'wove his way adroitly through the flak that followed', but was not best pleased his decision contributed to 'disturbing the working relationship between the board and the management'.

Grade's spat with Cowgill over *Dallas* had also embarrassed Milne in front of the governors. A decision about the licence fee was then pending and Rees-Mogg and Young found the whole thing ludicrous and politically very ill timed. Soon after, they had lunch with Milne and made this very clear. Milne had so far left Grade to his own devices but now he insisted on showing the remaining episodes. Grade used the first *Wogan* programme to announce his climb-down. But the whole affair left a nasty taste. Grade's high profile may have had its virtues but in this case he had again managed to upset the delicate relationship between the board and the management and had done nothing for the credibility of the BBC. This episode had marked the start of a certain cooling in the relationship between Milne and Grade.

Milne was becoming concerned, as Cotton admits, about the high profile Grade enjoyed. 'Alasdair felt Michael was getting too much publicity.' Cotton tried to reassure him that this was of no consequence. 'I was employed to run the television service but I didn't have to run it myself. I gave Michael the credit. The BBC was going through a mad period anyway. We had come across a government that didn't like us and was going to do something about it. They wanted to try and create a situation where real power in television fell into the hands of like-minded people. If they could manufacture that they wouldn't have all these problems with all these nasty programmes criticising them.' In such a situation, Cotton saw Grade's high profile as an interesting, if not worthwhile, diversion.

In any case, Cotton had his celebrated 'young brother relationship' with Grade which he sees as 'When life is going fine you don't need it. But I know if I turned up on Michael's doorstep and said, "Michael, I am in the shit," he would drop everything and help me. He knows I would do the same.' Milne had no such rapport and he thought the rave reviews Grade had received over his ratings success had an element of luck attached. Having to cope with the backlash of some of Grade's decisions, while no more than irritants, was beginning to get to Milne.

Apart from the *Doctor Who* and *Dallas* rows, Milne had also had to rein Grade in over drama. In March 1985 Grade had had to reverse his controversial decision about moving a number of classical dramas in the Play of the Month slot, including *Antigone* starring John Gielgud, from BBC 1 to BBC 2. Milne recognised that BBC 1's production of classical plays had been partly overtaken by the BBC 2 Shakespeare cycle which he had himself initiated. Milne had also not been pleased by Grade's abandoning the long-standing BBC commitment to the single contemporary play on BBC 1 and had made him change his mind. That such differences should have arisen is, perhaps, not surprising, but they underlined the very great gulf in the two men's backgrounds (Winchester and Oxford versus the London Palladium) and that while Milne was steeped in the BBC culture and was very much a corporation man Grade, for all the kudos he received as a great scheduler, was still essentially a loner and an outsider.

Milne refuses to discuss Grade, limiting himself to the cryptic observation that 'I'm not a great admirer'. His brief references to Grade in his book *DG: The Memoirs of a British Broadcaster* suggest he did not care for his high profile or his leaving the BBC.

Michael Bunce feels that the differences between the two men widened as the BBC became enmeshed in rows and reflected their very different views of the organisation:

'When Alasdair was DG, Michael did not have much time for a corporate bureaucracy. He was only concerned with the television directorate. Michael did not see his role, whether to run the channel or run the television service, as a corporate role. He saw that as a leadership of a particular sector of the BBC without taking on board all that the BBC stood for. If you are running the corporation you have to see things from the corporate perspective: sometimes that is the same and sometimes it is different. Michael would not even accept that there were ways of doing things other than the ways he was doing them. He was very bullish about the attitude to a whole host of things, like *Real Lives*. He is very outspoken and often assumed that making a great noise about something was going to achieve his end. There are different ways of achieving your ends and being up front and loud in lobbying doesn't always achieve the best results. So Mike would be inclined to bang on and steam ahead without recognising that different people in different ways needed to be consulted and to know what was going on. Alasdair's views on Michael reflect that particular sense.'

Although Grade could never be Milne's man he was still useful to him and as the Milne–Rees-Mogg saga developed Grade became a beneficiary. This arose in the summer of 1986 when Milne, just as with Singer previously, engineered the removal of Dick Francis. One of the longest serving of BBC executives, Francis had been with the corporation for twenty-eight years and on the board of management since 1979, first as director of news and current affairs and then as managing director of radio. He was known as a man who spoke his mind freely but was not universally liked. He had fallen out with Milne in a spectacular fashion over the reorganisation of radio and the building of a new radio centre at Langham Place. In January 1986 Milne asked Francis to retire early, offering him the managing directorship of VisNews, the BBC equivalent of promoting a troublesome backbencher to the House of Lords. Unlike Singer, Francis refused to go quietly and insisted on addressing the board of governors. It was summer by the time the meeting took place and Milne had to cut short a holiday to return to meet the governors. Rees-Mogg, appalled at the way Milne was handling the affair, insisted that Milne, in the presence of Francis, explain to the governors why he wanted him sacked. He then had to sit and listen while Francis argued his case. In the end Milne got his way but another nail had been hammered in the coffin that was being prepared for him.

Rees-Mogg would have liked to have fired Milne then. As he now says, 'Milne should have gone either at the end of *Real Lives* or when he fired Dick Francis.' But Milne hung on and the Francis saga opened up a route to the top for Grade. Milne decided that Wenham should replace Francis. Rees-Mogg violently opposed this move, describing Wenham as a cynic, a man of no conviction and a disastrous choice.

Milne had to compromise and got Wenham accepted only on the condition that David Hatch, who was already Controller of Radio, should be brought in alongside him as Director of Programmes (Radio). Wenham's departure from Television Centre meant that his job as Director of Programmes had to be filled and who else could do it but Grade?

Milne may have had increasing doubts about Grade, unhappy about his penchant for publicity, but he had to weigh up other considerations. There was Grade's success as a scheduler and Cotton, with whom Milne did have an excellent rapport, was pushing for him. However, giving Grade the job would also mean putting him on the board of management and here Milne was keen to balance Grade. This he did by bringing Hatch on to the board as well. Milne felt that Hatch, a roly-poly figure full of laughs, whom he clearly admired, 'was a good counterpoint to Michael'.

On 19 June 1986 the governors met in Cardiff and ratified Milne's changes. On 7 July Grade replaced Wenham as Director of Programmes.

The post of Director of Programmes was as curious one, a job created for David Attenborough by Hugh Weldon. Wenham had seen it as 'a grand personnel function, the television equivalent of the managing editor of a newspaper who is often the man checking expenses and running the administration. Also, he was meant to be a super editor of journalistic content, a sort of clearing house, so suddenly there were't four documentaries on fly fishing being made at the same time.' Such confusion was always possible in the BBC.

Once on the same Monday night, both *Panorama* (which Wenham then edited) on BBC 1 and *Horizon* on BBC 2 showed programmes about mental health. Director of Programmes was the spare wheel of the system, meant to avoid such duplication. It was not a vastly creative job.

If this sounds unexciting, the compensation for Grade was that it gave him direct programme control over both channels and he also retained his job as controller of BBC 1. Ironically, his career was now following Milne's, for he too had doubled up these roles for a time. In a sense it also fulfilled Cotton's old plan to have one man controlling both channels. Grade did not have the formal title Controller of Television – McDonald was still at BBC 2 – but his new appointment and his retention of his old title gave him all the powers to do such a job. Given the publicity that had accompanied his appointment as controller, one would have expected an orgy of interviews, but Grade greeted his appointment with silence, a silence which was almost more eloquent than any publicity. It suggested that Grade recognised that Milne did not always appreciate his high profile.

Not that Grade did not celebrate his new powers. He did so by travelling to Mexico for the World Cup. If his contretemps with Cowgill had shown the colours of the new gamekeeper, Mexico revealed that Grade wore the cloak of the BBC man very well. The World Cup was being shown on both BBC and ITV. But before the contest the BBC and ITV had signed a concordat about splitting the matches featuring England. In such sporting competitions, television channels lay great store by the tag 'exclusive' and the pride of place is taken by England's matches. In the first round the matches had been split two to one in the BBC's favour between the channels and John Bromley was sure he had a deal that 'if England got through we [ITV] had the first pick'. England, after some difficulties, did get through and the first match in the second round was against Paraguay.

Just as ITV were getting ready to televise the match an argument broke out in the broadcasting centre in Mexico into which Grade was, inevitably, dragged. The BBC played the imperialist media role it loves so much, particularly when it comes to such sporting occasions, and announced that it was going to televise that match as well. The British public, it said, wanted to see it on BBC. There was some merit in the BBC argument. When in the past both the BBC and ITV have shown the same events, such as Cup Finals or royal weddings, more people watch then on the BBC, as if that were the authorised version.

The argument became very heated and Grade stepped in in the role of the arbiter. It had so often been Bromley and Grade; now in the broadcasting centre in Mexico it was Bromley versus Grade.

'You know we agreed this three months ago,' said Bromley, waving in front of Grade the piece of paper signed by both the BBC and ITV.

'I don't accept that,' replied Grade. 'None of that sports concordat is legal. Anyway, I have decided I am going to show it.'

Bromley was aghast. He was now being subjected to the same treatment that Grade had dealt out to Gerry Loftus when, with Bromley's help, he had planned 'Snatch of the Day'. For some time the two long-standing friends argued with one another, with Bromley feeling not a little foolish: 'There I was waving my piece of paper and back at base camp they are saying, Bromley, you are getting screwed. But it made no impression on Grady. Of course we could also show the match and we did but we had lost the exclusivity.'

Grade in his new role had preserved the BBC's self-appointed status as the guardian of the nation's viewing habits.

In one of those ironies that life continually throws up, as Grade took charge of his new responsibilities he became caught up in a curious controversy whose origins lay with a decision Milne had taken some four years previously. It has become known as the Falklands play controversy and was quite the most bizarre episode in Grade's time at the BBC.

In 1982, Milne had addressed a meeting of the now defunct Writers' Luncheon Club. Among the other guests was the playwright Ian Curteis, whose drama *Suez* Milne proceeded to praise in his speech. It had been a three-hour blockbuster, straddling the *Nine O'Clock News*, which put Eden's case during the 1956 Suez crisis and told the story from Eden's point of view.

Curteis wrote to Milne to thank him for what he had said, and added an afterthought that in a few years he'd like to write a parallel play about Mrs Thatcher and the Falklands War, from her viewpoint. To Curteis's consternation – he felt it was too soon after the event – Milne jumped at the idea and wrote that he wanted to go ahead without delay.

He passed instructions down to Plays Department which commissioned the screenplay, granting Curteis unique conditions of contract – veto over casting and choice of director, for instance – that could have been conceded only by the Director General's personal intervention.

Curteis was pleased. He felt that, in the avalanche of reporting the Falklands war, the reason why Britain had to fight it had become obscured and distorted in large areas of the media, and media coverage had turned into a vendetta against Mrs Thatcher. It seemed right that the balancing view should be put, and this was consistent with the BBC's obligation to be even-handed in matters of controversy.

He was excited by the subject. A distinguished-looking man with a track record of over 120 credits for plays and films in British and American television, he has four times been nominated for the coveted BAFTA Best Play of the Year award. Above all, he prides himself on his craftsmanship.

In April 1986, he delivered the final draft of his screenplay to Plays Department and the Director General. It was warmly received and scheduled for recording in January and BBC 1 transmission on 2 April 1987, the fifth anniversary of the Argentinian invasion. Cedric

Messina, doyen of BBC Plays producers, was brought out of retirement especially to make it and David Giles, director of many notable BBC Classic Serials, assigned to direct it. It was to be a major event.

Grade had little to do with these preliminaries but on 6 June he presided over a meeting in his office to give the official go-ahead and authorise the budget. Although he had a script, Grade claims he had not then read it. He said later he could not read everything and was content to rely on the professional judgement of the highly distinguished team making it.

Two months into pre-production, the new Head of Plays Department, Peter Goodchild, decided to send copies of an early draft of the play to Grade and Cotton. Why he delayed so long, and why he did not send the production draft, is unknown. Cotton read it and hated it. Many theories have been advanced about the reason, but the one which gained most acceptance was that put forward by the *Sunday Telegraph*, who quoted a senior colleague of his: 'He was damned if he was going to allow Mrs Thatcher to get the credit for the Falklands all over again.'

Cotton sued the newspaper for libel, later allowing his action to lapse – after his solicitor had been sent the evidence, but not before the *Telegraph*'s solicitors had seen a statement made by a close relative of Cotton's: 'Bill is True Blue, but the one person he simply cannot abide is Margaret Thatcher.' Certainly, he has described her to the author as 'screaming like a fishwife'.

It is not always realised that the BBC does not own the copyright of any television play it produces and transmits. That is retained by the writer, who remains legally and morally responsible for what it says. What Cotton should have done was to contact Curteis, using whatever he felt was the most tactful reason, and say quite openly that he was cancelling the production. But this did not happen. Instead, the BBC followed a tortuous, almost Byzantine process so that Curteis began to realise something was going badly wrong only through winks and nods – the winks coming from the new Head of Plays, Peter Goodchild.

Goodchild's had been a curious appointment for the BBC. A graduate in chemistry, he had spent most of his time in the science features department and had got the job because nobody in the drama department wanted it. It had been offered by Wenham to Trodd, who regretted turning it down as soon as he heard Goodchild had taken it. 'If he had said it was going to Goodchild I would have accepted.' Curteis had clashed with Goodchild over a trilogy of his plays, *BB and Joe*, which

Goodchild had suddenly cancelled virtually without explanation. Mindful of this, Curteis sought to build bridges with him, inviting Goodchild and his wife to lunch at his home in Gloucestershire.

On a hot summer's day in July Goodchild came for lunch, wearing a straw hat and without his wife, but no bridges were built. He raised several questions about the script which quite troubled Curteis. It is a long-standing convention in the BBC that any changes to a script should always come through the producer and director. Goodchild not only violated that but also raised questions which, in essence, Curteis saw as affecting the historical accuracy of the play. Curteis was particularly worried by suggestions that Mrs Thatcher may have fought the war to gain party political advantage. At a separate meeting, without Curteis present, Goodchild put the same points to the producer Cedric Messina, who rejected them.

Not to be put down, Goodchild then wrote officially to Curteis, saying that his points 'must be addressed' or the production would not proceed. Producer, director and writer were united in resisting this.

Curteis was puzzled by Goodchild's behaviour – when challenged about some of his points Goodchild rarely presented proof – and formed the impression that someone was pulling his strings, that there was a 'shadowy presence of someone else . . . staying hidden for the moment, for whom Goodchild was acting as a messenger boy.' But who could that someone be? Milne had written to him, 'Your work has enriched the BBC'; Grade had given the go-ahead. Initially Curteis thought the puppet master might be Cotton, who had refused to return his calls or answer his letters.

It was in the middle of July when Curteis, unable to get much joy out of Cotton, approached Grade direct.

On 19 July Grade returned Curteis's call. Fiercely loyal to his mentor, he had changed his position since the 6 June meeting. He made four points to the playwright, two of which Curteis accepted, the other two points he could not agree to. One of them concerned doubts Grade had about the relationship between the sinking of the *Belgrano* and the timing of the Peruvian peace initiative, one of the great controversies of the Falklands War. (The view of those who opposed the war and saw it as a glorification of Mrs Thatcher was that the *Belgrano* was deliberately sunk to make war inevitable). Curteis did not agree with such an interpretation. His final point was more fundamental. Grade, Curteis writes, 'questioned the propriety of writing and producing such a play at all'. It was this last remark that made Curteis now wonder if it were Grade who was Goodchild's puppet master.

Was he? Certainly within the BBC Grade made no secret of his new position on the play. About this time, in a late-night meeting with Milne, Grade not only told him he thought the play was dreadful but offered to deal with Curteis himself if Milne did not. Milne assured him he would write to Curteis. Three days later, on 21 July, Milne, responding to pressure from Grade, wrote Curteis a 'Dear Ian' letter which said that both Cotton and Grade had 'reservations' about the play (although, as we have seen, Grade's feeling had become more than mere reservation). But even now, instead of taking the bull by the horns and saying that the play was not liked by two of the BBC's senior management – who intended to over-rule the drama professionals – and therefore could not be done, Milne fell back on a spurious reason: that he had decided not to make the play because an election was looming – if it was made now and then an election intervened it might not get shown for nine months. In such circumstances Milne felt an expenditure of £1m could not be justified.

The reasoning only exposed Milne to contradiction. In a meeting with Curteis the previous month, he had been confident that an election was unlikely before 1988; now he felt it might come just as the play was being screened in 1987 and it would not be politic to show it. Curteis wondered what could have happened in the intervening month to make Milne change his mind. Had Grade got to him in the meantime? Curteis, perhaps not surprisingly, began to form such suspicions.

Just as Curteis was beginning to suspect that he was being told less than the whole truth, Grade was beginning to take a more active interest in the whole subject of BBC drama. As we have seen, in his first years at the BBC plays had not played a large part in Grade's repertoire; even Milne had to admonish him about that. But that autumn he seemed to be on a mission to promote drama. Grade set much store by *Première*, that autumn's drama series, billed to be shown on Sunday night and featuring such things as the South African *Death Is Part of the Process* and Dennis Potter's six-parter, *The Singing Detective*. He found the series particularly useful to deflect criticism that he was just a populist. Whenever journalists or critics would point to the fact that he had taken BBC ratings up by going downmarket, or that he had made BBC 1 a soap-dish for the American networks with *Dallas* on Wednesday and *Dynasty* and *Dynasty II* on alternate Fridays, he would point to the fact that he had invested significantly in indigenous drama and that he indeed reversed the process of switching resources away from drama.

The pride of the season was a series of plays called the *Monocled Mutineer* by Alan Bleasdale which sought to narrate events surrounding the Etaples Mutiny of 1917. Although based on real events, the play was fictional. However, it was advertised by the BBC as 'an enthralling true-life story', a phrase which Grade later publicly stated was his choice. It was only when the press began to pick holes in the alleged facts that Cotton admitted it did not represent what had actually happened but 'the greater truth . . . about the First World War'. The right, particularly the right-wing press, jumped on this as evidence of the grossly left-wing weighting of BBC drama.

The Monocled Mutineer was not the only controversial drama Grade supported. He was also keen on a play about the Falklands War by Charles Wood called *Tumbledown*, considered by some to be anti-war. Grade took such an active interest in it that he was ready to abandon the normal budget ceiling of £390,000 per screen hour to get the play made. This allegation was soon the subject of much malicious gossip in the right-wing press and Curteis says, 'I have always found Grade's excessive promotion of *Tumbledown* an interesting psychological phenomenon. That he personally backed it right through the system, breaking the normal budgetary bounds and getting it on (entirely with BBC licence-payers' money, which is unusual – the normal form would be a co-production) come what may, argues the same sort of anti-authority-figure approach with a touch of frenzy about it.'

By now Curteis felt as determined to fight Grade, Cotton and the messenger Goodchild, as Mrs Thatcher had General Galtieri and he started a spirited correspondence with Milne and Cotton about his play. He also began preparing a case to be presented to the governors. However, before he could do this, Stuart Young died. Three days after Young's death the BBC transmitted *The Monocled Mutineer*, which just added salt to Curteis's wound. In September 1986, Norris McWhirter of the Freedom Association broke the story of the Falklands play and soon afterwards news of *Tumbledown* was picked up by the press. What had started as a small problem in the drama department was becoming a *cause célèbre*.

Even then, the matter might have been partially resolved had Grade allowed other television companies to produce the play. But when Sir

John Wolff of Anglia Television read the script and told the *Standard* he wanted to produce it, Grade rang him to say that the BBC was not going to release the remaining seventeen months' copyright licence it held on the play. Interestingly, this was one subject for which Grade was not keen to get publicity. He told Anglia, 'This call is not for the press.' As the right saw it, this was conclusive proof that the BBC was dominated by left-wingers who hated Mrs Thatcher and that is why they had blocked a play favourable to her, representing one of her greatest moments. Norman Tebbit, who was leading a campaign against what he saw as BBC bias, came to lunch with Milne and the governors, citing the Falklands play to prove his point.

But is it quite as simple as that? If there was a conspiracy, Grade hardly acted as a conspirator. His dislike of the play was open and clear and he claimed it was based on artistic grounds. In October at the Tory conference in Bournemouth, Peter Ibbotson, Grade's chief of staff and speech writer (BBC wags said he also did the thinking for Grade) descibed it to Tory MPs as 'a terrible play', with two-dimensional characters, and one that could not be produced.

On 2 October Grade himself held a press conference for selected journalists at Television Centre and claimed that the real reason for the cancellation was not the possibility of an election but the laughably poor quality of the script. 'There was absolutely no commitment to production or transmission on this project. I respect the Prime Minister. All the alterations we proposed to Curteis had been to protect Mrs Thatcher.'

None of this calmed Curteis, and nor, perhaps, was it meant to. Coming on the heels of the cancellation of the earlier productions without explanation, he, his wife and four children (one an adopted West Indian boy) now faced a catastrophic financial position. He determined to fight what he saw as professional malpractice of a high order – not only to stave off his bank, but also because the play is dedicated, in print and on screen, to the 253 British servicemen who were killed in the Falklands. A practising Christian, it seemed to him grotesque that the reasons underlying their deaths – which is what the play is about – should be improperly suppressed by people who had never worked in drama and whom he suspected were lying to him. His complicated story of BBC intrigue rings true. There was a cock-up, certainly, but was it more than that and how much of it was Grade's fault?

Ken Trodd, who is as representative of the left in British drama as some believe Curteis is of the right, thinks 'The main pont about the Ian

Curteis episode is that it was a cock-up by the BBC but it didn't start as a cock-up by Michael Grade. The essence of the cock-up was that Curteis managed to persuade Alasdair Milne to commission a Falklands play. Curteis was able to hold Milne to that. Down the line they were lumbered with something they never wanted. I read that script and that play would have been much, much more propagandist right-wing than any leftist play ever has been. It was never persuasive and acceptable as a piece of work. It went so far because the boat was being pushed out by the Director General. Also, this is the place which at any one time has seven or eight contradictory patterns, the left hand does not know what the right hand is doing. In a sense, on the sixth floor you can be as removed from actual programme-making as the man on the Central Line, although it is only one floor up from the drama department. The same thing happened to *Brimstone and Treacle* [by Dennis Potter]. They never got to know about it until it had almost happened. Controllers are involved with next week's schedule. They are not to do with long-term planning. Grade as a boss figure can remain very immune but such is the way the BBC system works that once it became a *cause célèbre* he had to take an interest.'

According to this view, Grade walked into a situation not of his creation and, probably, found himself lumbered with it. Yet he showed great passion against the play, much more than would be called for from a man solving a problem not of his own making. His handling of Curteis and the whole affair also throws an interesting and revealing light on Grade's character. So adept at publicity, normally so eager for it, he shunned it during this affair. In addition to his vow of silence to Anglia, his letters to Curteis were marked 'Private And Confidential – Not For Publication' and when Curteis asked permission to publish them, he refused. Grade the publicity man now seemed frightened by it. It revealed that Grade, like all of us, wanted publicity when it suited him, when it was favourable to him. If the publicity was unfavourable then he, like most others, shunned it.

Grade also chose to give Curteis's allegations a simple tabloid interpretation of left versus right. Curteis's case against Grade is more complicated than that premise allows. But Grade viewed Curteis's attack in party political terms. After the dust had settled on the public dispute, Grade wrote Curteis a letter we are not allowed to reproduce. Curteis replied 'You ask me if I voted at the last election' (the 1987 election, which had seen Grade get quite close to Lord Young, who ran the Conservative campaign.) Curteis, rightly, replied that the question was a 'red herring' and was keen to emphasise that his argument against Grade was not that he had party political bias but that he apparently believes that 'the role of the broadcaster is to challenge and question the actions of the state'. Whatever the true intentions of the broadcaster, under a Conservative government such actions are bound to appear left wing.

Curteis says: 'One running theme in his professional life seems to be his hatred of all "authority-figures", whether living or dead – ignoring the fact, of course, that he has become one himself. I don't think Grade is in any way a party political animal. But this often makes him blind to the political effect of a decision as was the case here. But that is the price you pay if you want to be King of the Trendies as he is sometimes called.'

'King of the Trendies' may be putting it a bit too strongly. The journalist Bryan Appleyard, who has made a spirited defence of him, says that Grade is hated by the intellectual snobs and trendies precisely because he is not one.

'Trendy people have loose, dark suits and shirts. Grade wears red braces and socks, striped shirts, light suits and a mid-seventies haircut. He also smokes fat cigars, evoking his uncle, Lew, and all the old theatrical traditions that the new inhabitants of the new media thought they had overthrown.'

Certain clothes may be among trendies' signature marks but are not the only ones. What is undeniable is that when it came to making choices in drama or dramatists, Grade's decisions coincided with those of the trendies. Within the BBC and the television establishment, where the balance of opinion was definitely against Curteis, it did Grade no harm to take such a stance. Curteis could be labelled a cranky right-winger and Grade dismissed the whole thing as a subject on which they were fated to disagree. It was all *rashomon*, he said – different ways of looking at the same subject.

Perhaps the real clue to this whole affair lies in the possibility that Grade may have been bounced into a position which once taken he felt obliged to defend. There is a peculiar loyalty factor in Grade and having decided to support Cotton he could see no way of backing out. In that sense he was not so much Goodchild's puppet master as the boss backing his underling. Curteis insists that at no stage was he attacking the BBC, but only three individuals who seemed to him to be undermining and betraying much of what it stood for, from within. But perhaps the most telling verdict on the whole Falklands play episode came from Lord Annan, Chairman of the Annan Committee on the Future of Broadcasting, in a debate on broadcasting in the House of Lords.

Hansard records him (25 May 1988): 'I thought Mr Curteis's play was gripping television material when I read it . . . There are rumours that the BBC staff hated it because it was patriotic and favoured the Prime Minister. I must say, from what happened afterwards, in all the rows that followed the cancellation of that play, I think there was something in that. Some of the top brass of the BBC were devious and dishonest on that issue and displayed no more understanding of the ethics of broadcasting than an earwig.'

A year after the Falklands play controversy another incident concerning a controversial playwright would demonstrate how easily Grade could be forced into making some very important decisions after virtually no time to think or reflect. The moment also illustrates the chaotic way in which the BBC drama department works. This time Grade was seen to support Dennis Potter, that most fashionable of modern British television dramatists.

The actual incident concerned an episode from *The Singing Detective* which showed a scene where a boy watched his mother making love – guaranteed to offend right-wing pressure groups. Trood, who was the producer, describes what happened:

'His attention was drawn to it only on the Thursday or the Friday before the episode was to be screened on Sunday. There was a press leak. So there was a crisis. Jonathan Powell, then head of drama, Jon Amiel, the director, and I were all involved. Potter kept out of it. We had a long meeting in Grade's room. He thought about it, he weighed it all up, saw the pragmatism of it, the genuine technical difficulty of changing something at that short notice.'

The series had been produced on a very tight schedule because of the limited availability of its star Michael Gambon, and by the time it was due to be screened in November 1986 only the first episode had been edited. The director was editing each episode just days before it was to be screened. So that Friday afternoon, episode three, due to be screened on Sunday, had just been finished. Amiel was working on number four and told Grade that if he had to take time out to cut this scene then that episode would not be ready for the following Sunday.

'It would have been appalling', says Trodd, 'if Michael's courage had failed. But it did not. But then he was almost in a box from which he couldn't escape.'

Grade, or course, was a fan of Potter's. He was keen that the Dennis

Potter season should include *Brimstone and Treacle*, which had been banned by Milne in 1976 and which he decided to screen in 1987. His decisions on Potter and Curteis had been taken instinctively and both reflected the prevailing BBC and dramatic sentiments. It was Curteis's fate that these were so dramatically opposed to his own.

Ultimately, too, the overall outcome of the Curteis incident did Grade no harm at all. If anything, as he took charge of the additional responsibilities of Director of Programmes, his image as the open man of the people grew. He initiated the popular series *Crimewatch* and started the *Open Air* programme. He may have wanted to keep what he wrote to Curteis secret but he was keen that the BBC should be open to criticism. In the past programmes critical of BBC output had not been successful because the people responsible for those programmes had not fully participated. But Grade ensured, says Bunce, 'that if there were complaints about BBC programmes in television then the people responsible for making them should appear in that programme. With Mike in charge they were required to appear and answer to their critics. He was very eager to open up the corporation to the public. He was very good on public platforms; he was very good in discussions and dialogue and wished to be involved in them.'

He also got involved with Tim Bell, Mrs Thatcher's PR adviser, about improving the BBC's image. And there were also further scheduling triumphs, as with *EastEnders* previously, when he again built on platforms provided by others.

Roger Laughton, who had responsibility for daytime television, had bought *Neighbours*, an Australian soap. Grade scheduled it just after the news at lunchtime, then repeated it again at 5.35 the same evening. The idea was to help the *Six O'Clock News* and for it to inherit some of the *Neighbours* audience. However, it did not quite work out that way. Instead, there was an 'echo effect' on the children's programmes that preceded *Neighbours*. They began to attract more viewers as people tuned in to wait for their favourite soap. But the concept of showing *Neighbours* twice a day worked brilliantly and soon its scheduling was being hailed as almost as great a triumph as that of *EastEnders*.

By this time the very landscape that Grade worked in had changed radically. Stuart Young's death had opened up the BBC succession: Who would replace him as chairman of the governors?

Rees-Mogg had gone and been replaced as vice-chairman by Lord Barnett, the former Labour minister. This was almost one of the last acts of Stuart Young, who had used his brother Lord Young to approach Barnett, a neat illustration of the bipartisan approach in British politics. With Young's death Barnett himself was in the frame as successor along with Lord King of British Airways and several more unlikely names.

Rees-Mogg was also seen as a possible candidate, but although Downing Street consulted him, he decided not to go for the job because of the antagonism that had built up towards him during the *Real Lives* controversy. Instead, he actively promoted Duke Hussey, a close friend, a Somerset neighbour and, like him, a Somerset cricket supporter. Hussey, who had been chief executive and managing director of Times Newspapers during the long strike of 1978–9, was at first just a bit reluctant but Mrs Thatcher was very keen he should take the job. William Waldegrave, whose sister Lady Susan is married to Hussey, rang to make this clear and Douglas Hurd, who had replaced Brittan as Home Secretary and who had offered the job to Hussey, emphasised that it was the Prime Minister who was, in reality, offering him the job. Hussey agreed. Rees-Mogg saw Hussey's appointment as completing the job he and Young had begun. The BBC needed to be sorted out and Hussey was seen as the man most capable of doing that.

The first job Hussey had was to deal with Milne. His contract ran out in July 1988 and there was an option for a further period. Despite all his problems Milne was optimistic his contract would be extended and at a lunch with Hussey he raised the subject of the extension. Hussey said, 'It's not the right time to talk about that.'

A few weeks later, on Thursday, 29 January 1987, one of the regular fortnightly meetings of the governors took place at Television Centre. The meeting ended a few minutes before lunch. As Milne was waiting to go for lunch he was summoned by Hussey and Barnett. Milne began to suspect something was afoot. The BBC secretary, Patricia Hodgson, who acted as messenger, had addressed him not as DG but as Alasdair, something she had never done before. She had good reason.

As Milne walked into the chairman's little room where the blinds were drawn to keep out the sun, Hussey said, 'I am afraid this is going to be a very unpleasant interview. We want you to leave immediately. It's a unanimous decision of the board.' It was some time before Milne realised that they wanted him to resign. The decision had been taken in the previous two weeks but it had been brewing for almost two years now, ever since *Real Lives*. Amazingly, Milne had just not seen it coming.

In the usual fashion the BBC advertised the job and three hundred people applied although, television being such a small industry, there were only half a dozen candidates worth considering.

Checkland as Milne's deputy was a front-runner; Wenham was another strong candidate; and there were extenal candidates: Anthony Smith of the British Film Institute and Jeremy Isaacs, chief executive of Channel 4. David Dimbleby, a television presenter, also applied.

Grade was not much taken by any of the candidates but it was Dimbleby's application that aroused him. He made no secret of the fact that he thought Dimbleby would be a disaster. When Hussey seemed to favour Dimbleby, Grade let it be known to the press that if Dimbleby got the job he would leave. For some time now Cotton had been pushing Grade as a future Director General, although he did not think he could get the job this time. But he felt he should put a marker down and when Grade rubbished Dimbleby's application he told him, 'If you are going to make a comment like that, you'd better apply for it yourself. It will do you good. You might get it next time. You can fish for something else for a while.'

Personally it marked a significant moment for Grade. All other jobs had come to him. This was the first one he had ever applied for in his life.

The interviews were fixed for 26 February and Grade was the last of the six candidates to be called. He was also the least likely to succeed. He was not, recalls Sarah, confident; 'he really didn't think he would get it. But he didn't think much of the opposition. I think he would have liked it. He was serious about applying but he knew he wasn't going to get it.'

The television establishment favoured Isaacs and so did Barnett. Wenham was certain that 'Isaacs would win hands down'. But the interviews began to give some clues as to how the governors were thinking. Wenham was asked whether he would like a separate news and current affairs department, an area which had created most of the problems for the BBC. Wenham replied no, arguing it would be a tremendous drain on resources. The mood of the governors was that a separate department was needed and Wenham's answer, probably, fatally damaged his cause. But perhaps the greater damage was caused by the fact that the times were wrong for Wenham. He had long been tipped as DG but he suffered from having a background similar to Milne's. He was seen as too close to the world of the producers and somebody more detached was deemed more desirable.

In the BBC that Rees-Mogg had wanted and Hussey planned for, this was a disadvantage. Checkland, although he had no programme experience and was an accountant by training, gained by comparison. Wenham could not believe that 'the BBC would turn its back on Isaacs who had such a lively track record', but for some of the other governors he was too much of a risk and Barnett's vote for him was checkmated by Hussey's in favour of Dimbleby. In this stand-off Checkland emerged, in the cricketing phrase Hussey liked, as a safe pair of hands.

Cotton, having encouraged Grade to apply, was not surprised he did not get it. Even had he been a governor he would not have given Grade the job; he saw it as a Grade sighter for a successful application next time round.

Sarah was relieved he had not got the job. 'He would have liked to have led the BBC with its global outlook and with the government; he would have enjoyed that. I think he can be quite visionary when it comes to broadcasting. But he would have got away from the things he liked best. He would have been useless at the day-to-day grind of it.'

But Grade could not escape the grind so easily and the Checkland appointment set up a chain reaction which within a few months was dramatically to change his life – yet again.

Checkland's first move, made early in March 1987, was to bring a man into Grade's life to whom he had bidden goodbye in Paris almost six years before. Although Grade could have little suspected it then, this man was now to play a crucial role once again. Checkland was well aware of the governors' worries about news and current affairs and sought to remedy what seemed a chronic BBC problem, one that he knew had eventually destroyed Milne. Convinced there was nobody suitable in the BBC, he looked outside. Through an intermediary he approached John Birt. They arranged to meet at the Howard Hotel. Birt was just about to take up the managing directorship of LWT, which came with attractive share options, but at his meeting with Checkland he was impressed by Checkland's briskness of purpose. Within minutes he was talking about pay and what Birt would be expected to handle. Birt, as we have seen, had once been rejected by the BBC. To be courted in this fashion was very flattering.

However high a broadcaster may go in commercial television, he or she does not feel fulfilled without some experience of the BBC. Usually commercial television executives start life at the BBC, then get lured away. Birt, like Grade, was reversing the process and savoured the moment. Also, the post of Deputy Director General which Checkland offered seemed to place him in the ideal position for when the top job once again became vacant. He accepted.

The weekend Birt joined the BBC saw the first casualty of the old Milne guard. Wenham was told the new management wanted to separate news and current affairs and also the regions from his radio control. He went to see Checkland.

'We had a conversation about moving on. It was an analysis of what I thought of the way they wanted to run the organisation and its need of me, whether there was anything challenging I might do. If they had been desperate to keep me they would have done something, but they didn't.'

This, probably, should have been a warning sign for Grade of how the new management's thoughts ran. But Grade saw little reason to worry. Checkland's appointment of Birt did not appear to affect him. If anything his route to the top seemed assured, just as Cotton had said it would be. True, Cotton was not entirely happy with Checkland's appointment but he felt that Checkland, being a financial man, could only work the financial magic – and how long would that last in the BBC? However, Cotton himself was due to retire in 1988 and Grade was his natural successor. Soon this was confirmed when Grade was made Managing Director (Television) Designate. This would make Grade the second most powerful person in the BBC, next only in practice to the DG. Often in the BBC the next job after this was that of DG.

At this stage the Grade–Birt relationship seemed to be set on an even keel, although in nominal terms Birt was Grade's superior, a reversal of their LWT roles.

Wenham supposed that 'Michael was quite content with Birt coming in. The impression I got was that Michael saw Birt coming in and looking after the journalism, the difficult end, and he would be left on the Westway to get on with what he likes at the entertainment end of the channel.'

The problem was that Grade had totally misunderstood how Birt saw his job. By the summer of 1987 Grade began to realise that Birt meant to exercise the powers his title nominally gave him: Deputy Director General, not just a glorified Head of News and Current Affairs.

'Michael,' says Sarah, 'knew that John's other title was Deputy Director General. However, what he thought was he would exercise that role only when Checkland was away. That's very different from being Deputy Director General all the time. So he did not give it much thought. Michael is not very clever at the politics. He did not think he would have to report to John. When it became clear that was the case, the two of them didn't talk to each other. They retrenched. Michael Checkland should have stepped in. It was weak of him not to explain to both Michael and John what their respective jobs were. In the end what happened between John Birt and Michael was bad management by Michael Checkland.'

The geography of the BBC did not help. Birt's office was next door to Checkland's on the all-important third floor of Broadcasting House, that part of the building where the carpets are lush. (On another part of the same floor where programmes are made and journalists and editors work the carpets are distinctly threadbare.) Grade was based in Television Centre.

'Who', as Sarah asks, 'is going to be closer to the ear of power?'

From his LWT experience Grade should have known that Birt's basic approach was very different to his and that they were bound to clash.

'Michael,' says Sarah, 'will look at a problem and go for a solution instantly. That is that. And on to the next job. John thinks out a problem from every possible angle. John will go through figures, reports. He will see every single side.'

So, through the summer of 1987, various niggling little problems arose between the two men and a battle quickly developed between the long-term planner and the man of instinct.

Since then both men have tried to play down the differences. Birt denies them, claiming that the cuttings of the period which outlined some of these differences are not reliable. Grade has always said that they are the best of friends.

Wenham has no doubts there was a serious rift between the two men: 'I don't think it is remotely true that there were no differences between Birt and Grade. I think there were a number of differences. John Birt's view was that his job was not simply to look after news and current affairs. It was the whole range of policy. This included the documentary field which was not technically part of his immediate area of control and this, in itself, was regarded by Grade, I think, as a provocation. But Birt saw his job extending to drama scripts and even dramas which might be deemed to be a little bit challenging or different, therefore, in a sense, having control over the totality of what was going on BBC television. This, I think, led to a degree of friction during that summer. If Michael Grade initially welcomed the appointment he went off the idea quite rapidly. The message I was getting was Grade saw Birt working outside the role he originally was meant to have and encroaching on Grade's sphere.'

Birt showed his hand at the first programme meeting he attended, when a new play was being discussed. Birt, mindful of what had happened with *The Monocled Mutineer*, asked, 'Can I ask whether there is any fictional portrayal of any living person in this play?' This was the first inkling Grade had of how wide Birt saw his remit and how he would encroach on his domain. But instead of resisting, Grade withdrew.

'Michael', says Sarah, 'may be instinctive, judgemental, but he doesn't like confrontations at all. Never has. Never likes shouting matches.'

Grade's instinct is to seek a non-confrontational way out – which often means flight. He had done this at Stowe, he would do it again with Lynda, and this is exactly the strategy with which he approached Birt.

Through the summer of 1987 Grade seemed to be seeking a way out of the BBC. At the time journalist Mark Jones was involved in helping with the programmes Grade was devising to make the BBC more accessible to the public and noticed a curious thing. 'Grade was as friendly and approacheable as I had been led to believe. But there seemed to be an end-of-term feel about it, as if he was planning to leave.'

Suddenly the press, which for three years had been singing his praises as the man who had rescued BBC 1 and would lead the channel into the nineties, was now linking Grade with various jobs.

Some rumours suggested he might rejoin ITV and others that he might join forces with Richard Branson in trying to secure a new franchise. On 2 August 1987, Richard Compton Miller in the *Daily Express* wrote yet another fulsome piece on Grade headlined: 'THE FAVOURITE NEPHEW IS PUTTING AUNTIE IN HER PLACE.' Unlike most articles about him, it was not based on an interview, but Miller appeared to have been briefed and made references to two areas of Grade's circumstances that would suddenly begin to take on greater significance. Miller reported that Lord Burnham had complained that he and his wife hardly ever saw Michael and Sarah although they lived next door to them in Beaconsfield. Grade's father-in-law appeared miffed that Michael did not shoot, ride or have any country pursuits and that he and Sarah were glued to the box and the video. That is, when they were even at home. Often Sarah was away in America but she was quoted as saying, 'Absence really does make the heart grow fonder in our case.' Remarks that were soon to haunt her.

The most revealing passage in the piece, though, was at the end. Miller was sure that Grade was unlikely to defect to ITV's higher-paying Big Five, but noted that the arrival of John Birt had stolen some of his fire. Then, in conclusion, he quoted a BBC mole as saying, 'Michael has his sight set on becoming Director General,' adding, 'He is not interested in taking over from Jeremy Isaacs when he leaves Channel 4 next year.'

Use of such moles is a very old journalistic trick but was this perhaps a coded message about Grade's thinking, a suggestion that Grade was again restive, looking for change?

It is the reference to Channel 4 that is most puzzling, for nothing in Grade's previous career had suggested he might go there. However, now that channel seemed ever more in Grade's thoughts.

In September he spoke at the Royal Television Society in Cambridge. This place, as we have seen, has played a crucial role in Grade's earlier career. It was here in 1981 that his intention of going to America was first aired by Tesler to Brian Young; here in 1983 that Wenham had begun the soundings that were to lead to Grade's first BBC job. Now Grade himself was speaking and his theme was Channel 4. The channel's future was being debated, parliament would have to decide how it should be funded, and Grade jumped into the debate. The BBC did not much care for his doing so. It was, in strict theory, of no concern to the BBC but Grade insisted and suggested that the channel, instead of continuing to get its revenue from the ITV companies, ought to be privatised. This was a controversial view, more so as it was given by the man designated to become the next managing director of BBC Television. Was it more than Grade sounding off?

At least one Channel 4 executive believed this was not a thoughtless remark but that deep planning lay behind it. That executive was Sue Stoessl, who was in charge of marketing and public affairs at the channel. Through much of the previous summer she and Grade had discussed the question of his applying for Isaacs's job. The two had worked together at LWT where Stoessl had helped Grade prepare the schedules. They had re-established a working relationship shortly after Grade had returned to the BBC. Every now and again he would ring her up to get 'the overnight ratings' on certain programmes. The BBC does not care for such instant ratings, preferring to wait for the weekly ones, but commercial television does worry about them and Grade sometimes used Stoessl to obtain figures from Thames or LWT.

That summer the conversation widened. 'It would be one of these conversations we would have. He would say, "Can you find me the ratings for so and so?" I would say, "Are you going to apply for Jeremy's job?" He would say, "No, I don't think so, it will always be Jeremy Isaacs's channel." Next time he rang me to ask about the ratings we would talk about the matter again.'

The conversations were touched by banter, inevitable among old colleagues, but as the summer wore on they became more frequent. It seemed to Stoessl obvious that 'when Birt had moved to the BBC Michael wasn't going to stay there. It wasn't a question of not getting on. It was a status problem. Michael didn't think he was going to have to report to him and he found he had to.' This, she argues, made him turn to Channel 4 and use the Cambridge speech as a job application.

'A lot of people thought it was a job application. I don't know why he made it but it could have been part of seeking a high profile. What you do to get headlines is make that sort of speech. You get somebody to write you a speech that says that. It could have been Michael's way of letting the world know he was interested. What better way to make a job application?'

This may make Grade out to be much more Machiavellian than he is, but at the time he was not contractually bound to the BBC. His BBC contract had expired in August. In October, Checkland, worried by this, held what the BBC call an executive lunch and over the hors d'œuvres offered him another five-year contract. In a sense it was a formality; Grade was due to take over as managing director in under five months, but even so Grade did not commit himself straightaway.

Also about this time Wenham began to hear from sources close to Downing Street that it was not inconceivable that Grade might move to Channel 4. There is no suggestion that Downing Street had any part in what was to follow and it would indeed have been scandalous, as Anthony Smith has said, if it had. But Grade, the Falklands incident well behind him, was now part of the political circle close to Downing Street, drawn there by Lord Young and Tim Bell, and it is possible that the talk amongst them came back to Wenham.

Wenham says, 'Conversations had been going on and I wouldn't be at all surprised if the roots of it go back into the summer when he thought, "I'd better open up another option in case I don't like things here".'

The need to 'open up another option' became more pressing in the second week of November when there was the final row with Birt. This had to do with the selection of controllers for BBC 1 and BBC 2. Cotton had never reconciled himelf to Checkland's appointment and he was quite appalled by Birt. The two men were soon to fall out in a quite spectacular way about the scheduling of *Newnight*; now he wanted to keep Birt as far away from Television Centre as possible. Cotton thought he had arranged it so that he and Grade would sit on the panel to appoint the controllers of BBC 1 and BBC 2 but Birt insisted on sitting on the panel as well. It was unusual to have an active deputy director general in any case; to have such a person sitting on a selection panel was, Grade felt, quite outrageous. It was the final, clinching proof of Birt's vaulting ambition. The need to open up other options was becoming quite crucial.

On Tuesday, 10 November Grade sent a fax to Pamela Reiss, his loyal statistician: 'Can you give me some information to show that Channel 4 is downmarket in profile?' For Reiss that was no great problem. She believes that all television is basically downmarket. Reiss had research which proved that it was a myth that Channel 4 was a young, upmarket station. 'Upmarket or downmarket does not really apply in television because it is a mass medium. On a typical week everybody watches something on all four channels. In sheer numbers there are more old people and downmarket women watching everything, but in profile terms it may be different.'

Reiss quickly faxed her reply to Grade along these lines. To her it may have seemed like a standard piece of research but it was to be the last piece of research she ever did for him. Information she had provided would form the basis for yet another dramatic twist to the Grade story and one of the most extraordinary events in British television.

Grade was now ready to make a call that was to change his life, yet again.

X

MR A. N. OTHER

I have a dark horse, darling.
RICHARD ATTENBOROUGH, talking to Anthony Smith

*I had nothing against Michael Grade, but the procedure
followed was ungentlemanly, not how we had been told
the choice would be made*
JUSTIN DUKES, managing director of Channel 4

THE PHONE CALL THAT GRADE MADE that Tuesday was to Sir Richard
Attenborough. His film about Steve Biko, *Cry Freedom*, had just been
released and the ostensible reason for the call was to discuss a documentary the BBC wanted to make about the film.

But Grade is an inveterate gossiper and a 'subtext' (the word Grade
would himself later use) developed between the two men as talk about
Biko veered to talk about something very different and much closer to
home.

They began to chat about who might become the next chief executive of Channel 4. This had been in the air since February 1987 when
Jeremy Isaacs had come to the Channel 4 board and asked for permission to apply for the job of Director General of the BBC.

The board was not sure why he wanted to apply for the job. Board
members believed absolutely in Jeremy, they rarely questioned what he
did and readily gave him permission to apply. As we have seen, Isaacs
failed to get the job. The BBC rejection 'devastated Jeremy', says John
Gau, then a director of Channel 4. 'He went into the application with
too high expectations and he was poleaxed by the rejection.' Wenham
might have found it difficult to believe that the BBC could turn its back
on him, a man with such a track record, but the time was not right for
him. For Isaacs, a sensitive soul used to the adulation and the almost
ceaseless rapture of Channel 4, the rejection cut deep, more so as he
reflected that an accountant, a man with no programme experience,
had been selected in preference to himself, then being hailed as the most
original broadcaster in British television.

In a sense, the rejection should not have mattered and Isaacs should have recovered from it. He could just have stayed on at Channel 4. No modern British broadcaster has been so identified with a particular television channel as Isaacs with Channel 4. Tony Smith may be seen as the father of the channel but Isaacs was the creator, the man whose personality, skill, vision, intelligence and television expertise made the channel.

Not since the early days of the BBC and Lord Reith had one man so stamped his personality on a particular broadcasting medium as Isaacs had on Channel 4. He saw it as his baby and all those who worked for the channel held him in a mixture of love and awe that was truly remarkable. The board were as much in the thrall of 'dear Jeremy' as the programme makers, who delightedly recounted stories of how Jeremy watched every Channel 4 programme before it was screened.

Had Isaacs decided to put the BBC rejection behind him and carried on at Channel 4, nothing more would have been heard about it. Certainly no board member would have seen it as an excuse to get rid of Isaacs. That was just unthinkable.

In the early years of the channel Isaacs had had to cope with Edmund Dell, its first chairman, and had not much enjoyed that. This former Labour minister had never liked Isaacs, felt the television establishment was foisting Isaacs on him and would have much preferred John Birt. Relations with Dell had degenerated so much that Isaacs had very nearly parted company with the channel within a year of its birth. But now Dell was gone, Dickie Attenborough was chairman and he was just as devoted to Isaacs as the programme makers. Everything seemed set fair for the continuing reign of Jeremy Isaacs.

But that was only the outward impression. What hardly anyone outside Isaacs's immediate circle knew was that for some time he had been quite keen to leave Channel 4. In January 1986, his wife of twenty-eight years, Tamara, had suddenly died of cancer and he felt it was a time to move: move home, move jobs. In December 1986 it became clear that the Royal Opera House wanted a successor to its general director Sir John Tooley, although his term was not due to finish until the summer of 1989. Isaacs's love of the opera is famous, Tamara had loved it even more and in December 1985, just before her death, Jeremy had been made a governor of the Royal Opera. Now he was approached to succeed Tooley. The very day in January 1987 that he and Sir John Sainsbury, who was taking over as chairman, agreed they could work together, Milne's resignation was announced. Isaacs decided to put the Opera offer on ice and go for the BBC. He had not told anyone at the Channel about the Opera while his application for the BBC was common gossip in the London media world.

So when the BBC rejection was followed by news that very weekend that Isaacs would go to the Opera a lot of people saw it like Gau: 'Jeremy, stung by the BBC rejection, decided to leave Channel 4 and go to the Opera House. He told the board he ought to set an example, nobody should stop too long at a job and five years as chief executive of Channel 4 was long enough.' Dell wanted him to go straightaway, but Isaacs could not. Tooley was not due to leave for almost another two years. In any case, he probably did not want to give Dell the satisfaction of choosing his successor. But this introduced another strand into the complex web. Dell, who left in July 1987, had been succeeded by Richard Attenborough. Isaacs had put up Sir Peter Parker's name but at the last minute the IBA had turned down his application when he refused to undertake not to participate in any political activity in the forthcoming election. Isaacs had to accept Attenborough. The elements of a classical tragedy were being assembled.

Isaacs had justified his decision to move to the Opera on the grounds that nobody should stay at a job for more than five years. Some members of the board could not understand what was so magical about working at a job for five years. But, they reasoned, Jeremy was Jeremy, he had made up his mind to go and that was that.

However, what Isaacs did not realise was that he was placing the board in the position of the electorate in a safe seat where the sitting member of parliament is suddenly elevated to the House of Lords, thereby forcing a by-election. Recent by-election evidence suggests that the electorate, forced to go to the polls in what they feel is an unnecessary election, react by rejecting the party they have always voted for, almost as if to say, 'Serves you right for foisting this on us.' There is just a suggestion that the Channel 4 board was in that mood: Jeremy had forced this upon them and, well. . . .

Attenborough formed a small sub-committee of the main board which was authorised to select the next chief executive, a sub-committee which comprised, besides Attenborough himself, Paul Fox, John Gau, Carmen Callil and George Russell. The composition of the committee was to prove significant.

Attenborough was by now a colossus of the British film and broadcasting industry, having with his film *Gandhi*, as it were in one bound, broken free from his stereotype of playing sturdy British sailors and other sundry characters. He now ranked with David Lean and David Puttnam among the great British film-makers.

Fox, although known in the industry as Eighteenth-century Fox, was a television elder statesman. Gau, who had been passed over for Hart in the early eighties as controller of BBC 1, was established as a significant independent programme maker. Callil and Russell were the television outsiders. Callil, although a highly respected book publisher, was little known in the television industry. Russell, a businessman and chief executive of Marley, a public company, had just taken over Attenborough's job as vice-chairman of the channel when Attenborough succeeded Dell as chairman.

In the usual fashion the job was advertised, although Attenborough and his committee knew full well that this was just a formality. There were only a handful of realistic candidates and a short list could have been jotted down on the back of an envelope. Television is a small, intimate world where everybody knows everybody else, everybody drinks with everybody else; advertising the job was just going through the motions.

However, the intimate circle of television and its very gossipy nature made Attenborough fearful of the interview process. To see so many familiar television faces trooping into Channel 4 would immediately start the gossip mills rolling. Also, many of the candidates requested privacy. He decided that they should not be interviewed at Channel 4's headquarters in Charlotte Street, but in hotel rooms in central London. The Ramada Hotel in Berners Street, a short walk from Charlotte Street, and the Churchill in Portman Square were chosen.

The secrecy was carried to such an extent that the rooms in the Ramada Hotel and the Churchill were not booked in the name of Channel 4, nor was the hotel allowed to advertise that Channel 4 was holding a conference by displaying it in the hotel foyer as is done when other companies or institutions use hotels in such a fashion. The members of the committee were told that they must arrive separately and just walk up to the reception and give their names.

'It was,' recalls, Fox, 'cloak and dagger, almost as if we had code names. We were told go up to the reception and discreetly mention "I want so and so" and you were somehow expected secretly to find the room.'

The predictable result was worthy of a script that Attenborough might well have rejected had it been presented to him: what was meant to be a subtle John Le Carré thriller assumed aspects of a *Carry On* farce.

At the end of one interview session Fox emerged into the hotel lobby to find the whole lobby lit up for filming. David Green, a Yorkshire film director, was filming the *The Great Train Robbery* and he immediately recognised Fox. 'Hello, Paul. How are you?'

Fox had to acknowledge him and felt a fool going through such a charade. 'There were these electricians standing there and television directors and they had seen everyone coming and going and I thought the whole thing had been blown.'

But somehow it was not blown. The charade did serve a purpose. Almost nothing about the cast list of candidates leaked to the press and by the time the sub-committee assembled for its final session on Friday, 13 November, Attenborough had managed to preserve secrecy in a world which naturally abhorred it. At 3.45 that afternoon the final candidate from the short list, still following the elaborate secrecy rules laid down by Attenborough, came for interview. This was Anthony Smith, widely regarded as the father of Channel 4.

Smith had a special relationship with Attenborough. In a sense, Attenborough was his boss as he was also chairman of the British Film Institute of which Smith was director. In February, when Smith had applied for the BBC job, Attenborough had helped him prepare his application. Some of the candidates, including Wenham, had the impression that Smith had virtually been promised the job. Smith denies this: 'It wasn't quite like that.' But between job adver-tisements had come a fateful ride in Attenborough's green Rolls-Royce.

When Edmund Dell left Channel 4 in June 1987 there had been pressure on Attenborough to take over as chairman. As we know, several names had been suggested but it was clear Attenborough could have the job if he wanted.

As they drove, Smith tried hard to dissuade Attenborough from taking it on. 'Don't do it, Dickie. You can't do it. You are terribly overworked. You work unbelievably hard. You have been unwell. You'll kill yourself.'

Attenborough shot Smith a quick glance and then said, 'There is only one reason I would take the job, darling. If I become chairman you will have to become chief executive when Jeremy goes.'

Smith did not quite see this as a cast-iron promise to make him chief executive but he felt secure that, should Attenborough accept the chairmanship, he stood a very good chance of getting the job. He and Dickie had 'a kind of long-term vision about the channel'.

So Smith came to the Channel 4 interview that Friday evening with this conversation very much in mind and with a job application that was a retouch of the one that Attenborough had helped him prepare for the BBC.

Applications for such jobs are detailed and properly prepared. Smith wrote how he saw his life, what he had done, but whereas for the BBC job he had written about his plans for the BBC, now he wrote about his plans for Channel 4 and why he felt it was right for him as well as for the job that they should come together.

The interview seemed to go well and Smith, a small, intense man, could have been forgiven for thinking that he would succeed Jeremy.

However, when Smith had departed and the sub-committee began to assess the candidates, it was by no means clear that he was the obvious favourite. The candidates who had trooped into the rooms at the Ramada represented the cream of television executives: apart from Smith, there was Brian Wenham, Philip Whitehead, Roger Graef, Hugh Williams, Will Wyatt, Alan Yentob and a string of Channel 4 internal candidates led by Justin Dukes, managing director of the channel, Liz Forgan and Naomi Sargeant. Curiously, there was only one ITV candidate who had come forward: Richard Creasey, then with TV-AM.

Smith had given a good account of himself but the feeling of the sub-committee was, as Gau recalls, 'that it was no longer the time for Tony. A new generation of broadcasters was emerging and there was a sense his moment had gone.' Roger Graef was a good representative of this new generation: he had made an excellent presentation, and there was a small lobby for him. There might have been a lobby for Alan Yentob but he had become the Controller of BBC 2, a job that Grade had pushed hard for him, and he had rung that afternoon to say he was no longer interested.

The strongest internal candidate was undoubtedly Justin Dukes. There was quite a lobby for him from within Channel 4 and Dukes had been given impetus by Attenborough giving him the impression that he stood a good chance.

'Dickie,' says Gau, 'tends to do that. "Apply, darling, apply, I am sure you stand a great chance." He built up the poor man's hopes.' Gau did consider Dukes, the 'unsung hero of the creation of Channel 4'. But he suffered from one major disadvantage: he was not really a television man, he did not have experience of either making programmes or even of being involved in television programming. He had come to Channel 4 from the *Financial Times* and to appoint him would confirm what Gau saw as the recent and depressing trend in television of giving the top jobs to salesmen or accountants. Every top job in ITV recently seemed to have gone to a person with a non-television background and Gau, a man steeped in television, did not like that.

Smith had left at 5 p.m. By 6.30 p.m. it was clear there was no strong candidate around whom the committee could unite. The talk had gone backwards and forwards, without conclusion. For television executives used to quick decisions they were displaying a great deal of dither. Then Attenborough suddenly said, 'We are clearly not agreed. I have kept this to myself but there is one other candidate.'

'Who's that?' asked Fox.

'Michael Grade,' replied Attenborough. 'He has said that if drafted he will be willing to serve.' Before the astonished sub-committee could catch its breath, Attenborough told them of the phone conversation he had had with Grade on the Tuesday, how Grade had probed him and how he had told him that they were finding it difficult to get a replacement for Isaacs.

'That's absolutely wonderful,' said Fox. 'We must talk to him.'

Gau was just as pleased. 'We were all astonished when Dickie told us. But on the whole we were excited. Michael was involved in programme making. He is a charismatic figure. It is a hard act to follow Jeremy but from the Channel 4 point of view it needed somebody with a bit of chutzpah. Michael had that.'

But where and how would the committee meet Grade? How could it be kept a secret? Attenborough suggested they interview Grade next day at twelve o'clock at his home in Richmond.

Fox had never taken kindly to the secrecy imposed by Attenborough and now expressed his irritation. 'That's a ridiculous idea, Dickie. Richmond is a hot bed of the BBC, an awful lot of BBC executives live in Richmond. We are bound to bump into them on a Saturday morning. How are you going to smuggle Michael in?'

'Leave it to me,' reassured Attenborough. 'Don't worry, I'll get him to the house.'

Fox's fears were confirmed almost as soon as he arrived at Attenborough's house. That day, as an additional precaution, he had decided to drive himself, leaving behind his chauffeur provided by Yorkshire Television. He parked nearby but just as he emerged from his car he was seen by Bob Roland, a BBC television executive.

'What are you doing here in Richmond? This is not your part of the world,' said Roland.

Fox, who was virtually outside Attenborough's home, could not very well lie but tried to pass it off as nothing. 'Oh, I have a meeting at Dickie Attenborough's house. I am going there.' Fox was after all on the Channel 4 board and a meeting between the two men need not be seen as sinister. Roland's suspicions were apparently not aroused and Fox, breathing a sigh of relief, knocked on Attenborough's front door.

Meanwhile, in west London, another little drama was taking place. Callil who lived in Notting Hill Gate, did not know where Attenborough lived and George Russell had offered to give her a lift. But she had recently moved, Russell went to her old address, missed her and arrived on his own. Eventually Callil had to hail a taxi to Richmond.

Despite all this, the principal character made it without detection. Attenborough had told Grade to tell his driver, Bill Ansboro, to take the car straight into Attenborough's garage. Only then was he to let Grade emerge from the car. A connecting door from the garage would convey the prospective chief executive into Attenborough's home without detection from anybody outside.

Finally, at about twelve, the committee assembled in the extension to Attenborough's house which acts as his office to talk to Grade. The setting was informal; the interview was not.

Unlike the other candidates Grade had made no formal presentation (he was not a formal candidate), but he faced the most serious question of them all. The others were committed to Channel 4. Grade was a declared opponent. All those interviewing him that day were vividly aware of his comments in Cambridge in September. How could this be squared with his now becoming the chief executive of the channel he had proposed be sold off?

Grade's Cambridge remarks were much on the mind of Gau, who questioned him closely on them. Was he still in favour of privatisation? The Channel 4 remit was to provide programmes to cater to the minority tastes which the main television channels did not. Would the remit be safe in his hands? Grade had always been identified as a mass broadcaster. His BBC reputation was that he had pushed up ratings. How would he adjust to a minority channel where it was not ratings but the response of very specialised tastes that mattered?

For Grade such questions posed few problems. He had figures from Reiss to show Channel 4 was not quite as upmarket as it made out. As far as the wider philosophical issue was concerned Grade, as we have seen, has never found it difficult to change his views. He readily recanted his previous statements on Channel 4 and was quick to assert that he was a Channel 4 man and the precious remit of the channel would be safe in his hands. However, even by Grade's legendary chameleon standards the conversion in Attenborough's house was remarkably swift. To an extent Attenborough and his committee wanted to believe that he had recanted. Grade did all he could to help them.

Fox may not have seen Grade as a younger brother as Cotton did, but he had always been an admirer. Callil, who was just getting introduced to the world of television, instantly took to him. Callil, an Australian by birth, has the reputation of being one of the toughest executives in publishing, a lady skilled in creating reputations and well known for her publishing enthusiasms. These included such diverse people as her 'two princes', as she calls Tariq Ali and Imran Khan, one a lapsed revolutionary, the other a cricketer turned sex symbol. Grade, in his own way, was a splendid addition to that list.

Gau, while aware of Isaacs's great broadcasting achievements, felt that it was time someone took charge at Channel 4 who could bring some order to it. 'Jeremy had this philosophy of "let a thousand flowers bloom". He was a libertarian of the old school. But this meant that the channel itself was run in a whimsical way. It was a bit disorganised. Jeremy had vision but visionaries are not the most practical people. He was inclined to run it by the seat of his pants. People within the organisation found it difficult, some times independent producers found it impossible to get the phone answered. Channel 4 had stopped being pioneering country; it was more a settled country. Vision is all very good but people like to know where they are headed. People need a system.' Gau saw Grade as a strong executive who would bring method to the creative chaos Isaacs thrived on.

By early lunch time the committee had come to the unanimous conclusion that Grade was their man. Attenborough's first thought was for Smith. The London Film Festival was just about to start; Smith was at the National Film Theatre making the preparations when he was summoned to reception to take a call. It was Attenborough.

'Darling,' said Attenborough, 'there is a dark horse. I can't tell you.' As the call was being made the dark horse was being hustled away as secretively as he had come, via the garage into his car.

That day Grade was due to fly to Los Angeles on an annual buying mission. Sarah, whose job meant she had to spend almost half her year in America, had already left for Los Angeles on the Friday. As Bill Ansboro drove him back to London Grade pondered what he should do. He could not very well go to Los Angeles for the BBC when he was planning to leave. Nor could he go home. The news might leak and he might be besieged. So he did what would become known as his John Stonehouse act: go to ground and disappear for a time. As he always does on such occasions, he took refuge with Anita in Hampstead to clear his mind for the dramatic developments he knew would follow. It was now up to Attenborough and the others to deliver.

The sub-committee's decision had to be ratified by the full Channel 4 board which was due to meet on Monday evening. But that was not expected to be a problem. If there was to be a problem it might come from the IBA, which as the guardian of the ITV system needed to approve Grade as well. As Fox was the only ITV executive on the committee it was agreed that he would try to get the IBA's approval.

He rang Lord Thomson, chairman of the IBA, at home in Kent with the news about Grade. Thomson wanted to know what the other ITV companies thought of it and Fox spent some time that Saturday ringing round his fellow ITV managing directors. Fox reported back to Thomson that ITV would welcome the news of Grade's arrival with three chairs. 'The ITV companies,' he told Thomson, 'would throw their hats in the air. Michael Grade (a) away from the BBC and (b) joining Channel 4 could only be good news.'

Thomson readily agreed to ring his fellow IBA members including John Whitney, Director General of the IBA and, says Fox, 'to his eternal credit he spent the weekend, Saturday evening and Sunday morning, phoning all the members of the IBA in order to get their approval.' By early on Sunday the coast was clear for Grade.

Fox, feeling pleased that he had delivered the ITV companies and that the IBA had also approved, rang Grade at his home in Beaconsfield to give him the good news. Grade, as we know, was not at home. However, he had not told the housekeeper he had gone to Anita's. She was still under the impression he was going to America and told Fox that he was on his way to the airport. This phone call was to introduce a curious twist to the story.

Grade was due to be accompanied to America by Ibbotson. That weekend he had been waiting patiently for Grade at Heathrow airport. As the time to board the plane came and there was no sign of

Grade he rang him at home. The housekeeper answered and told him, 'If you see him, will you tell him Paul Fox is looking for him.' This was the first indication anyone outside the committee had about what was going on. Until then Ibbotson had been thinking Grade had just missed his flight; now he began to suspect that there was more to it than that.

For Grade the missed flight and the suspicion in Ibbotson's mind were of little concern. He needed to be away from it all. If his decision to join the BBC had been agonising, so was this one. The three nights he spent at Anita's he could barely sleep and a good deal of the time was spent talking to Sarah in Los Angeles. Sarah knew that Channel 4 would provide a way out from the confrontation developing at the BBC, a confrontation she felt Michael was bound to lose. Taking the job would also mean keeping in touch with creative people, working with programme makers.

There was also the question of how Michael would inform the BBC. He decided to write a letter of resignation to Checkland and asked his driver to make sure that it would be delivered to Broadcasting House on Monday evening at seven. That is when the Channel 4 board was due to meet to ratify his decision and he wanted the resignation to co-incide with that. By then the IBA would also have formally approved his appointment. Everything seemed to be going according to plan. Attenborough and he had discussed the details of the contract and it had been arranged that Grade should meet Attenborough at 5.30 on Monday evening at the Hyde Park Hotel. There he would meet with the IBA and hear the news at first hand.

It was only when Grade arrived at the hotel shortly before 5.30 that he began to receive the first hints that Attenborough's carefully scripted plans were meeting with some resistance. At the Hyde Park Hotel he expected smiles and congratulations; instead there was a very white-faced John Whitney and Attenborough himself looking most disturbed. There were lots of comings and goings. This did not look like a celebration, more an attempt to avert a crisis. Grade quickly sensed that there was a problem. The certainties of the past forty-eight hours were suddenly vanishing.

The problem was something, or rather someone, nobody had thought of: Jeremy Isaacs. He had not been privy to the selection process or the weekend's drama. The first he heard about it was on Monday and he immediately wanted to confront Attenborough. However, Attenborough, who is famous in the industry for being hyperactive, was that day chairing a lunch at the National Film Theatre for Jean

Rouch, President of the Cinéma Tech Française, and it was not easy to get hold of him.

Finally, Isaacs's office rang Tony Smith to arrange a room at the NFT where Isaacs could meet Attenborough. Given his schedule for the rest of the day, Attenborough cut short his lunch, missing the coffee although not the dessert, made his excuses and went to the special room that Smith had organised for the meeting with Isaacs.

It was a unique confrontation between two men who symbolised so much in British film and television. Isaacs was a mixture of rage, despair and helplessness. The news of Grade's appointment had come as a thunderclap: how could Dickie appoint Grade? It was like inviting the Antichrist to high church, a betrayal of all that Channel 4 stood for and that Isaacs and the others had fought for. Had not Grade just a few weeks previously called for Channel 4 to be privatised?

Attenborough explained Grade had recanted. But, countered Isaacs, if a man can recant so quickly, how could anybody take him seriously? Isaacs was a member of the full board and clearly it was not going to be as easy and painless a meeting as Attenborough had thought.

However, for the moment the row was confined to the two men. Smith knew nothing of what transpired but later heard that Isaacs cried and so probably did Attenborough. 'But then Dickie always cries, so that's nothing.' As Attenborough was leaving the NFT he encountered Smith, who could see he was terribly upset. He told Smith, 'Darling, I can't tell you who it is but I feel for you.'

When Grade met Attenborough he was still feeling bruised by his meeting with Isaacs and was clearly quite shaken. He had clearly not anticipated the venom of Isaacs's rejection. Grade, expecting a coronation, had found a rebellion, and as his natural tendency is to avoid confrontations he told Attenborough that he was prepared to withdraw, given the hassle.

Attenborough wouldn't hear of it. Relations with Isaacs were ruined; in any case they had to find a replacement for him; and there was no question of a Grade withdrawal. They had come too far now to turn back.

Grade, however, still faced a ticklish situation. What was he to do with Bill Ansboro? By now it was nearly 5.30 p.m. and Ansboro would be leaving Television Centre at any minute for the drive across London to Broadcasting House to deliver Grade's resignation letter to Checkland. But with Isaacs so furious, the Channel 4 board looked likely to be difficult and it would be very unwise to send the letter only to find he had not got the appointment. Grade frantically called his secretary to try to stop Ansboro and she just managed to catch him as he was about to go down to the Television Centre car park.

So far the only person outside his immediate circle to be told about the appointment had been Cotton. 'I was pretty devastated when I heard he was leaving. He said, "I would not sign the contract without you seeing it, without talking to you." '

On Monday evening, as the Channel 4 board were meeting, Grade contacted Cotton again. 'Let me talk it through with you.'

The two men met for dinner at the Mamas Chinese restaurant in Richmond. Cotton asked, 'Michael, answer me one thing. Do you want to go?'

'Yes, I do,' Grade replied.

'In that case,' said Cotton, 'I will talk it through with you but I have no intention of trying to talk you out of it. If you really, really want to go, then you must.'

As the evening wore on, what emerged were Grade's fear and loathing of Birt's unbounded ambition, feelings that Cotton had begun to share, and his dislike of being second-guessed. In the three days of retreat at Anita's house Grade had stopped to think about his career, where it was going for the next three to five years. He did not like what he saw ahead at the BBC. Channel 4 represented a very attractive alternative.

Cotton could appreciate why Grade wanted to leave. 'As I understood it the offer to be his own man, rather than be caught up in what was apparently going to be a lot of in-fighting, was attractive. Also, the people at the centre are better situated than the people on the outside. Michael was at Wood Lane working harder than anybody else, but insulated from the people at the centre who were busy sorting out the things, playing politics. You can lose out in that process. Michael was astute enough to realise that.'

The dinner may have begun as a means of trying to persuade Grade to remain with the BBC; it ended with Cotton almost endorsing his going. By ten that evening Grade had decided for sure that his future was no longer with the BBC.

By this time the Channel 4 board meeting at Charlotte Street was in near uproar. Attenborough had reported to the full board how the sub-committee had unanimously recommended Grade, how the IBA had blessed his appointment and that he himself had settled the contractual details with Grade. Fox, Gau and the other members of the committee had looked on, feeling pleased. They had not been privy to the NFT confrontation between Attenborough and Isaacs and had expected the board meeting to end in mutual congratulation. But suddenly Isaacs got up and said, 'I disagree with that.' There followed, to the astonishment of Fox and Gau, an impassioned denunciation of the choice of Grade and a plea to the board to reject it. They had never seen such anger, such passion.

Fox was the first to react. 'Come on, Jeremy. Stop behaving like this. If you do not like Michael, then who do you recommend?' Isaacs had no answer. In fact this was the crucial weak point in the case Isaacs was trying to build against Grade. In the months preceding his departure Isaacs had given no indication of who he wanted to succeed him.

Fox sees this as one of the key issues in the whole drama. 'The point is Jeremy had not suggested a candidate himself. Who was Jeremy's candidate? He had not in any way said to the board I suggest my successor is X, Y, Z, Justin Dukes or Tony Smith or whoever. Jeremy hadn't done that.'

Gau agreed with Fox. 'For nine months, at no stage had he said, "This is the person you should have." Now to denounce the person we had selected was a little surprising.'

The whole process had been forced on the board by Isaacs's unilateral decision to go after five years.Gau and the others had worked hard to come up with a name; to see him now being criticised by Isaacs was a bit rich.

The board still felt a deep sympathy for Isaacs. He had recently lost his wife and some felt that explained his unexpected passion.But the board, that had for so long accepted everything that Isaacs had suggested, could not agree with him this time. He was the king no more. They decided to endorse Attenborough's choice. Isaacs insisted that his vote against the decision, a minority of one, be recorded.

As this decision was being taken, London's gossipy media world was at last beginning to trade rumours and stories about the successor to Jeremy. In his characteristic style, Attenborough had rung the leading candidates and told them, 'Darling, you were wonderful, but there is another candidate.'

That Monday evening Wenham was sitting drinking with Melvyn Bragg in his office in LWT. All the candidates and several noncandidates – Bragg himself had been mentioned as a possible choice – were phoning each other furiously to discover who the dark horse might be. So far the name of Grade had not occurred to anybody. As far as they knew he was in Los Angeles. But amidst this welter of phone calls Wenham spoke to Ibbotson and it emerged that Grade was not in Los Angeles. He had missed the flight.

But he was not in his office either. Also, on the Sunday he had missed the party at Alan Yentob's house to celebrate his appointment as Controller of BBC 2.

So where was he? It did not take Wenham, who has perhaps the shrewdest brain in television, long to work out what had happened.

The unthinkable had come true. The dark horse was Michael Grade.

Wenham's first thought was Smith, poor Tony, who, he thought, had already been promised the job by Attenborough. Smith had just got back to his flat in Piccadilly when Wenham called. Just as after an accident people remember the trivia, so later Smith would recall that Wenham had an unlikely drinking companion (in fact, Bragg is not such an unlikely companion for Wenham), but his words are imprinted on Smith's memory.

Wenham said, 'We have just worked out who it is. It is Michael Grade.'

'Don't be ridiculous,' replied Smith.

'No,' insisted Wenham. 'He was supposed to go to America and he didn't turn up at the airport. Ibbo [as Peter Ibbotson was known to friends] doesn't know where he is.'

Smith was due at a dinner party at the writer Susha Guppy's home in Chelsea. Asa Briggs was also there. They all said to Smith, 'They must have appointed you.'

Smith smiled, shook his head and said, 'No, it is Michael Grade.'

The guests could not believe it. 'How can it be?' they chorused almost in unison. To them it seemed as if the Devil himself had been invited to lead the service. Asa Briggs, the great historian of the BBC, was dumbfounded.

Smith returned home quite devastated. 'I said, may God forgive them. Dickie got very upset about it. He doesn't like the idea that he is not on God's side. Later Dickie and I patched it up.' Smith, who has since moved to academia and become President of Magdalen College, Oxford, now takes a philosophical view of the whole affair. 'I am sure all people who are good friends of mine behaved properly. My understanding with Sir Richard antedated even his acceptance as chairman or even the formal offer of the chairmanship to him. I never expected him to do anything more than what is good for Channel 4. Once he was chairman of Channel 4 he had certain obligations to work in the interest of that channel and I hope that he served them, just as I do in my job here. I am president here and I have to behave as president. I don't think Sir Richard behaved improperly. He probably thought that someone who was an even better candidate came along and that it was his duty to appoint him. The question is whether Mr Grade was the right person in terms of the nature of the channel and the predicament in which it found itself.'

By dinner time on Monday, of course, the news had already leaked, or at least a part of it, and the *Daily Mail* carried a story of Grade having a row with Birt and walking off to Channel 4. The *Daily Mail* thought it of such importance that it led its front page with the news: ANGRY GRADE MOVES TO CHANNEL 4. While many of its details were wrong, what was significant was that the *Mail* considered it more important than the crisis in the Soviet Union and the growing opposition to Gorbachev. This was a measure of how Grade had captured the public, or at least a section of the tabloid, imagination.

Although the story had leaked, Grade would still have to be formally presented to the press. That night Sue Stoessl got a call from her press office telling her the news and that a conference had to be arranged for the next morning at eleven. Stoessl could barely contain her surprise and sense of shock.

The press conference was to be held in the Channel 4 cinema. Stoessl arrived early the next morning and began ringing round to make sure everybody would be there. 'My job was to get him through the press conference.' Stoessl would not have been surprised to find Grade a bit apprehensive but was impressed by how well he carried it off. 'He didn't look nervous.'

But not even Grade could avoid the laughter that followed his attempts to explain how he had so quickly changed from a man who wanted to sell off the channel to one who wanted to be its saviour.

In contrast to the almost flawless performances Grade normally gives at press conferences, for almost the first time in his public career he seemed hesitant. He denied rows with Birt but when he was asked why he had left the BBC it took Grade four takes and some prompting from Attenborough before he came up with the right answer. Peter Fiddick, reporting the conference, could not remember Grade ever being so hesitant. Nor was he really comfortable when asked about the recantation of his views about the channel.

At one point, exasperated by the questions, he snarled, 'Some parts of the channel are very precious.' Grade, the master of the press conference, was beginning to lose his cool and forget his one-liners. Nor was he better pleased when it was suggested that his salary of £82,000, a 42 per cent increase on his BBC salary, had something to do with his move.

The press conference, like all such modern conferences, was in two parts. After the formal proceedings Grade gave a series of one-to-one interviews with selected journalists and provided much of the additional background for the story. For this Grade needed an office and Attenborough suggested he used his.

Stoessl took Grade up to the second floor where all the leading Channel 4 executives have their offices, including Isaacs. 'I took Michael to meet the various people who were on the floor. Head of finance David Scott and Frank McGettigan, general manager. They all lived on that floor.'

Grade and Stoessl had just passed Justin Dukes's office when Isaacs emerged.

Isaacs had sat in his office while Grade held his press conference. Now as he heard him outside he came out, looked at Grade and said, 'I'm handing on to you a sacred trust. If you screw it up, if you betray it, I'll come back and' – Isaacs had meant to conclude by saying 'thump you' but as he looked at Grade his eyes rested on Grade's Adam's apple and he said – 'throttle you.' Isaacs's lips were smiling but there was no laughter in his eyes and his words were spat out. Stoessl could feel the animosity and was struck by how shaken Grade was. This was the moment, if ever there was one, for one of Grade's masterly one-liners. But for once the master of the smart-arse remark had nothing to say.

The big question mark was over how the Channel 4 staff would react. Mike Bolland, who was assistant director of programmes and had played a major role in creating its entertainment profile, was in Los Angeles on the same buying mission that Grade was supposed to have been on. Not being BBC, the Channel 4 team stayed not at the Bel Air but at the Four Seasons. The subject of who might be their next chief executive was almost as obsessive a concern as the winner of the Grand National might be to most housewives.

David Elstein had organised a sweepstake of possible candidates and the choices were varied. The news came through as Bolland and the Channel 4 team were in the offices of Gilsen International and the shock was so total, Grade was so unexpected, that only one man had entered his name in the sweep. He was Andy Allen and he did so only because he had put down his choice as A. N. Other. Grade had not even been a 100–1 outsider in the Channel 4 Next Chief Executive stakes.

The BBC maintained a formal politeness about Grade's departure, issuing the regulation press release. But as if like a commentary on the Grade era, that evening it also announced that a pair of red braces Grade had contributed to the BBC's Children in Need appeal had been auctioned for £150.

X I

HIGH CULTURE, LOW POLITICS

*Michael Grade takes on the coloration of the institution
he serves*
ANTHONY SMITH

*I get the impression that at Channel 4, Michael is parked,
waiting to move*
CHARLES DENTON, Zenith Productions

SOON AFTER GRADE HAD TAKEN OVER at Channel 4 and Isaacs had moved to
the Opera House, Lew Grade turned up at Covent Garden. Isaacs,
intrigued by his presence, went up to his box and introduced himself.
Lord Grade looked at Isaacs and said, 'Mr Isaacs, you don't have to
worry about our Michael. He'll be all right. He can do anything. If they
appointed him head of the educational channel, he would do that.'

Later, as Isaacs delighted in narrating the incident to friends, it
quickly became a popular story in the gossipy London media world (it
even made the diary column of the *Financial Times*) and was a
favourite dinner-party piece for those who felt that Grade at Channel 4
was an outrage. For them the Lew Grade anecdote seemed to sum up
the whole philosophy of the Grades: have smile, will travel.

As it happened, Grade's move did seem to fit the temper of the
times. Other unexpected media appointments were being made, outsiders not on short lists were selected as editors of the *New Statesman*
and the *Listener* and it seemed as if the whole sixties and seventies
system of inviting applications for such jobs would soon become
redundant. But the glee with which Grade's critics attacked his
selection also suggested that the chattering classes saw Channel 4 as
occupying a special place in British culture.

The *Guardian*, which in contrast to other papers had doubts about
Grade, wrote that the channel had 'truly advanced the gaiety, variety
and depth of a television-watching audience'. Sceptical of Grade's
change of heart about the future of the channel, it warned that he had
'built a lustrous – but different – reputation in another part of the

forest . . . He is not, on that record, the most obvious choice for Channel 4. He competes by doing the same things better, rather than by doing different things . . . But there is just the hint – in the chopping speed of Mr Grade's appointment – of the old football manager's musical chairs. Here's a desirable, disaffected property on the market. Snap it up. Enjoy the headlines and the dismay of rivals and then work out what you actually need much later. We shall see; and we hope to see no change.'

It is no surprise that the *Guardian* should have taken such a stance. For if Channel 4 has a newspaper equivalent, then it must be the *Guardian*; indeed Anthony Smith's famous article that helped lauched the channel was written for that paper. The *Guardian*'s stance indicated that Grade had gone to the most ideological, committed television channel in the country, one that had what may be called (and many of those who make programmes for it still do) a certain 'right-on-ness': concern about ecology and the environment, faith in 'small is beautiful', the Third World, women's rights and various other issues, all wrapped around a conviction that these could be mirrored through a very different kind of television. For the devotees of the channel, Grade's smile and red braces were not a charming eccentricity but a provocation and, like the *Guardian* leader writer, they could not believe he was a true convert. The channel that thrived on zealots now feared it was in the hands of a man who could change his views with one telephone call or a press conference.

The charge of being a vulgarian with no fixed view was an old one and had been expressed in different ways. Thus Rees-Mogg pictures Grade as having a Californian cast of mind, by which he means a mind capable of absorbing every passing fad (Grade's friends respond with the tart observation that Rees-Mogg has an antiquated mind that is hardly worth considering); others, like Anthony Smith, see it as Grade's chameleon-like attitude, able to adapt to the colour of whichever institution he serves.

However, the anti-Grade sentiment that welled up as he now prepared for Channel 4 was different. It was starkly personalised as Isaacs (high culture) versus Grade (populist). Almost from the very day he took over at Channel 4 he was put on the back foot by having to defend himself against Isaacs. Much as Cotton marvelled at how well Grade rode press criticisms, the Channel 4 attacks cut him to the quick and he resented what he saw as the tabloid view of his work. Within a day of his taking over at Channel 4, on 4 January 1988, in his first press interview, in the *Independent* as head of the channel Grade was forced to defend himself, claiming that although Jeremy's reaction may have been understandable (he was 'giving his child away'), it was nevertheless based on 'a very simplistic characterisation of me in the popular press'. Just because he had pushed up the BBC's ratings, he was branded a vulgarian.

Nearly three years later, in an interview in autumn 1990, Grade was still being forced to respond to Isaacs. 'Jeremy was accepting a sort of tabloid view of my work. If anybody had studied the work I had encouraged and commissioned at LWT and the BBC, they couldn't possibly have concluded that my arrival at Channel 4 was the end of the world.'

Isaacs's fierce and openly expressed views also mirrored emotions within the organisation and Grade was soon aware of the depth of feeling his appointment had caused at Channel 4. It had been greeted, as Mike Bolland recalls, with 'tears and weeping' and not since his first job at the *Daily Mirror* had Grade gone to work faced with such indifference, if not downright hostility.

This was also his first job where there was no mentor to guide him. Here there was no John Bromley, Billy Marsh, Cyril Bennett or Bill Cotton. He had to find his own way.

The situation was made worse by the fact that Grade could not immediately take over. Given the circumstances of his appointment, Grade should have walked in through one door as Isaacs went out through another. Attenborough's selection of Grade amounted to a coup, but of a curious kind; it was as if the tanks were on the lawn while the old leader still clung on inside the palace.

For almost two months Grade was made to wait in the wings. Isaacs was not due at the Opera House until January 1988 and over Christmas 1987 Grade could do little but improve his golf. After every round he would love to banter with Bill Cotton that while he was improving his handicap, Cotton was waging a futile battle with Birt, but the delay made his eventual takeover at Channel 4 even more fraught. What made it potentially very embarrassing was that little more than two weeks after Isaacs had threatened to throttle Grade he was required to spend a weekend with him discussing the channel's future.

Channel 4 had decided, long before Grade had even been a speck on Attenborough's horizon, to have a skull session in the first weekend in December. This was to be at Nuneham Courtney near Oxford with the board, commissioning editors and the management committee of the channel meeting to discuss its future. For Grade this was to prove as momentous an occasion as the one at Selsdon all those years ago.

Grade drove up on the evening of 4 December, heard Isaacs speak and then joined him and the others for dinner. The following morning he addressed the gathering. Many at Channel 4 had wondered how he would react; some were meeting him for the first time. Whatever hurt and disappointment he felt about Isaacs were well hidden in an immensely skilful speech. If this showed the distinct stamp of Ibbotson, who now wrote nearly all Grade's speeches, it also indicated how well Grade could strike the right note even on an occasion potentially so full of pitfalls.

The previous day Isaacs had laid down the first principles that guided Channel 4. Grade, sounding as eager as any Isaacs devotee, now said, 'We listened yesterday to Jeremy's eloquent and passionate statement of first principles. I listened very carefully indeed and concluded at the end that my job is not to question those principles, and I do not question them.' In the printed text the words 'very' and 'not' were underlined. No convert could have been more zealous.

Despite this genuflexion to Isaacs Grade still managed to raise the odd note of dissent. Was the channel producing distinctive enough and high enough quality programmes at the popular end of the schedule? Why was the channel showing *The Far Pavilions* mini series 'in which the lead American actress is white but has been blacked up to look Indian?' (A potent point in a channel so concerned about racial minorities.) He ended the speech with what he described as the Grade family motto, 'loosely translated from the original Yiddish: "If at first you don't succeed, you're fired."' Then, while his audience laughed, he, with a flourish, went off to play golf.

Adrian Metcalfe, then commissioning editor for sports and features, was at the conference and could not help but admire the way his old friend handled the situation. 'Michael sat in, listened to everything, did a round-up speech and came over as charming and engaging.'

The audience he faced was not totally hostile. Not everyone at Channel 4 disliked him on sight. Mike Bolland may have been as surprised as the rest by his appointment and was aware that 'at Channel 4 there were tears, and weeping and wailing. But despite this I was quite keen that there would be somebody who would be big enough to take on the job. Jeremy was a very strong, a very inspirational figure. All the people who were on the list to replace him were actually rather pale by comparison. At that level I was actually quite pleased that Grade was coming.'

Some of this admiration for Grade came from the feeling that whatever else he did he would always project a high profile for the channel. So while Isaacs's throttle-you warning may have made Grade react to events, rather than take the lead as he liked doing, he quickly showed that he could still use offence as the best defence strategy when it came to publicity.

In this Grade was helped by the BBC. The very week he took over at Channel 4 the Birt–Cotton row emerged in public. Birt gave *Newsnight* a fixed time slot: 10.30 p.m. Previously it had been very much a movable feast, any time between ten and eleven. Not only did Cotton disagree but he learnt of the decision at a press conference. For Grade the BBC row was too good an opportunity to miss.

So far he had said nothing publicly about his problems with Birt but the day after he arrived at Channel 4 he talked to Sue Summers of the *Independent*. 'Bill is a precious asset to the corporation,' he said. 'There has to be something deeply wrong when a man of thirty years' experience, success and loyalty is treated in that fashion.'

This reaction showed Grade at his best. He came over as a loyal friend defending an old colleague who could not defend himself, but he also used the occasion to suggest that for all the negative publicity about his arrival at Channel 4, the real problems were with the organisation he had left. The headline over the Summers's piece was 'FORECAST OF STORM CLOUDS OVER THE BBC' and the accompanying piece on the *Independent* media page read 'Who runs the corporation?'

Grade also used the interviews to signal that his endorsement of Jeremy at Nuneham Courtney did not mean everything Isaacs had put in place would be sacrosant. Weekend, arts, education were all areas that would require changes and he was scathing about 'too many sloppy programmes that are not as well crafted as they might be'. As he had done at the press conference announcing his appointment he also now argued for complementary scheduling with ITV which would bring to an end both channels showing sport or drama at the same time. This could not present a greater contrast to Isaacs, who saw the channel as not only completely divorced from ITV but as a station whose scheduling would always be very distinctive.

Grade's first weeks sharpened the contrast with Isaacs. He was more public, always willing to provide the headlines and never afraid of controversy. Less than a month after he started, Channel 4 was acutely embarrassed by a documentary, *Some Mother's Son*, in the series *Merely Mortal*. This showed an interview with a man called Clive who claimed he had served with the British army in Northern Ireland, seen a colleague shot and had shot a teenager at a checkpoint. But the man had been a fantasist and the makers of the film had not checked out his story. Grade moved quickly to defuse the situation, letting it be known he was 'angry', getting Liz Forgan, his deputy, to reprimand the producers and broadcasting a quick apology. Even the programme makers were impressed with the speed and decisiveness with which he acted.

Then, mindful of his experiences with Curteis, he earned brownie points from the right by deciding not to screen a film that was critical of the career of Sir Arthur Harris, the controversial wartime C-in-C of Bomber Command who had planned the fire-bombing of Dresden. Alan Sapper, the general secretary of the ACTT, saw it as a 'blatant political censorship' but Grade was dubious about a film that seemed to mix fact with fiction and was praised by Max Hasting, editor of the *Daily Telegraph*, for resisting the temptation to present a 'half-baked political broadside as historical truth'.

In early March Grade attended his first British Academy of Film and Television Awards (BAFTA) as head of Channel 4. This event is one of the most glittering of television nights and Grade grabbed the headlines by attacking Yorkshire Television's decision not to screen the awards ceremony. Yorkshire, miffed because its programme *The Falklands War: The Untold Story* had not been nominated, decided to show the film *The Sting* instead. The decision had been taken by Paul Fox, Grade's old friend, who was just about to leave Yorkshire to take over the BBC job Grade had vacated. Grade himself was talking to the ITV companies about complementaty scheduling with them but, oblivious of all this, he denounced Yorkshire's decision as 'deplorable' and as an 'insult to the British film industry'. He was roundly booed by the audience but it had ensured that the next day's headlines were about Grade rather than the BAFTA winners.

Not even all this publicity could mask one problem and ironically this was the one Grade had himself identified back in the summer when he had told Stoessl he wouldn't be applying for the Channel 4 job. It was just so much Jeremy's channel.

Metcalfe appreciated the dilemma this posed for Michael: 'Jeremy was such a stong, cohesive person. He has employed everyone and what held us together were the quirks of Jeremy's personality. This was the glue that held us. Michael didn't fit into that. It was fairly intimidating coming to Channel 4 where a group of people had worked very closely for a long time. So when Michael arrived it put their backs up a bit; they didn't speak his language.'

The first person to realise that Grade spoke a different language was Rosemary Shepherd, who ran the children's programmes. She was a curious woman. Although she had been hired to do programmes for young children she had an obsession with teenagers. She would constantly nag Isaacs about doing something for that age group but every time she raised it with Isaacs he would just bark at her and say, 'You get the job for under-fives right and then we will start worrying about teenagers.' Despite such rebuffs he valued what she did and just before he left he had increased her budget to £5 million.

Shepherd assumed Grade would react like Isaacs, so when they met she said, 'I don't think we should be doing programmes for under-fives because we don't have the resources for it. We should be doing programmes for eleven to thirteen-year-olds.'

She had played right into Grade's hands. He was less than enamoured with the educational programmes and said, 'I agree about the first bit; not about the second bit.' So children's programmes and Rosemary Shepherd went.

Shepherd could be said to have had a death wish about her. She introduced herself later at the Edinburgh International Television Festival as formerly of Channel 4, currently with BSB, which made that sound like a very temporary post, as indeed it proved to be.

Grade's decision to axe *Mavis On 4*, a daytime programme presented by Mavis Nicholson, was more controversial. The programme, broadcast three times a week, was watched by a million viewers and had powerful friends, among them Richard Ingrams who in his influential *Observer* column castigated Grade. Nicholson herself was very put out that she did not even receive a note from Grade that her programme was being axed, just an abrupt call from Thames, the company that made the programme for Channel 4. Grade felt that with the televising of parliament he needed more daytime slots and the axeing of children's programmes and *Mavis On 4* would help in that. In any case, he could point to the fact that all this had done wonders for the ratings. When Isaacs has left Channel 4 was getting about 8 per cent of viewers; within two months of Grade's arrival this had risen to 11.7 per cent.

Such ratings measurements are like snapshot polls, one contradicting another. It should be remembered that the programmes had all been made by Isaacs and in Channel 4's case ratings are a double-edged sword. For the channel to get too high a rating might seem to contradict its remit of catering to minority tastes not served by the other channels. Isaacs had bridged this divide rather well. Grade was soon made aware that his reputation as a ratings specialist merely widened the philosophic divide separating him from the 'Isaacs channel'.

On 15 March 1988 the Channel 4 board met to confirm Isaacs's departure. The next day, Jane Thynne in the *Daily Telegraph* ran a prominent story asking, 'Is Michael Grade departing from the script?'

Unnamed Channel 4 executives spoke of their sadness at the axing of Shepherd and Nicholson and others wondered whether Grade had not 'taken the first step down the path towards a schedule which may be perceived as catering for the white middle class'.

The government White Paper on broadcasting which would set out the options for the channel was expected in July and, Thynne wondered, were the changes a prelude to the privatisation of the channel, something Grade had advocated in September, changed his mind about in November, but might be reverting to in March?

In reality, the privatisation problem was a red herring. The rumours that fed the story were caused by the fact that Grade's changes were now creating a disaffected class of Isaacs's children who had flourished during his reign and now resented what Grade was doing.

The most entrenched was Michael Kustow who ran the Channel's arts programmes. His *State of the Art* was unashamedly elitist and Grade refused to recommission it. Kustow, backed by Isaacs, saw arts on television as a performance. Channel 4's arts programme had started with a television reworking of *Nicholas Nickleby*, Laurence Oliver in *King Lear*, Aeschylus's *Oresteia* and Brook's version of the epic *Mahabharata*, all theatrical productions adapted for television. Grade had a more conventional, limiting view of how arts should be presented on television. He liked arts programmes of the type that the mainstream channels favoured: single-subject programmes as presented by *Omnibus*, *Arena* or *The South Bank Show*, at the same time each week.

Kustow versus Grade was another version of high culture versus vulgarian argument or, as one Channel 4 producer told the *Daily Telegraph*, 'Michael Grade wants to get away from an image of Channel 4 arts as being programmes about Armenian mime.' The philosophical differences between the two men would have always made them incompatible but the arguments about what is an arts programme opened up a breach which has never healed.

More worrying than this for Grade was the quarrel he had apparently picked with Liz Forgan. She had been at the channel since it had started, having moved there from the *Guardian* where she had been editor of the women's page. The *Guardian* women's page has acquired a certain position in British cultural history, its start in the seventies coinciding with the rise of campaigns for women's rights. Forgan, while not wholly identified with the Jill Tweedie *Guardian* woman, had been typecast unfairly – as women in the media often are – in that mould. As she was not 'gorgeous and pouting' and since she rather disarmingly describes herself as 'short and fat', she had become typecast as 'headmistressy' or 'head girly'. Forgan's disappointment at not getting Isaacs's job was intense but with Grade not being a programme man she was confident she stood a great chance of becoming director of programmes and that offered some compensation.

Within days of taking over, Grade arranged for them to have lunch and they met in Forgan's offices over sandwiches washed down with a bottle of claret. He quickly came to the point. 'I want to be my own director of programmes for a year, to see how things are done.'

Forgan could barely conceal her irritation. What increased her uneasiness was that Grade did not even hint at whether she might get the job after a year.

For the chief executive to be his own director of programmes was the acid test for the Channel 4 insiders. The very first decision of the Channel 4 board, made even before Isaacs had been appointed, had been that the chief executive was also to be head of programmes. The Channel 4 devotees had been very proud that theirs was the first television company where the chief executive was actually in charge of the programmes, not an accountant or an administrator or a bureaucrat. And in his Nuneham Courtney speech Grade had suggested he would follow Isaacs's example. However, Forgan's fears were groundless.

Although this crucial decision was in the Isaacs mould, it was an unlikely one and Grade did not stick to his resolve. Instead of staying a year as director of programmes he stayed barely a few months. Changing his mind as quickly as he had made it, he decided that he would be far better off not doing the job and Forgan, to her delight, *was* made director of programmes.

The decision raised a storm of feeling. Anthony Smith, who had been on the board that had decided that the chief executive should also be head of programmes, saw it as the first step on the road to bureaucracy. 'Once you do that, you bureaucratise the whole notion of Channel 4 and for me it dies. It means the chief is an administrator and it becomes harder and harder for someone to throw aside all the programme decisions and say, "Such a wonderful programme idea has come, let us throw everything away and do this instead." You can't do that if you are not the boss.'

Other critics, particularly those inside the organisation, saw it in more Machiavellian terms. 'He has always been happy to have women in high places,' says one executive then highly placed in the organisation. 'To have Liz as the first woman director of programmes of a national network is good for his image and the fact she has comparatively little television experience is very good for him.' Even if he was not motivated by such considerations Grade's move did give him a firm ally in Forgan and was also a useful political step.

This was not an insignificant factor, for Grade's change of mind was probably driven by the fact that the very structure Isaacs had created was now falling apart. Under Isaacs there had been a neat division between him and Dukes; Isaacs as the chief executive was involved in programming and Dukes as the managing director ran the business end of the company.

Dukes had been devastated by Grade's appointment. As the deputy who had been spurned he was, in any case, in an invidious position. The manner of Grade's appointment made it worse. He felt strongly that Attenborough and the board had acted in an 'ungentlemanly manner', having assured him that all the candidates would be known, then producing a surprise one literally at the last minute.

Dukes had wanted to leave straight away. But Attenborough called him over to his home in Richmond and pleaded with him: 'Darling, you must stay. Jeremy and Michael are poles apart. If you leave it will create a very serious vacuum, a very serious discontinuity in the channel. It will jeopardise everything you have achieved in the last seven years.'

Dukes was persuaded to stay on for another six months and handle the transition.

The six months were to prove purgatory for Dukes. 'It was like a prison sentence. I was very bored and I would have preferred to be free. You can choose with whom you work. I chose to work with Jeremy, but not with Michael.' While he did not blame Grade for the manner in which he was chosen he has nothing but contempt for him. He sees him as 'a creature of our times. The sort of person who has risen inexorably through the eighties. Jeremy could be selfish but he had vision and courage, his abilities outweighed his disadvantages.'

Grade's success in securing more publicity for himself and the channel in his first few months than Isaacs had done in almost seven years only filled Dukes with distaste. He sat in his office, unhappy, sullen, wishing to be free, removed from what Grade was doing and wondering, 'I suppose if I got up every morning and thought what can I do to get publicity, I would get as much as Michael Grade does. But that is not my style.'

By the summer of 1988 Dukes's Attenborough-induced prison sentence was over and in September he finally left, publicly pretending it was an amicable split but privately confident that eventually Grade's hype could not last. At Nuneham Courtney, playing the Isaacs convert to the full, Grade had said, 'I see little need for any radical adjustment to the operation structure which Jeremy and Justin have evolved and which seems to serve the channel's needs effectively.'

Now, with both men gone, Grade decided to alter that structure quite radically. He decided he didn't want a managing director. Even at the conference there had been talk of a wider representation on the board and Grade decided to create three extra directors. The three who had tendered for the job of managing director joined Grade and Forgan on the board as executive directors: Frank McGettigan, general manager; David Scott, finance; and Colin Leventhal, acquisitions and sales. Also joining the board were John Willis, whom Grade had poached from Yorkshire as controller. Mike Bolland was made deputy director of programmes.

All reorganisations put noses out of joint. The head of engineering who did not make the board left and Sue Stoessl began to feel that the warning given by journalists on the day she had guided Grade through his first press conference might well prove true. After that press conference, as Grade was talking to people over drinks, several of the serious journalists asked Stoessl, 'What are you going to do now?'

Stoessl replied, 'What do you mean?'

They replied, 'He will bring his own staff in.'

Stoessl dismissed it. 'That will not affect me.' Now, watching Grade's changes, she was not sure.

Metcalfe was the worst hit by the changes. In a reorganisation in 1986 by Dukes the channel had been grouped under five department heads: arts and entertainment; education; features; drama and marketing, with Metcalfe who was sports editor also becoming head of features with religion and children's programmes under his wing as well. This hardly made much sense and Grade moved him back to just straight sports editor. When Grade arrived Metcalfe had thought their old friendship might help him settle in the hostile Channel 4 world. 'I felt protective and wanted to form a bridge. I didn't succeed.'

The problem with the reorganisation was that Grade had introduced an additional layer. Bolland as controller of arts and light entertainment took in all film and series purchasing, but his brief did not include dramas. This was still headed by David Rose who was allowed to keep his empire. There was, however, no relationship between any controllers and drama. Rose was to report directly to Grade, despite the fact that Grade was supposed to have no input in programming. Grade's decision not to be director of programmes suggested he also wanted to be a pure administrator. Although he didn't want to know about programming he still wanted to schedule, his great joy. This, as Bolland says, 'made a complete nonsense' of not being director of programmes.

Perhaps this explained a certain lack of touch which marked some of Grade's initial moves. First he disbanded the scheduling committee that Isaacs has started, consisting of Sue Stoessl, Gillian Braithwaite-Exley (head of planning), Liz Forgan and Mike Bolland, but then a month later he reformed it.

Such events are not uncommon in any organisation but what made them disturbing was that Grade was being indecisive when he had a reputation for being decisive and his changes were building up organisational resentments. Perhaps, as Sarah, says, 'At leading the charge himself, he is not that hot. When it comes to executive and office back-up he is at one remove. He is just not interested. When it comes to institutional leadership I don't think he is very good. Writers, actors and performers love to be appreciated and nurtured. He is terribly good at that. He understands instinctively what they are going through. When it comes to creative leadership there is nobody better than Michael.'

Already Grade was beginning to feel the strain of leading Channel 4. The initial months, recalls Sarah, were 'proving more stressful than America. It was more or less a repetition of the same pattern.' But the worst was yet to come. In October 1988 he went to the National Film Theatre to be interviewed by Anthony Smith. Smith, who was retiring from the BFI, had already quizzed Isaacs and this was to be the first opportunity for Grade to address just the kind of critical audience he needed to win over.

Grade should have realised that by going to the NFT to be interviewed by Smith he was entering his enemy's territory. Smith may have come to terms with Grade snatching away the job he had been promised, but he could not get over the feeling that Grade at Channel 4 was 'a very depressing moment in British cultural history'. He kept thinking back to Grade's press conference when he had publicly recanted his views about Channel 4. For Smith it had echoes of Richard Nixon during Watergate. 'It was a wonderful phrase worthy of Richard Nixon: that was then, this is now. I have changed scenes. When you consider that we had been fighting for Channel 4 for twenty years, the idea that the whole of the enterprise we had given so much of our lives to bring about had been handed over to someone whose conversion was not spontaneous but induced as a result of becoming chief executive was deeply depressing.'

Smith still believed in his role as the founding father of the channel. 'I had the right to expect the second chief executive would be someone who would be a zealot for the cause of Channel 4, since all the founding board, whether they came from ITV or BBC, were all zealots of Channel 4, if not at the start then certainly at a very early stage they acquired the commitment.' Smith saw the NFT interview as a chance for Grade to 'make it clear that his conversion, though somewhat peremptory, actually went deep and he believed in the long-term interest of the channel.' He wanted to give Grade this opportunity and see how he reacted.

The interview began innocuously enough, following the pattern of such interviews. Grade was asked a range of questions about television, starting with the role of BBC governors in the light of the *Real Lives* drama. Smith reserved the deadly question for last. That is when he asked Grade about his vision for Channel 4. How did he see its remit?

'The reaction was quite extraordinary. He couldn't formulate a reply for a few moments. He couldn't construct a sentence. I said, "I am sorry, Michael, am I giving you a hard time with the question?" He said, "No, no," but he was completely unable to answer, he was very flustered, which was very unlike him.'

Eventually Grade did construct an answer and said he had no particular vision about the channel. It all sounded very hollow. As is usual on such occasions there was a drinks party afterwards where the person interviewed mingles with the audience. But Grade, normally so gregarious, who revelled in such occasions, did not stay for the party. He seemed so upset by the question of vision that he left as soon as the interview was over. This as much as his hesitancy convinced Smith that Grade's recantation was a public performance and he could not believe his faith in the channel went very deep: 'So I continued to be depressed about that and about his intellectual and emotional predisposition to deal with his job.'

In many ways, of course, it was unfair of Smith to sak that question. In his previous interview he had asked Isaacs the same question and received a wonderful reply that made it clear why Isaacs was considered a visionary. But Grade has never been that and has never pretended to be. Indeed, Grade has a great antipathy to such intellectual exercises. The journalist Bryan Appleyard has written that 'Affable and accountable he may be, but his rationalisations are all functional. He is never caught out in a generalisation other than his belief in independent broadcasting.' Grade, like George Bush, has this vision problem, except he does not see it as a problem.

Even Grade's office at Channel 4 emphasised his excessive neutrality: shaggy plants, light wood, cream blinds, carpet squares and spotlights, six TV sets, one computer and the motto 'collaboration' in showy script framed over the meeting table. Contrast this with the same office when Isaacs occupied it: Tom Phillips's portrait of Elgar with Union Jacks and cartoons galore, Mel Calman's little man hoping Channel 4 wouldn't be too good for him, Mark Boxer's smoothies pondering, 'I suppose this audience of one Channel 4 is down to must be Mrs Whitehouse,' with Alan Parker sympathising, 'Running a sodding, effing, blinding TV channel isn't easy, you know.'

If Grade had a creed it was, as Appleyard says, 'a kind of expertism'. Even if he could he would never generalise the way Smith wanted him to, Appleyard has suggested that what, probably, annoys intellectual snobs is Grade's 'professional reluctance to say very much'.

Certainly the NFT episode, like the earlier Opera House incident between Lew Grade and Isaacs, was further grist for the anti-Grade lobby. The whispering about Grade the vulgarian grew even louder in the wine bars of Soho and Fitzrovia where, as Grade himself was to lament to Appleyard later, the endless question posed over the white wine was: What is this populist up to? What further ruin does he plan for the channel?

All this does seem conclusive evidence of what Appleyard has called tha 'elaborate and insidious snobbery' which had been at work ever since Grade came to the BBC from LA. His move to Channel 4 had merely given it 'a new, more virulent anti-Grade' form. Smith rejects this, denying that he was trying to trap Grade into the high culture versus vulgarian argument.

'That is a very tabloid view of the story. I don't take a high culture view of the role of television. Channel 4 was constructed in an era when high brow and low brow divisions had broken down. In Channel 4 the new cultural settlement of the sixties was institutionalised. It predicated its entire existence on the notion that every individual belonged to a multitude of audiences and that every audience was composed of a multitude of small groups. Channel 4 didn't apologise for being minority, it redefined minority. Divisions between high and low brow are still there but they are shadowy and unimportant. That is very much the context of the eighties. Look at Tim Bell or the Saatchis who are patrons of high art but also high-quality advertisers. In some ways they are parvenus. But then the eighties were an era of parvenus. We are all parvenus. We sometimes belong to non-parvenu organisations, so people can represent revered institutions like the BBC or Oxord colleges.'

Yet Smith, after the trauma of Channel 4 rejection, retreated to Oxford, becoming President of Magdalen College. It is inconceivable that Grade could become president of an Oxford college, even if he wanted to. When the contrast was pointed out to Smith, he laughed, saying, 'Grade can retreat to Hollywood,' thus providing a clue to the vast cultural gulf that separates them.

Perhaps we shouldn't join Smith in being so hard on Grade. Just as he was stumbling over words at the NFT he was stumbling in his private life. The autumn of 1988 was not only a period of professional worry, it also marked a profound personal change. The marriage he had put such faith in was about to break up and as with his first marriage it was Grade who did the breaking.

So far Sarah Lawson has not figured much in our story since the night she found inspiration in Kalil Gibran to help Grade decide on the BBC offer. One reason for this was that she was often not in London. Taffner had offered her a job in London but then her company was up as a joint venture based in England and Los Angeles, which meant shuttling back and forth doing the transatlantic television business and spending up to three months in LA. Sarah was acting as a sort of inter-mediary between the US and Engliand, encouraged by the belief that she knew it over here as well as she did over there, in some ways a sort of one-woman Hanson of the television world.

The arrangements seemed to suit both Sarah and Michael. 'I was incredibly daunted by the fact that I was in the profession and I was Michael's wife. I didn't want to pitch to broadcasters over here. In any case I was never the orthodox BBC wife. In the early days after coming back from the States both of us rather rebelled.' Sarah found Britain far behind the States in its appreciation of women's rights. In 1985, as Michael moved into the BBC, Sarah was quite shocked to discover that wives 'were still something of a sub-standard species in the BBC'.

So, although they had the most standard of domestic existences, liv-ing in a house in the country, a short hop down the M40 from the BBC, it was hardly conventional suburbia. As Sarah grew more involved in her work and Michael in his they became more and more the caricature yuppie couple always on the phone. 'I used to say we only see each other properly between midnight and 6 a.m. I would get off the tele-phone at midnight and he would get up at 6 a.m. to go to work.'

There was one occasion when Sarah, who was at home, wanted to speak to Michael but did not know where he was.

'So I rang him in the car. And his driver picked up the phone and he said, "He is still at home." And he was. He was upstairs in the bath. This was just indicative of two people whirling around fairly fast and not getting to see each other. I think the sort of lifestyle I led was like being a whirling dervish; two whirling dervishes was kind of tough.'

Often their only time together was at public occasions and far away from home. In May 1988 Sarah and Michael briefly met up at the 41st Cannes Film Festival. Even this was to be a swift reunion as Michael had to dash off to Switzerland for the Golden Rose of Mon-treux Awards. If anything, it looked as if they might have even less time together, for Taft Entertainment with which Sarah had worked had crashed, and she had now set up her own film and television company. This would mean spending several months away from London.

By the middle of 1988 it was clear that something had to give. In an attempt to try to spend more time together they decided they would move and in July 1988 bought a house in the exclusive Clarendon Close just off Hyde Park. For a time the move seemed to work and despite Michael's job and Sarah's travelling they spent more time together. But this togetherness lasted only until October when Sarah realised that the marriage needed more than a change of bricks and mortar to hold it together.

Michael had met another woman, Patti Marr, who worked for BBC Pebble Mill. He had met her in the summer while doing a programme about his *Mirror* experience in the BBC series *First Job*. 'Michael started having this affair in October and when I came back from America we talked about it and he really felt he couldn't continue in the marriage, which was a shame. I think we could have sorted it out. But he really didn't want to. Michael initiated the break.'

Interestingly, a few months before this the film *Fatal Attraction*, about the perils of adultery in a modern marriage, had been released. Grade had attended a lunch at the Savoy and, sitting at the same table as Richard Ingrams, had said how he wished Mary Whitehouse could be forced to see the film, because although it was violent it had the highly moral theme that husbands should be faithful to their wives. Ingrams, who had never liked Grade and liked him even less when he took his friend Mavis Nicholson off the screen, had found the point fatuous and delighted in making fun of Grade. Now in real life Grade was in the middle of something like a *Fatal Attraction* situation.

In April 1989 Michael moved out of Clarendon Close into a flat. For a few months he and Sarah had kept the split private and, with Sarah working from Clarendon Close, for a time they 'did this bizarre shuffling. I was in the country and coming to work in the house in Clarendon Close and he was here going to Channel 4.' But in May the charade had to end and the couple formally split.

Almost a decade before when Michael had been wooing Sarah it had been sixty on his side, forty on hers. But now it was Sarah who pined for Michael, still loved him and continued to do so for some time. She still felt the marriage, despite Michael's adultery, could be rescued. There is something almost puritanical in the way she saw it: 'It was our responsibility to try and look at it.'

But Michael just did not want to. He had closed the chapter and once he does that he rarely goes back. It was so with Penny and Lynda and now with Sarah. The actual steps were different in each case but the ultimate process was the same. Sarah, who had once felt Michael had seen himself as a Professor Higgins to her Eliza Doolittle, now felt just as 'humiliated' as Eliza had by her rejection. 'It was rejection without a chance, judgement without a trial, which I think is deeply unfair.'

For Sarah, of course, there was no Freddy to turn to and once the tears had stopped there was a deeper despair.

'I cried a lot when I broke up with Michael . . . You go through a period of feeling incredibly guilty at not having been the model wife.'

But then Sarah calmed herself down. She had had little to do with Penny; now she spoke to her and discovered that Penny too had anguished about not being a model wife. The two ex-wives consoled each other. Talking to Penny made Sarah realise that 'it is jolly tough being married to Michael Grade. There is a lot of the absentee landlord about it and you still have to pay your dues. It has its rewards, Michael is a very interesting, very funny companion, but you don't get an awful lot back.'

What made it worse was that 'He doesn't appear a worrier and he doesn't give out signals when he is worried. It is only when it has got to the crisis stage that he realises something is wrong. He doesn't even know himself until it is all too late which is one of the sad things about us breaking up. He never really knew until it got to that stage, then it was too late. He doesn't open out. He doesn't tell people what he is thinking or what he feels. He has to be told. I had to tell him. It is a terrible burden on somebody else. It is tough being a mind-reader. It is all tied in with his not being very good at protecting his back politically. Michael is very potent in his needs. He always gets what he wants. But it can be a private process. I had the day-to-day running of the relationship, financially and org-anisationally. We didn't have a joint account. He wanted me to do that. But at the end of the day what Michael wants, Michael gets.'

At the start of the marriage Sarah had been quite keen on having children but Michael had decided it was not a good idea. Now Sarah was grateful they hadn't had any. 'The timing was not right. After several years in England we hadn't got our act together.

'Failed marriages,' says Sarah, 'arise because people aren't communi-cating. When we came back to England that was the turning point. There was huge misunderstanding and there was a lot of pressure on two people, neither of whom managed adequately to provide a safety net. When that becomes the case, when neither really under-stands what the other is going through, you begin to grow apart. That is when the day-to-day communication starts to ebb. It is very, very difficult to get it back. You have both got to work at getting it back and Michael was not prepared to do that.'

Sarah's regret soon after was over the way Michael ended the marriage: 'Michael chose a way out which I would not have chosen, that is to cut and run rather than have a go at making it work. At the time of the split I had huge regrets. But you don't destroy a good friendship because you are upset. He wouldn't have gone off unless he had his own reasons for it and he was unhappy.'

If Michael had regrets about the break-up he was good at concealing them. He had, after all, initiated it, but almost a year later friends would think he had a delayed reaction to the end of the second marriage. The process was not without pain and he would refer to the upheaval when things got tough at Channel 4.

By the early spring of 1989 several of Isaacs's men had begun to leave Channel 4. Dukes had already gone; now Kustow and Metcalfe followed. Grade had just two questions for Metcalfe when he came to him in February to say he had been offered a job by Eurosport. 'Are they paying a lot of money? Are you going to take it?'

Metcalfe answered yes to both. 'Good, all right. Goodbye, then.'

The once great friends parted like distant acquaintances.

As television departures go this was about standard. Metcalfe's favourite story about how abrupt such partings can be was when Roger Moody, number two to Jonathan Martin, head of BBC Sports, left. He had an offer from BSB, told Martin, then decided to sleep on it. Next morning he told Martin he was going to take the job but since Martin had a busy summer ahead [the World Cup and Wimbledon] he was ready to delay his departure to see him through those. 'Fair enough,' said Martin, then picked up the phone and rang Security. 'Can you send somebody here, Mr Moody is just leaving.' So Moody, who had worked for the BBC for twenty years, left in half an hour.

Both Kustow and Metcalfe departed because they wanted to. Grade was more instrumental in getting Stoessl out. In March Grade told Stoessl he was going to advertise for a head of press, he wanted to strengthen that role and wanted the press to work directly to him.

'But I work directly to you now, Michael,' protested Stoessl.

'I want someone who works more directly, someone whose function will be just to do press,' replied Grade. (Stoessl had a much wider remit which also covered research, marketing and advertising.)

'What would you want me to do?' Stoessl asked.

'When we get a sales director you can work for the sales director,' replied Grade.

Stoessl knew this was the end of the road. She had no intention of working for a sales director and decided to negotiate terms to leave. By April she had gone.

Although the job had to be advertised, Grade planned to have Stoessl replaced by Keith Samuels, the BBC press officer with whom he had worked very well at Television Centre. But Samuels could not be prised away from the BBC and eventually another candidate was selected.

So by spring 1989, yet more senior Isaacs executives had departed: John Cummings, commissioning editor for youth programmes; Naomi Sargent, commissioning editor for education, and now Stoessl. In the programming side only Forgan, Bolland and the venerable Rose, who, was widely regarded in a special light, remained. Although it it not unusual for new chief executives to carry out changes, this was more than a spring-clean and at odds with Grade's promise in his Nuneham Courtney speech that he saw no need to make organisational changes. It was also quite a haemorrhage for a small, experimental channel based on intimate work patterns.

The departure of executives was matched by the loss of programmes that had made the channel so distinctive: *The Comic Strip*, which had won the channel its first big international comedy award, the Golden Rose at Montreux, had moved to BBC 2; the satirical sketch show *Who Dares Wins* had gone and so too had *Saturday Night Live*. Grade justified all this as the process of change. He could point to the changes he had already made, such as the introduction of all-night television, and in any event he saw Channel 4 as 'a nursery rather than a grocery. We like to develop our own. Inevitably when they get big, they'll either stay or get knocked off. That's the game, isn't it?'

The game in the wine bars of Soho and Fitzrovia, where those who had left joined the disaffected who remained, was to raise further questions about Grade's suitability to run the channel. Such feelings found focus in *The Sunday Times* on 23 April 1989. In a long article headlined 'PARADISE PARALYSED' and based on talks with some twenty producers and executives, the paper wrote about how the channel which Isaacs had seen as a paradise for programme makers was in trouble. The basic problem, it alleged, was that Grade had taken his eye off the ball.

This was quite the most damaging attack ever on Grade and his response was furious and characteristic. Unfortunately for *The Sunday Times*, the article had begun with a minor error. Channel 4, it said, had started in 1983 (it was 1982) and Grade wittily used this mistake to build his reply, denouncing the paper for using selective facts, failing to research properly and seeking 'to construct' a crisis where there was none. Grade took issue with the writer's claim that Channel 4 had been created as a paradise for producers. 'It was set up to extend the choice available to British viewers, to offer programmes of a range and interest unlikely to be provided by the rest of the commercial sector.'

Yet there was some merit in *The Sunday Times*'s accusation that Grade had taken his eye off the ball. His eighteen months at Channel 4 had begun to chip at the most enduring of Grade myths: the one of his being a workaholic.

Bolland realised this fairly early on: 'I used to have an office that was directly opposite his in the building next door and I could peep into the window. We had heard all this about how at the BBC he would be in at eight in the morning and work until nine in the evening. There was never any sign of that at Channel 4. He would rarely come in before ten, long after I did. He is not the workaholic people have been led to believe he is. We would wait for him at a screening, look out of the window and there he would be outside holding a television press conference, the great self-publicist.'

Grade would even miss the Monday morning scheduling meetings; sometimes there would be a schedulers' meeting without the great scheduler. It mattered little because, says Bolland 'things got changed on a whim anyway'. This was one of the reasons that was later to prompt Gillian Braithwaite-Exley to leave. Nor did Grade attend very often the important programme review meeting every Thursday morning when the previous week's programmes were examined. The only meeting he religiously turned up for was the finance meeting held every fortnight. However busy his schedule, he never missed that.

Grade is sensitive about his workaholic image and grows very resentful if people question it. 'It is', says one insider, 'the image he likes. He goes crazy if you suggest he is not a hard worker.'

However, Stoessl is not surprised the myth has crumbled. 'Indeed he is not a workaholic. He might be a workaholic if he is doing something he really enjoys. But he doesn't enjoy his present job. So often he sits in his office and is on the phone most of the time.'

Valid as this criticism was, in many ways Grade's critics were taking him to task for not doing something that he had never intended to do. Having decided not to be his own director of programmes he had withdrawn from the one area that had made Isaacs special. The Channel 4 belief was that Isaacs saw every film before it was screened on the channel and while this may have been an exaggeration it indicates how pervasive his influence was felt to be. Grade did not match that, did not want to match it, and scheduling in a minor key as the channel required clearly did not motivate him. His energies were concentrated on what he saw as his main preoccupation: saving the channel.

In the autumn of 1990, when this battle was well and truly over and Grade could claim victory, he would declare that this 'long and exhaustive campaign has been pretty well my sole occupation since I came to Channel 4'.

If, as *The Sunday Times* had said, his eye was off the ball about what went on in Channel 4, then this was because the eye was on the wider politics of television and had been almost from the first day.

So while Grade as programmer and scheduler may not have made much of a contribution at Channel 4, Grade the broadcasting politican was just coming into his own. His political remit covered a wide front, as was evident from his answer to *The Sunday Times*'s criticism. He concluded his reply with this barbed comment: 'Perhaps *The Sunday Times*'s proprietor realises this only too well.' The suggestion here was that the article had been motivated by the fact that Rupert Murdoch, proprietor of *The Sunday Times*, knew very well how important Channel 4 would be in the 1990s and how great a thorn in his own plans for satellite television.

Grade was returning to a theme Milne had taken up in the last days at the BBC when *The Times* had fulminated against his running of the BBC and he had countered by saying it might be motivated by Murdoch's own media interests. Milne's attacks had read like a defensive reaction. Now as Murdoch launched Sky which his newspapers, with 40 per cent of the market and extending from the *Sun* to *The Times*, vigorously promoted, Grade took up the cudgels on behalf of broadcasters who felt that Murdoch's closeness to the government and particularly Mrs Thatcher was allowing him to get into a dangerous monopoly position.

It is a role far removed from any Isaacs would have been comfortable with, but it was a natural one for Grade. His attacks on Murdoch's media concentration would run almost parallel with his efforts to preserve Channel 4.

Grade's attack on Murdoch was also an indication that he was assuming the role of Mr Broadcasting. The position had been vacant since the departure of Hugh Greene as Director General of the BBC in March 1969. His successors at the BBC had been competent but colourless. There was nobody at ITV who could do it. In general, the broadcasting voices were too divergent, and Grade began to see his job of trying to save Channel 4 as a splendid platform from which to become the industry's self-appointed spokesman.

Grade had a dry run at this in the summer of 1987 when, still at the BBC, he had led the fight against a proposed extension of the Obscene Publications Act designed to bring broadcasting under its remit. At one stage he suggested the Act might end up by banning *The Jewel in the Crown* and *I, Claudius*. Then suddenly, four months into the campaign, chairing the Milton Committee, he quit saying, 'I don't think it is reasonable to argue that broadcasters be outside the Act.' The recantation was so severe that later even he admitted that 'the campaign did us a lot of damage.' The change of heart left the broadcasters devasted; Grade's critics whispered about him being a rent-a-quote broadcaster, but in situations where broadcasters made the news, rather than just reported it, his willingness to provide the media with a sound bite was undeniably handy.

Right from his first days at Channel 4 Grade seemed to define a remit for himself which was nothing less than the case for preserving the present government-regulated television system. Within weeks of getting to Charlotte Street he went to America to attend the annual American Television Programme Convention (NATPE). On his return he sent a letter to *The Times*, still considered a prestigious showplace for the views and opinions of those who matter, about the horrors of children's television in the States: Do we, he asked, really want schoolchildren to compete for top prizes of $25,000 a week in quiz shows? This, said Grade, should be a warning to anyone who wants to dismantle the regulatory framework that now exists.

In May 1988 it was announced that Sir William Rees-Mogg [now Baron Rees-Mogg of Hinton Blewitt] was to head the Broadcasting Standards Council. This was the government's response to growing concern about sex and violence on television. In the previous summer

Michael Ryan had perpetrated the ghastly massacre at Hungerford and it was said he had been turned to violence by watching *Rambo* films on television. In fact, Ryan never had, for the simple reason that had it never been shown on television. But nevertheless the myth prevailed and there were suggestions that that the BSC might preview programmes 'of special concern'.

Grade had consistently opposed the idea of the council, Rees-Mogg's selection provoking a special fury. Grade pictured Rees-Mogg as having a 'contempt for producers' and made clear his own contempt for him. He could not forgive him for his role in the *Real Lives* controversy and asked, 'Is this opinionated ex-editor of *The Times* a figure of reassuring impartiality? Or is he simply the ideal man to carry out a predetermined task handing down his patrician wisdom from his country seat in Somerset?'

Grade was well aware that by setting himself up as Mr Broadcasting in this way he was like a boxer who holds out his jaw; sure enough, his attacks on Rees-Mogg provoked an angry response, not from Rees-Mogg but from others.

Perhaps predictably, Ian Curteis, writing in the *Standard*, saw it as the sort of 'violent, personal attack' that the 'excitable' Grade specialised in and denounced it as 'the howl of those who should know better'. Auberon Waugh suggested that perhaps William Rees-Mogg should publicly cane Grade and 'if the correction is shown on late-night television, it will be a source of comfort to those who actually enoy watching violence, as well as an effective warning to the Michael Grades of this world that violence hurts'.

Grade was not to be put off. In August, when the composition of the Broadcasting Standards Council was announced, he wondered what collective wisdom the 'great and the good at the BSC' would bring to broadcasting which the BBC board of governors and the members of ITA did not. But his special anger was reserved for the fact that its members were all quite ancient. 'I do not quite see how a council whose average age is sixty is going to understand what Channel 4 is about. They are totally out of tune with our audience. The average age of a Channel 4 viewer is about forty.' There are, Grade pointed out, 'no writers on the council, there is nobody with professional expertise in the management of broadcasting on the council'.

Curteis may have found all this offensive but at least one well-known body, the Oxford Union, saw it as good knock-about fun and on 17 November 1988 Grade was invited to propose the motion: 'The government does not appreciate the strengths of British broadcasting.' He was to be opposed by Douglas Hurd, then Home Secretary, Professor Norman Stone, the right-wing historian, and Rees-Mogg's son Jacob who was then a student at Trinity. Grade realised this was far too good an opportunity to miss and that the debate could do much to add to his growing stature.

So far all Grade's speeches had been written by Peter Ibbotson who, although still at the BBC, would send across his drafts on Amstrad disks which would then be corrected in the Channel 4 press office. However, for this occasion, his first visit to the Oxford Union, an honour Grade valued greatly, he decided to change his speech writer. Ibbotson, while good on the politics of television, could not write witty speeches and a witty speech was what he needed.

Grade hired Mark Lawson, by now the *Independent*'s television critic. Lawson, a sharp, clever journalist who had also been the political sketch writer for the *Independent*, had in the past turned down offers from politicians to write their speeches. He did not mind writing speeches for other prominent people but he wanted to be sure they could deliver them. With Grade he could be sure.

Lawson's speech was a minor classic of its kind and Grade, delivering the Lawson-scripted one-liners with devastating effect, scored a great triumph. He had been preceded by Stone, who tends to speak softly and could hardly be heard by much of the audience. Grade began his speech by making fun of Stone and then in a veritable *tour de force* demolished both Rees-Mogg's Broadcasting Standards Council and the arguments of Stone and Hurd. On analysis, the speech contained no great original thought except a general defence of the status quo in broadcasting – Grade came out in favour of the existing BBC/ITV duopoly – but, listening to it, the undergraduates could not contain their mirth. It was undoubtedly the speech of the evening and it won the day. The man brought up in 'that dangerous place for revolution, the London Palladium', as Grade has put it, had converted one of the supposed bastions of intellectual thought.

Grade had attacked Stone when he was out of the room and this considerably angered Curteis, who was there and felt it was unfair and typical of Grade. But neither this nor the witty reference debunking Hurd and his thriller-writing career did Grade any harm. Within months Hurd appointed him to chair a working party on crime set up by the Home Office.

Hurd's decision met with surprise and no little derision from Barry

Sheerman, Labour's front bench spokesman, who wondered if Grade was 'after a knighthood'. But as far as Grade's image went the appointment served only to emphasise that he was a broadcaster distinct from all others, in effect Mr Broadcasting.

The report, issued in December 1989, concluded that Britons have a higher fear of crime than their European neighbours, even though actual crime rates may be the same or lower, and blamed a too-frequent publication of crime figures and television programmes like *Crimestoppers* and *Crimewatch* for increasing anxiety. If it made no lasting contribution to the debate about crime, the report did earn Grade rare praise from Auberon Waugh.

By this time, of course, Grade was in the middle of the battle to secure Channel 4's future and had established the team he needed to support him. This meant getting Peter Ibbotson. The appointment of Paul Fox to his old job at the BBC in the summer of 1988 had provided the opportunity. Fox was reported to have said, 'I do not need Ibbo to think for me' – a remark that was relayed with much relish by Grade's enemies. That Ibbotson does all the thinking for Grade is perhaps too extreme an assumption but his analytical, cool mind was what Grade coveted. While Grade could present the Channel 4 case, he needed someone who could construct it for him. The two men complement each other splendidly. Ibbo is a thinker, not much of a presenter; Grade is a wonderful presenter. Ibbotson, as *Broadcast* magazine put it, 'has a keenly political mind, but in a scientific rather than baby-kissing sense: he is thoughtful and analytical in his approach, carefully shifting through issues to identify strengths and potential trouble spots. As for doing things, he leaves that to others; dealing with people is not his strong point, and he is often described as a bit distant, even cold.'

The great contrast in the two men is in their sense of humour. Grade is famous for his, Ibbotson is just as well known for not having one. In the film *A Very British Coup*, a prize-winning *Film on 4*, his name was shown as an MI5 mole. The film's researcher claimed that it was just one of the names she found in the telephone directory and had stuck it in. Ibbotson was not amused.

Peter Ibbotson had come into prominence defending the BBC against libel and other attacks from its critics. As a former producer of *Panorama* Ibbo had been involved in screening *Maggie's Militant Tendency* which Tory MPs claimed libelled them. The matter was eventually settled out of court; Ibbotson, given the choice of apologising or paying his costs, apologised. Since then he had gained vast experience in arguing the politics of broadcasting and getting used to broadcasting controversies, having been seconded, in 1985, to work on the Peacock Committee which was looking into the future of BBC finances.

Ibbotson's relationship with Grade, initially formed when Grade came to the BBC, had become closer when he was appointed Grade's deputy in 1987. In November 1988 Grade formalised it by persuading him to leave the BBC and join Channel 4 as a consultant. *Broadcast* commented, 'It's his mind he wants and needs, to help secure a future for C4. . . . Ibbo wrote most of Grade's speeches and helped him steer clear of trouble. As one friend puts it, "Grade had the instincts which Ibbo could articulate."'

Grade had to show some delicacy in making the appointment. Forgan, who was increasingly at Grade's side, rated her own political savvy, which was said to be similar to Ibbotson's, but Grade presented Ibbo as complementing rather than usurping her and the two were pictured as a formidable combination behind Grade and ready to meet any challenge thrown up by the government.

One thing that Ibbotson did not have to teach Grade was to acquire the nimble feet politicians require. He had in his very move to Channel 4 shown a dextrous ability to change his views. As the battle for the channel developed he was to display this again and again. Since his celebrated recantation Grade had publicly and vigorously argued in favour of preserving Channel 4's status whereby ITV companies financed the station and the Welsh fourth channel by contributing seventeen per cent of their advertisement revenue, in return for which they sold Channel 4 airtime and kept the revenue. Grade made the case against privatisation with all the classic zeal shown by the convert and in presenting his first annual report as chief executive he said, 'We are not asking for guarantees, just a percentage.' Grade's claim was that 'Channel 4 is clearly paying its way. We need no subsidy, no charity to run this operation.'

In late September 1988 Grade and Attenborough had spent about forty-five minutes telling Hurd how unwise it would be to tinker with the station's present form of funding. Grade also warned Hurd that he would be unable to fulfil the channel's legal duty to cater for minorities if the government legislated to privatise: 'Programmes like *Channel 4 News*, *The Bandung File* and our new weekly arts programme will not be sustainable.'

The reference to *The Bandung File* was somewhat ironic as the programme was soon to be killed, with its death provoking great anger amongst those who produced it. While much of this anger was directed at Grade, the desire for change was more on the part of its commissioning editor, Faruokh Dhondy, rather than a Grade fiat. But such contradictions had never worried Grade – or his enemies – and in this war he knew that what mattered was the initial fusillade. The details could look after themselves. In October Grade travelled down to the Tory conference in Brighton, which was returning there for the first time since the IRA bomb plot to kill Mrs Thatcher. He wanted to gauge what might be in the White Paper the government was about to issue on TV deregulation.

The guessing game about what the White Paper would contain had been going on since early summer and reached its climax at Brighton. In June the *Daily Telegraph* had led with a front-page story which began, 'A radical plan to make BBC 2 and Channel 4 available only to viewers with satellite TV dishes is being examined by the government.'

According to this report, Douglas Hurd and Lord Young, the then Trade and Industry Secretary, had told the chairmen of the BBC and ITV of this and of plans for establishing six new commercial television channels in the 1990s. At Brighton there was less talk of this than that the government would not only sanction a new Channel 5 but link its finances with Channel 4. This option appears to have attracted Grade. His public posture remained that he wanted to preserve the present funding, but privately he gave the impression that he saw the combination of Channels 4 and 5 into a potent force as a welcome development: another ITV but separate from and in competition with it.

Indeed, Channel 5 was much in Grade's mind. A month before Brighton he had been at Edinburgh for that year's International Television Festival and on the hotel's registration form he had put under the question 'next destination?': Channel 5.

Richard Last in the *Daily Telegraph*, who had likened that year's festival, the last before the White Paper, to 'attending a funeral before the corpse had properly expired', spoke of Grade's interest in Channel 5 and it became something of a festival joke to talk about Michael's interest in running Channel 5 should he tire of running Channel 4. This was heightened when at Brighton Grade was seen speaking to the Thatcher inner circle, arguing that a combined Channel 4 and 5 would make good sense. Sarah Lawson is convinced that had the government legislated for a combined Channel 5 and 4, 'he would have become a shareholder in Channel 5. This would have gone some way to solving his need for money – the great drive in his life.'

The White Paper on Broadcasting was issued in November 1988 and proposed to remake commercial television: replace the ITV system with Channel 3 and settle the future of Channel 4. Channel 4 seemed quite secure, at least as far as the remit went. The White Paper judged that Channel 4's programming remit had been a 'striking success' which must be sustained in the future. The debate was about how to fund the channel. Here the White Paper presented three options: it should be privatised; it should have a link with the proposed Channel 5; or it should become a non-profit-making subsidiary of the newly formed Independent Television Commission (ITC), selling its own advertising separately from ITV, but with a minimum level of income as a guaranteed backstop.

Much as Grade had liked the Channel 5 option he soon realised that this was never an attainable objective. He was now attracted by another option.

In February 1989, accompanied by David Scott, he went to the House of Commons to present oral evidence to the Home Affairs Select Committee, which in the wake of the White Paper was concentrating on the future of Channel 4. The committee already had Channel 4's written evidence; now in the oral questions and answers Grade made it clear that any link between Channel 4 and Channel 5 was not on the agenda. Instead Grade favoured the White Paper's second option of Channel 4 selling its own advertising but with a minimum level of income as a guaranteed backstop.

This option was not welcome to all and particularly not to the television companies. They accused Grade of wanting to have his cake and eat it. David Elstein, director of programmes at Thames Television, charged Grade with giving up the game even before it had begun. Once Grade admitted that the status quo could not be maintained the relationship between Channel 4 and the ITV companies would dissolve. 'Pursuing competitive selling is signing the death warrant of the Channel 4 remit,' said Elstein. But Grade, undaunted, countered by saying that the ITV companies had 83 per cent of the market, Channel 4 was only asking for a safety net of fourteen per cent of terrestrial NAR while the channel was spending at the rate of fifteen per cent. Grade extended his lobbying to advertisers who had promised support but could not quite understand how the Channel's famous remit would affect them. Grade explained to them that while they may not want to advertise their BMWs in the middle of a minority interest programme, they might have to; there would be moments when the interests of advertisers and viewers would not coincide, that was the nature of the channel, and one that distinguished it from the proposed Channels 3 and 5.

Grade's energy and ability to project himself made him ideal for this fight. So while Ibbotson made the bullets, Grade fired the gun expertly: Grade at the Home Office conferring with Hurd, Grade at the House of Commons answering Select Committee questions, Grade at lunch with advertisers on the merits of advertising on Channel 4, all followed by quick press conferences to ensure the right headlines. In this he was the absolute master, aware that the man with the first sound bite held the day.

But how much of this was a real fight for the channel? How great a peril was Channel 4 in? Justin Dukes is convinced that it was something of a phony fight. 'I don't think Channel 4's status was in any danger.' While Dukes, given his views on Grade, is not exactly an impartial witness, and with hindsight a victory can always be made to look easy, there is some evidence to show that the channel was in less danger than Grade made out.

Even before the White Paper had been published, the *Sunday Telegraph*'s main feature article on 23 October 1988 was a long piece which saw the proposed changes in broadcasting as Mrs Thatcher's revenge on the television industry. Mrs Thatcher's anger with the media had been aroused, said the writer, by the television coverage of the murder of Airey Neave, her close adviser and friend. Following the murder a spokesman for the INLA which had committed the act was interviewed on television. It was then that Mrs Thatcher was said to have vowed, 'I will never forgive them.'

Now, in her third term, she was ready to settle scores. But while other broadcasters had much to fear from this the *Telegraph*'s writer was sure that 'With Grade now at Channel 4 the channel's remit to provide minority programmes is safe and the White Paper will guarantee that it has the financial base to continue.'

Not only was the *Sunday Telegraph* close to the Tory party but the article suggested briefings from good, influential sources actually in government. Ian Curteis may have denounced Grade some years before as being fundamentally anti-authority but he had developed good personal ties with those close to the authorities, in particular the Thatcher circle. Some of this was through his friendship with Michael Green, a wealthy entrepreneur, and this in turn led him to the mainly Jewish circle round Lord Young, then very close to Mrs Thatcher and credited with securing her 1987 election victory.

Green, a cousin by marriage of Lord Young, is sometimes referred to as belonging to the 'St John's Wood brigade' of rich, mostly Jewish entrepreneurs such as Charles Saatchi and Gerald Ratner who are jocularly referred to as the Kosher Nostra. As the fight for Channel 4 developed Grade had grown ever closer to them through Green. Grade, while not a traditional north London Jew, valued his Jewish connections as did Green and the two men often golfed and went on skiing holidays together.

Welcome as these links were it did not mean that Grade could abandon the public fight about the channel's future and he seized whatever opportunities there were going, not only to argue the case for the channel but to debate the future of British broadcasting, developing along the way an 'alternative White Paper'. If the fight for the channel was phony, then Grade showed uncommon energy in tackling it. The letters pages of *The Times* had become a regular Grade sounding board, as had the leader page of the *Daily Telegraph*. It was here, on 4 March 1989, that he launched an attack on Douglas Hurd's idea that there would come a time when there would be a rich diversity of television programmes all lined up like titles in a bookshop for people to choose what they want to view.

Interestingly, Hurd's views were a further development of the ideas that had prompted the launch of Channel 4. In his famous article in the *Guardian* on 21 April 1972 which had launched Channel 4, Anthony Smith had argued that broadcasting should be reshaped like publishing. Just as the written word had broken free from the taxed and licensed regime of the eighteenth and nineteenth centuries, so should broadcasting. But while Smith saw such an electronic publishing house as part of a National Television Foundation, founded by diverse bodies, Hurd saw it as coming out of the free market with the hope that diversity of channels would lead to quality.

Grade dismissed Hurd's idea as a 'nice conceit. It is reassuring. It lets us think quality will always out in the market place, that someone will always find a profitable niche opportunity to provide choice and quality. But it is a view of broadcasting as perhaps we would like it to be, rather than as it really is under the inexorable logic of the balance sheet.' While a book publisher can take a chance for the price of a small advance, high-quality television, much of it adapted from books, is expensive. The analogy just did not work. For those who pictured Grade as the American in British television this may have come as a surprise but he still carried the scars of his American sojourn and could not believe that a free-for-all would be beneficial. It also showed how much of a traditional broadcaster Grade really is, not only in contrast to Hurd but also to Smith. Grade is a man who has grown up in the cosy BBC–ITV duopoly and is most comfortable in it.

This world view of television also chimed in very well with the Home Office officials who, whatever their political masters may think, were keen to maintain much of the framework of post-war British television and particularly a commercial public service channel that could compete with the BBC. It did not take much for Grade to convince them that Channel 4 would not be able to keep its public service role unless its advertising sales were underpinned by a safety net of fourteen per cent of ITV advertising revenue. The officials took seriously their broadcasting charge and in many ways Grade's fight to secure Channel 4's funding was not so much Grade versus the government as one between the mandarins of the Treasury and the Home Office. Nigel Lawson, then Chancellor of the Exchequer, had been pressing for the channel to become more fully financially independent and the Treasury would have liked nothing better than to float Channel 4 off. But the Home Office, as the department responsible for television, carried the day and on 6 June 1989, when a Cabinet committee brought them together, the Home Office mandarins prevailed over the Treasury. Channel 4, it was decided, would have the safety net Grade had argued for.

Grade had won the major battle. Now some minor skirmishes remained. The most significant of these, or at least the one that received the most media heat, was a Home Office proposal that the planned trust to oversee the channel should be government-appointed. This trust could veto appointments to the new corporate board planned to run the company from 1993. The Home Office view was that since the channel was going to be like the BBC, then just as the government appointed BBC governors, so should it appoint Channel 4 trustees.

Grade did not see it that way. For him it was a dangerous threat, as became evident towards the end of December 1989 with the publication of the bill and its second reading in the House of Commons. Grade took up the cudgels. Attenborough threatened to resign and Grade pictured it as a fight as crucial as that to secure the funding. He saw the proposal as 'an ill-considered compromise solution, inserted as a *quid pro quo* to make up for not being privatised'. What he felt was most sinister was that this was 'a political veto' and one that would be exercised secretly.

Just before battle was joined there was a government reshuffle and David Mellor came to the Home Office to take charge of the bill. Mellor's arrival was a godsend for Grade. In his own way Mellor is a bit of a showman. He and Grade share a common love of football, Mellor identifying closely with Chelsea, where Attenborough is vice-chairman. Grade's ability to work Mellor was to prove crucial. One insider says, 'Michael worked David Mellor like a variety artist at the London Palladium.'

In fact, the debate over the Broadcasting Bill did to an extent develop like a variety act. Brenda Maddox caught the flavour of it as she attended the press conferences that accompanied its publication. It sent, wrote Maddox, 'all the old media faces scurrying around to debate the same old questions with the same old people before different microphones'. The best moment, Maddox reported, came at the Channel 4 press conference where the media game was to get Attenborough to repeat the resignation quote. Attenborough happily did so but he also added that his present term ran out in 1992 which made it something of a hollow threat, as the bill would not come into effect until a year later. So he was asked to repeat the resignation threat without the 'original dragging tail', and, recorded Maddox, he obliged, 'like a man cutting the ribbon twice for the cameras'. The star of the media show, however, was Mellor, who at his first press conference rebuked Richard Evans of *The Times* and Ray Snoddy of the *Financial Times* for exchanging a whisper: was this, he demanded, one press conference or two?

Grade was not totally eclipsed, though. He was as ever always ready with a quote and as the bill wound its way through the Commons and the Lords, the Grade sound bites filled the television studios. Such lobbying is a mixture of private talking and public posturing and Grade played the game well. As Charles Denton says, 'Michael in his years in broadcasting has picked up some valuable political skills and these he used very well during the debate about the Broadcasting Bill.' Much of this, like all parliamentary debates, was more noise and fury than actual substance but Grade could feel that he had done a good job. As the bill moved to the House of Lords, Grade, writing in the *Daily*

Telegraph on 5 June 1990, praised Mellor and the Commons standing committee for 'vastly' improving it. 'Channel 4 emerges with a workable structure to ensure its viability and vitality.' Grade had gone into battle hoping to get sixty per cent of what he wanted: 'That would have been a pass mark; over seventy per cent would have been a distinction. We ended up with seventy-five to eighty per cent of that we wanted.'

Everything seemed to be going well for Grade. The previous week he had been dining at Overton's, the expensive St James's restaurant just across the way from the Carlton Club. It was the night the IRA bombed the club, claiming they were getting at the British establishment. Grade, who always carries a portable phone with him, immediately rang the ITN newsdesk and gave such graphic details that they had a news flash in half an hour, an hour ahead of the BBC. ITN were very pleased and Grade's publicity machine ensured that the news made a suitable diary item.

But just then, with the battle for the channel seemingly over, perhaps the most dangerous argument, certainly the most controversial one surrounding the bill, arose. It came in the Lords when Woodrow Wyatt, now a lord, and Lord Ewing combined forces over an amendment that sought to include an impartiality clause. So far in his struggle Grade had felt that sometimes he was left to fight a lonely battle but the amendment did stir the rest of the broadcasters, who joined him in arguing that the clause would lead to massive vexatious litigation. Convinced that the clause, 'retrogressive and repressive', was the work of a small right-wing lobby, Grade said, 'It is vitally important to get the right wording so that the whole of the industry does not spend the next twenty years in and out of courts. The speed is far too fast for a piece of legislation designed to change the relationship between the politicians and the broadcasters.' If this was a bit of a hyperbole, there is little doubt that in the entire passage of the bill nothing raised quite such a storm.

How, broadcasters asked, would this impartiality clause work? If a pop star appeared on the Michael Aspel show and expressed a partial opinion, would there have to be a balancing programme? Could it lead to demands for balanced programmes on dog-fouling?

Lord Goodman had warned that the clause would become a lawyer's picnic; it certainly provided a media free-for-all as it dominated the headlines for a couple of weeks. Eventually the amendment was changed, although it still left the broadcasters facing tougher rules over impartiality with the Home Office justifying it on the grounds that it introduced some rigour into broadcasters' thinking.

There was a price for such public exposure and that continued to be paid internally at Channel 4. Just as the Broadcasting Bill was being published Grade faced his most severe internal crisis since taking over. Mike Bolland made it clear he could no longer work for the channel, which was the cue for widespread public attacks, ranging from the *Daily Telegraph* to *Broadcast*, on Grade about his role at the channel.

Inevitably this cast shadows on the political front and during the press conference discussing the bill, while Grade was attacking the government's right to veto members of the proposed Channel 4 trust, he was also having to defend his own leadership of the channel. Yes, he agreed, he 'would have liked to have spent much more time watching and talking about programme s but the first prioity has been the survival of the channel and I won't have achieved that until we get rid of this wretched veto'. Attenborough supported him, claiming, 'Inevitably, even in his bath, Michael Grade has to devote a considerable proportion of his mental energy to attemping to hold our position.'

Glib as this defence of his leadership of the channel was, the crisis that shook Channel 4 in the winter of 1989 was real enough. Mike Bolland told him he wanted to leave. He had been as steadfast by Grade's side as Forgan and if he had not initially welcomed Grade he had, at least, understood why the appointment was necessary. 'People in television often hire people duller than themselves and less able. Whatever else Michael is, he is not that.'

Two years on, that Grade charm had begun to wear thin. Bolland had realised that, while they were the same age, they seemed to come from different cultural generations. Grade's reference points are all from the Palladium, Bolland's from rock and roll, and Grade seemed to have missed a generation. 'Rock and roll doesn't seem to have happened for him. His life was more showbiz, more musical hall.' Entertaining as Grade's stories about life as an agent were, they had for Bolland a limited shelf life. 'Once you have heard the Michael jokes, or the stories about his time as an agent, you have heard them.'

Of course, such differences would not have mattered if the two mean had shared a common interest at the channel. But Bolland was mortified to find that Grade had little apparent interest in programming. 'I don't think Michael is completely in on the programming. He is not bothered about it until it happens. He is bothered if Alan Yentob signs up Ruby Wax. He is like Janet Street-Porter, loves to be quoted, something Jeremy didn't like that much.'

The preoccupation with preserving its status did not mean Grade completely ignored the channel. But like a man who picks and chooses from a buffet menu he picked his moments of intervention. This had been vividly illustrated in June 1989 when the BBC sought to poach Peter Sissons, who presented *Channel 4 News*, and make him Robin Day's successor as the presenter of *Question Time*. Grade played the high profile gamekeeper to perfection and in a typical television tug-of-war he threatened to hold Sissons to his contract. At one time, both the BBC and Grade claimed Sissons before Grade eventually gave way.

Such interventions, while providing the right media highlights, could do little for the running of the channel. The answer Grade came up with was: let's get away for a day, away from the office and do some thinking. One Friday in the summer of 1989 a planning meeting was held in Liz Forgan's garden. All those who mattered in the channel were there: Gillian Braithwaite-Exley, John Willis, Michael Grade and Bolland. The idea was to plan the coming season for the commissioning editors, starting at noon and working until the small hours of the morning. Dinner had been booked at a small restaurant near Forgan's house. But, recalls Bolland, 'the day was a complete farce.' John Willis was going on holiday and so had to leave early. Grade himself could hardly concentrate. He had just split up with Sarah and was looking for a place to live. 'If we did an hour of work that was a lot.'

The lost Friday had only succeeded in confirming Bolland's impression that the channel had 'no strategy, there was a lack of thinking. I didn't feel anybody was giving any coherent thought about what the programme mix should be.' Increasingly he felt marooned in a job he just did not like. 'I just found at the end of the day it really wasn't satisfying. I was elevated without any real influence. It also meant I was responsible for a hundred million pounds and the bulk of the channel's output in terms of airtime. It was a negative job.'

What Bolland really missed was commissioning. He had started the Jonathan Ross shows which had given him a great creative buzz. As a commissioning editor he could go out and find things. But 'being deputy director of programmes meant holding the balance between Michael, Liz and the commissioning editors. It was a very boring, very uncreative job. The problem was that the structure dissipated power. Nobody had it. What Michael had done was to give the two programme controllers more power and this meant there were too many chickens in the nest.'

As often happens when someone is unhappy in a job, Bolland began to fear for the future. Would he ever get back to programming again? He felt that he could not win either way in his present job: 'Once you begin to climb the ladder it is really hard to get off.' All these problems might have been solved if Grade had made Bolland director of programmes. 'I would have been able to schedule the channel. I found a committee member role unsatisfying.' Much as he respected Forgan personally, he had 'no respect for her in the programming sense. She is a newspaper person. She has skills that would make her a very good newspaper editor but she is not a director of programmes.'

But there was no way Grade could make Bolland director of programmes or give him a position that would help him feel free. However, he tried hard to keep Bolland. So hard did he fight that it took Bolland two and a half weeks to get out. 'Michael did fight very hard to keep me. More power, more money, more everything but not more room. More room was what I wanted.'

Grade seemed unable to understand why Bolland wanted to move. He concluded that it was money had made Bolland leave. 'Michael put it about they [Initial Television, the company Bolland joined] made me an offer I couldn't refuse. It was the only thing he could understand. He couldn't understand that somebody wouldn't want to carry on this exciting job with him. He couldn't get his head round that I needed a break from it. Everybody thought I was leaving for vast sums of money but that wasn't true. As the year progressed it became even more untrue as Initial Television went into receivership.' What made it worse was that in the press release announcing his departure it was stated that everything Bolland would produce did would be brought to Channel 4 first. 'It simply wasn't true. Totally wrong. I never had such a deal. I was not in a position to do that. By issuing such a press release Michael caused resentment in the independent community.'

While Grade could brush off previous attacks in *The Sunday Times* as biased, Bolland's departure was clearly a major turning point for the channel. The *Daily Telegraph* headlined its piece 'CHANNEL 4 MORALE SINKS OVER GRADE'S "LOW-BROW" SCHEDULE' and spoke of 'an all-time low in morale and disaffection over the leadership of its chief executive', somebody who was seen as failing the channel by being an absentee landlord. This was followed by an attack on Grade's style by Michael Kustow in

Broadcast magazine on 15 December 1989: 'Michael Bolland's resignation as deputy director of programmes and controller of arts and entertainment brings to a head contradictions in the post-Jeremy Isaacs channel, which it must resolve if it wants not just to survive through the nineties, but sustain and deepen the distinctiveness which is its whole reason for being. It would be an exaggeration to speak of a crisis but Bolland's departure certainly brings the channel to a crossroads.'

The previous week *Broadcast* had conducted a major investigation into Channel 4 and sounded the warning that there was a 'siege mentality' developing between the channel and the independent producers – many of whom were quoted as making critical remarks – leading to 'an air of mutal mistrust between the channel and independent producers which engenders a paranoid atmosphere in which producers are scared of expressing their concerns publicly for fear of reprisals.' As if to confirm this, neither Grade nor Forgan was available for comment.

An accompanying analysis comparing Isaacs's indian summer on 1987 with the first eight months of 1989 showed that under Isaacs there was more drama, less light entertainment, less imported product, whereas Grade had introduced more theatrical films and TV movies, mainly American, with fewer single plays or movies in the *Film on 4* slot. The major change was in light entertainment: no sketch comedy or variety in peak hours, more chat and in particular sitcoms from Hollywood. The growth had been in commissioned programmes: *The Manageress, Behaving Badly, Traffik* being among eight home-grown series, but these were not being watched by as many as for the series under Isaacs and none matched the figures for the great Isaacs original drama series *The Price* or *A Woman of Substance*.

Broadcast suggested Grade should take up the showbiz song, 'Next year it's gonna be different'.

In the past Grade's ability to do just that had worked brilliantly but it is a measure of the very different problems he faces at Channel 4 that singing different tunes led him back to the same problems. In the two and a half years since *Broadcast* made the suggestion, Grade has been unable to get out of the same groove. Kustow in his criticism had acknowledged that Grade had fought the external political battle brilliantly – he just felt the internal battle was more worrying. Yet not even he could have envisaged the sort of internal storm that would sweep over Grade in 1991.

At the start of the year is seemed unlikely that Grade would face any such problem. The channel's future had veen sorted out and Attenborough and Grade had formed a mutual admiration society in the channel's annual report. Attenborough: 'Our future circumstances have in no small measure been secured by his skills in helping shape Channel 4's terms within the Broadcasting Bill.' Grade: 'I pay tribute to the chairman and the rest of the board of Channel 4 whose continued support and wise counsel have ensured a continuity of purpose and direction which have served the channel well.' Grade was also confident that he had seen off the mutterings of the independent producers.

This is always a love–hate relationship, rather like that between a parent and a favourite child now turning into a moody teenager. The channel's existence had created the independents but there are just too many of them – some 750 when a viable figure would probably be a tenth of that number, and the turning down by a Channel 4 commissioning editor of an independent producer's idea can often seem more wounding and personal than a similar rejection by the BBC or ITV. By February 1991, as the recession began to bite and the Gulf War cast its gloom, making parts of central London appear as deserted as on Christmas Day, the independents had even more reason to feel aggrieved about the channel. It had confirmed budgetary cutbacks of £14 million due to the fall in advertising revenue. It had also announced that it would move from its present overcrowded offices in Charlotte Street to premises in Horseferry Road. Independents were staggered to learn that this would cost £80 million and would have to be financed by bank loans. Building projects are associated in many minds with budget overruns and this was seen as a particularly insensitive move at a time when the independents were being told to tighten their own budgets and lower expectations.

Grade had been aware that his relationship with the independents required mending and he had been seeking to do this. In February 1991 he addressed the independent producers at BAFTA, projecting Channel 4's future to 2003. The setting served only to emphasise the grim times. On a previous occasion the venue had been the Royal Institution (a much grander place than BAFTA) followed by luncheon at the Café Royal. Now all Grade could offer was a glass of 'BAFTA's best plonk', which, he confessed, reflects 'some of the short-term problems we now face.'

Grade tried to make up for this in his speech which was in the great Grade tradition, part self-congratulatory, looking back on the success of the battle to preserve the channel, part self-justificatory, bragging about how he was a different scheduler to Isaacs, and part a drum beat about the channel:

'That we are at the forefont of changes in taste.

That we lead and others follow.

That we offer the greatest diversity of programmes.

And that we take the biggest risks.'

The performance, while not entirely convincing, did leave some of the independents in a more bullish mood, which is what Grade intended. He had also sought to reassure them on one question: Was he now going to leave the channel? There had been persistent rumour that he was about to, but early in his speech he said, 'By the way, contrary to rumour, I intend to be at Channel 4 for quite a few years yet. I don't intend to be poached.' What the independents did not know and would not know for several months was that the channel had paid a high price for preventing Grade from being poached, a price that in the opinion of many had made this, the most unique British television institution, just like any other commercial company.

Grade leaving Channel 4 is, of course, an old sitcom. It has been running as long as he has been at the channel. Indeed, that has been one of the main problems with Grade at 4. If he has never been able to escape the shadow of Isaacs he has also never been able to convince anyone that he sees the job as permanent. Beginning with jokes about Channel 5 at the 1988 Edinburgh Festival Grade has done nothing to discourage the impression that his job as chief executive is a transient one. In Denton's memorable phrase, he is parked, ready to move out. But move where?

As we know, one of Grade's greatest motivations in life is money. Grade does not deny that – 'I've always needed more money' – but resists any suggestion that he would make another career move for money. He had learnt his lesson from America where, as we have seen, he went for money and it proved disastrous.

However, in the spring of 1990 the drive for more money and the chance to make money coincided rather neatly, or at least appeared to. While he had replaced Sarah with a woman who looked very like her, the break with her meant he had to find a new home. Sarah had been left with the house near Hyde Park and the apartment in Los Angeles – properties which she had bought with her own money – and Michael had to begin to look for yet another place he could call home. Initially Michael had stayed with his stepmother Audrey, then Patti and he had lived in a rented flat in central London. But this could hardly be a permanent place and the couple decided on a detached house in Hampstead as their ideal home. It was then that Grade appears to have realised that he just did not have the money to make the move. House prices then were still touched by the late eighties' madness and houses in Hampstead, never cheap, cost serious money. The realisation seem to have shocked Grade.

Donald Trelford, editor of the *Observer*, has known and admired Grade for a long time. 'It was after his divorce with Sarah that suddenly one day he realised he did not have the money to get what he wanted. For a Grade not to be able to do that is quite something; for Michael not to get what he wanted was a profound shock.'

The remedy was not difficult. Grade could certainly command a high price for his services in the market and with the ITV system up for auction this was the right time to move. His friend Michael Green, who had been gearing up his Carlton Communications to bid for the ITV franchises, had been talking to Grade for months about coming and working for him. Green, bidding for the Thames franchise, had seen Grade as crucial to his plans, with Green ready to offer a reported 'golden hello' of between £1 million and £2 million if Grade would head up his franchise application. (Grade refuses to confirm the figure, saying only that it was a seven-figure sum.)

One insider close to both men says, 'Michael was that close [he holds up the thumb and forefinger close together] to accepting. He thought about it very hard. But there was the insecurity. What if the bid failed? I think he also thought it was not a good idea to work with a friend and Green has a reputation for being a tough man to work for. But then, if you think about it, Michael is in quite a good position. He is the boss of the only television channel with a secure future.'

Grade could also resist Green because Channel 4 had come up with a figure which, while not a seven-figure sum, was comfortable enough to help him recover from the shock of not being able to afford the home he wanted. How precisely this Channel 4 offer came about remains a mystery. Months later, when the row was front-page news, Grade would confess to the Royal Television Society that contrary to popular rumour he had pre-empted the Green offer by approaching Atten-borough some months before Green made his bid, very possibly in November 1990.

'I talked to Dickie some time ago and said I was likely to get several approaches. I said, if you want me to stay, good, but if I take myself off the market we should have a negotiation. I told him I didn't want the market rate. I said I think you should make me an offer, and he did.'

Those close to both Grade and Green doubt if this sequence is quite right and Nigel Dempster reported in his diary that it was Green's offer that had so upset Attenborough that he burst into tears and flew back from Hollywood to make the deal with Grade.

Whatever the exact sequence of events, the fact remains that Attenborough agreed to give Grade a golden handcuff of £500,000. This was sufficient inducement to secure Grade to the channel for another five years with an enhanced salary of £144,000. This meant that in the four years since arriving at the channel Grade has seen his salary almost double from the £72,000 he had earned in his first full year in 1988. The salary figure was disclosed in the accounts but the golden handcuffs were only hinted at by Attenborough when in March 1991 he came to write his chairman's report for 1990. He spoke of his fear of losing talented executives to the ITV auctions and the need to 'hold the best executive talent'. This did not mean competing with the scale of inducements offered by the likes of Green but 'nevertheless, we are giving consideration to taking steps which the board and our share-holders, the ITC, consider reasonable to secure the services of our key people in the longer term'. Although nobody picked this up then, it meant golden handcuffs not only for Grade but also for his fellow executive directors Liz Forgan, John Willis, Andrea Wonfor, David Scott, Colin Leventhal and Frank McGettigan. They were given half a million pounds between them to prevent them being poached.

This had the smell of the deal Attenborough had made with Grade when he enticed him away from the BBC. The Channel 4 board, although some non-executive directors were uneasy, approved of it after Attenborough had worked out the details. The whole thing was overladen with the desire to keep it a secret. The plan worked for a time. Despite Attenborough's hint in the annual report, few picked it up, helped by the fact that in 1990 Channel 4 had decided to change its accounting year end from March to December, which meant the accounts for that year reported on nine months to 31 December 1990, making comparisons with the previous twelve months to 31 March difficult. A couple of leaks did take place. *Private Eye* reported a payment to Grade on 1 March, claiming that while other ITV com-panies sweated it out as to who might save their franchise, 'it is almost as if there has been a separate bidding process for the Michael Grade franchise'.

A few weeks later the story made the Dempster column, with Dempster claiming that the golden handcuffs were meant to help

Grade move into the house Patti and he had chosen in Hampstead. The diary item was accompanied by a cartoon showing Grade with cigars and braces wearing a tie with a large pound motif on it. But with the industry concerned about what might happen to the ITV companies, few took any notice of these leaks and, as Grade and Attenborough had hoped, the story got buried. Then in August, out of a blue sky, Grade suddenly found himself in the middle of controversy, attacked on two fronts.

Grade had travelled to the 1991 Edinburgh International Television Festival as the one man removed from the convulsions facing the industry. The ITV companies were in turmoil. With rumour and counter rumour about who had won or lost and with the final announcement not due until mid-October, Edinburgh in 1991 was for some like waiting for the hangman to appear, a cockpit of gossip and a seething group of ITV executives who feared for their jobs and their futures. Many ITV companies had not even turned up at Edinburgh while the BBC, headed by John Birt, who had been confirmed as the next Director General, was there in force but aware it faced its own moment of truth in 1996. Grade could look down on all this with Olympian disdain, aware that his own channel was secure and his own future tied up for another five years.

However, there was a debate scheduled about how Channel 4 would cope with its remit in the new set-up and here Grade faced a challenge from an old Channel 4 hand who, while ready to complement Grade on preserving the channel, had doubts about where he was leading the organisation. Roger Graef had been a founding director of Channel 4 and had, as we have seen, very nearly got Grade's job. Now at the Festival he articulated a widespread feeling that Grade might have won the battle for the channel's future but lost the war.

The contrast between Graef and Grade cannot be more stark. Graef is proud of his role as one of the founding fathers of Channel 4 and although he had applied for Grade's job he had done so 'not in order to get it. But I had gone for the job in order to tell them what I thought should be done with the channel. I was concerned that what we had started should be carried on.'

Graef had come to Edinburgh as one of the few independent producers willing to voice doubts about where the channel was headed – many others had doubts but were afraid of what any public broadcast of scepticism would do to their relationship with the channel – and saw himself in the centre of a chain of events leading to the role of public sceptic. The decision to sell advertising, he felt, set the channel down a slippery slope that would make it like any other TV station. 'All non-programme makers of the channel who were businessmen who wanted something to do felt this is what they should do because they wanted control over their own income. Channel 4 is not primarily a business, it is a cultural public service, made possible through a very British but brilliant piece of social and financial engineering. Once it sells advertising, it is just another company that is trying to keep its head above water.'

Graef was prepared to accept that Grade had saved the channel from privatisation, 'but nobody would ever know if it would have been possible to hold out for things as they were. She [meaning Mrs Thatcher] wasn't as interested in Channel 4 as in ITV. Michael did it very well. But would it not have been possible to keep the channel as it was?' Graef did not know and nor would anyone else now.

Graef liked Grade. They had got on well together when Grade had turned to Graef to produce *Signals* as an alternative to the Kustow-style arts programmes. It was quite a clever thing for Grade to do: get someone well respected in the arts world, who wants to break out of the arts ghetto and show how art affects ordinary people, but also wants to produce a show that is not obsessed with events as Kustow's were. Graef was solicited in a great rush – there was just a fortnight in March 1989 to prepare the applications. He had to be extensively wooed. 'I said no four times then agreed.'

The experience has left Graef disillusioned. 'Michael's whole approach to arts is that it could be rushed on the air in a fortnight, all of Kustow's programmes could be fitted into a slot. He said to me whatever we did the first three months would be terrible in *Signals*. He oversold it from day one as the big major arts programme. We were lumbered with his excessive hype for a programme that needed to find its way but which had its resources brutally cut back after we had been given the task to run it. Channel 4 was a very hostile environment. There wasn't enough time and there wasn't enough money. We were filling a scheduling need and trying to do it in a creative way and there wasn't room for that. I was trying to do something closer to *The South Bank Show* but take it further towards the general public. The programmes in the first series were cut from an hour to forty-five minutes for scheduling reasons; after the second year the show was cancelled for financial reasons. The whole thing had been rushed to the screen to beat *The Late Show* and it showed how Michael operates.'

So Graef, while praising Grade for fighting off the worst-case scenario of full-scale privatisation, feared that the challenge to sell advertising would mean that the station would cease being original and diverse and become boring and safe.

'Channel 4 is confident it can both sell and protect its present schedule. But there is no insurance against the future pressures slowly pushing out brave programmes for safer ones, as the competition from Channel 3, Channel 5 and cable grows. The cake of viewers and advertisers will stay the same or shrink. Only the difficulties of survival will increase.'

The precedent provided by other public service channels required to be funded by advertising is grim: none of them, whether in Europe or North America, has sustained its original programme standards in the face of competition anf Graef concluded, 'I fear we will have to fight to save Channel 4 once again.'

To an extent Graef's criticism was the old song: 'Look Ma, what he had done to Jeremy's garden.' Ever since Grade had taken over at Channel 4 his scheduling skills have been compared to Isaacs's. By instinct and upbringing he is a very different scheduler to Isaacs and this has been evident from the beginning. At one of the first scheduling meetings Grade had to decide where to place a dotty fifteen-minute programme. He put it on at midnight when Isaacs would have shown it at peak time. For Stoessl this was conclusive proof that Grade does not understand 'the way the audience of Channel 4 works. I explained to him the way Channel 4 get its ratings, it is after ten o'clock at night. It may be off-peak for the advertising industry but we built our ratings from ten o'clock onwards when nobody else is showing anything on television. If Channel 4 puts strong programmes then it will get viewers, whereas if it puts its best stuff between eight and ten, setting itself up against the stronger opposition of the major channels, it will not. The difference was Jeremy was totally, utterly committed to this channel, whereas Michael had knowledge of two channels, BBC 1 and LWT, and no feel for scheduling a minority channel.'

This has led Grade to schedule programmes, says Bolland, 'as if he is planning a variety bill: building up the evening viewing to a climax. That is where he is at home. There are one or two obvious ones like that at Channel 4, like nine o'clock on a Friday night where there is comedy, chat show, game show, maybe three hours of variety on television. But otherwise the trick at Channel 4 is to schedule so that the viewer can nip in and nip out as opposed to scheduling for the whole evening. I don't think to this day he is at home scheduling at Channel 4.'

But this scheduling argument is only one strand of a larger one: that Grade has led the station downmarket or, as Graef put in at Edinburgh, much of the channel's output is bought in, and is neither innovative nor distinctive'. Here again we have a familiar refrain: that Grade is too fond of America. The *Independent* put it another way, with a picture of Grade standing outside Channel 4 and the caption reading 'WAVING THE STARS AND STRIPES EVERY CHANCE HE GETS'. That under Grade the channel has been more welcoming for American shows cannot be denied. On the first Sunday in August 1991 the channel showed six hours of American material from 10.45 a.m. Every weekday at six children are drawn from BBC 1 and ITV with an American sitcom. Grade uses American sitcoms to entice viewers from the main channel, pitching them against the weaker current affairs slots: *My Two Dads* against *World in Action*, *Roseanne* against the news, *Voyage to the Bottom of the Sea* against Sunday lunch-time politics. *The Golden Girls* and *Kate and Allie* are also regular sitcoms for the channel.

Many of Grade's critics argue that such use of American series has reshaped the channel. 'He has,' says Stoessl, 'changed it to the way he thinks it should operate. Gradually he has built the audience for the channel by pumping it full of American material. Top Ten before he came and now is very different. Now there are thirteen American series in the top thirty programmes. There weren't thirteen American series in the schedule before he came.' It is not that Isaacs did not use American shows but there was a more discriminating mix and he loved exhuming old repeats which gave them a period flavour. Grade's preference for things American is understandable. European series such as *Black Forest Clinic* or *Châteauvalon* just do not transfer; even *Mission Eureka*, a sex-and-space European co-production series in whih Channel 4 invested money, has had to pushed in after midnight. And American shows are cost effective. An hour of original drama might cost between £250,000 and £300,000. Two half-hours of US sitcom could cost £10,000 to £20,000.

Grade can cite the success of Alan Bleasdale's *GBH*, an original drama series that was commissioned on his initiative, and has been quite the most talked-about series in recent years, although even this has not matched Isaacs's *The Price* or *A Woman of Substance* in terms of viewing figures. He can also justifiably point to the fact that Jeremy's wild cottage garden of a schedule needed weeding – what he has been doing is pruning and transplanting so that Isaacs's garden is easier on the eye and the diversity is more visible. Grade has argued that while

Isaacs increased audience share 'by "force feeding" the schedule mix with a blockbuster like *Woman of Substance* . . . our usual mix [is] better produced, more carefully scheduled, better packaged and more effectively promoted.'

The proof of the pudding lies in Grade's success in drawing audiences. In the first year that Grade was in charge, Channel 4's share of the audience declined from 8.9 per cent when Isaacs left to 8.7 per cent by the end of Grade's first year. But now the share is nearly ten per cent, something that Isaacs had hoped to achieve by 1985 but except for isolated periods never did. Also, those that watch do so for longer: for two hours twenty-two minutes a week, fifteen minutes more than in 1990. The problem with the channel is that attracting audiences is not its only rationale; as Graef says, 'Ratings are not part of the remit.' This may suggest that Grade is faced with a 'heads you lose and tails I win situation'. Whatever he does he will never be able to convince the critics – and they now form a sizeable body – that he has improved on Isaacs. In any case, many of his critics have made Isaacs something of a demi-god of television, all the easier given that he is out of it.

Grade dealt with Graef's sally jauntily and very effectively. Graef had spoken about how independents suggesting ideas to the channel had been told to aim for 'neat and tidy television', with 'remit programmes' considered a term of abuse. 'Who are these producers?' Grade wanted to know. Name them, give me specific names, tell me who they are! Unless you do that I cannot answer vague, generalised charges. Graef could hardly do that. He was fronting for the producers because many were afraid to speak publicly but Grade seized on this reluctance to name names as an example of the sour grapes criticisms you were bound to get from the independents who were not getting quite as much work from Channel 4 as they had in the past.

Grade went on to complete his apparent triumph that very afternoon when the Festival debated the effects of the new system and the job of central scheduler created by the ITV auctions. This means that the old floating poker game that schedulers played and which both fascinated and grated Grade will go. Instead of different network schedulers haggling over programmes every Monday, the new system will have one super network schedule laying down a central law. Such a proposal had been mooted by *Campaign* magazine back in the autumn of 1987 as a job that would be ideal for Grade when Grade was fretting at the BBC, keen to get away from under Birt. Now it was part of the new television dispensation was this the job for him?

That afternoon at the 1991 Festival Grade played the part of the Central Scheduler. It was of course play-acting, but done to devastating effect. Raymond Snoddy, introducing Grade, who was quizzed by the likes of Isaacs's old deputy at Channel 4, Paul Bonner, and others from ITV, made jokes at his expense. The debate was being sponsored by the channel but Snoddy had been told to make it clear that in real life Grade had no intention of applying for the job, he had a contract with Channel 4 for five years. Then Snoddy recalled asking Grade once whetrher he would ever apply for the job of chief executive of Channel 4 and Grade had replied, 'No, no, no, not interested in anything like that.' Bonner had wittily referred to Grade's love of money, saying as he began the mock interviews, 'This is a preliminary discussion, so there is no question about salaries.' But while both these jokes were much appreciated by the audience, Grade had overcome the laughter at this own expense with a commanding, polished performance which revealed him to be both strong-minded and a man who could laugh at himself. He even got in a good dig at Graef, referring to him, sarcastically, as 'my agent'.

There is no doubt that this was the high point of the Festival. Grade had found it a bore, lacking passion and anger. For this instant drama of how the new central scheduler might behave, Grade discarded his suit for red socks, denim jeans and shirt and stunned the delegates with what *The Sunday Times* called 'a wry, yet fiery performance'. With various senior ITV executives pretending to be the interview board, Grade's performance as the central scheduler was so masterly, if a bit Stalinist – the central scheduler, he said, would lay down the law and all the companies would have to follow – that not a few concluded that he was the ideal man for the job. One admiring BBC executive watching the mock rehearsal said, 'Michael is one of only two people in this country who could even begin to tackle it.' His only other competitor could possibly be Greg Dyke of LWT.

As Snoddy moved to sum up, Grade butted in for a last word, saying, 'I have the two outstanding qualities for the job: total megalomania and the common touch.' The hall dissolved into laughter and applause.

But play-acting in Edinburgh, however skilfully done, is one thing. Real life is different. And this was to hit Grade within weeks of his triumph at Edinburgh when the greatest storm he had faced since his move to Channel 4 broke on 12 September. On that day the *Independent* had a front-page story about Grade's £500,000 golden handcuffs. As we have seen, it was not exactly a new story. The *Private Eye* and *Mail* revelations of early March had not caught on; this one did. Much to the chagrin of the journalist who wrote the story, Maggie Brown, the by-line of the piece attributed it to Leonard Doyle, the paper's correspondent in New York. This gave it an even more exotic touch, although it was just an error. However, there was nothing exotic about the fuss the story created.

Anthony Smith wrote to the *Independent* denouncing the channel and claiming that the story of the golden handcuffs just showed how it had lost its way. The *Independent on Sunday* pictured the incident as a 'gold-plated mistake' and even Charles Denton, who sees himself as a friend of Grade's, did not think the channel had behaved well. Denton feels, 'It is legitimate for any individual in any profession to negotiate the best deal he can with his employers to get the best financial satisfaction. But I am not sure it was correct for Channel 4 board to be joining the same world. I am a supporter of Michael's right as an individual to negotiate the deal but it was a mistake for the Channel 4 board to join in that kind of debate. They were wrong to do so. It wasn't improper for Michael to suggest it, but it was improper for the board to progress it as they did.'

As luck would have it, the story broke just as the Royal Television Society was to hold its biennial meeting at Cambridge. These meetings have proved historic for Grade. Here in 1981 Tesler first discussed Grade's move to America; here in 1983 Wenham sounded him about the BBC; now he faced a different challenge. John Birt, who was organising the conference, had received a number of requests for an emergency debate to discuss Channel 4 and at Cambridge University's Faculty of Music a hasty debate was arranged for Grade to answer his critics. Friends had suggested he might adopt a softer tone but Grade would have none of it, the only concessions to the critics being an admission that perhaps it was his fault that he had not explained how the channel needed to change as it matured.

It was a typical Grade performance, with references to the fight to save the channel from privatisation and of the challenges ahead, combined with side swipes at his critics. Graef and Smith had revived the Channel 4 group and Grade ridiculed their efforts. 'Because Channel 4 enjoys a peculiar place in the hearts of the chattering classes from Muswell Hill to Magdalen College, they are alarmed. Doom and disaster are predicted on all sides. The remit is going. Innovation has ended. Channel 4 has lost its way. Well, I am sorry to ruin a good story.'

But the story was the golden handcuffs and although in his prepared speech he made no reference to them they dominated the questions from the floor and refused to go away. Back in London the Independent Programme Producers' Association met at the Bloomsbury Room of the Groucho Club and demanded Attenborough's resignation. Grade's own commissioning editors were aghast. At a weekly programme meeting Liz Forgan struggled to contain their anger about the golden handcuffs and finally on the evening of 16 September Grade himself addressed them.

At Cambridge it had been noticeable how under pressure Grade had made jokes about his Jewish upbringing, with many references to Olga. Many of them were funny, but they had a defensive ring to them. At this meeting with his own staff Grade was even more on the defensive as he explained how his divorce, loss of his house, and now his separation from Patti and need to find a house, had made him need money. Michael Green had offered him twice the money, he had told the board and they had given him the money. His only regret was that he had not told his colleagues earlier; they should not have learnt it from the press.

The speech did not completely reassure Grade's editors but they faced a dilemma. Did they want Grade to go? When Forgan asked the editors if they were trying to force him to resign there was no answer. In a sense this is Grade's triumph. He may not philosophically, as Graef says, be the man for the job – it is odd that as the man who always fought the concept of the channel he is now leading it into the new age. The problem for the critics is who replaces him? Graef and others try hard to argue that their misgivings are not personal but philosophical but Grade turns the whole matter into a personal loyalty test and there is no answer to the basic question of who can take over. This gives him the opportunity to dictate when and how he goes.

Grade has repeatedly made it clear he has no interest in the central scheduler's job, a job that might have been made for him. At Edinburgh, while accepting the accolades, he declared, 'I would rather sweep the streets than actually take on the job of central scheduler for real.' For Grade, after running BBC 1 and Channel 4, it would be a demotion and in any case it would not address his need for capital. But then, nothing in British television could. That is the central dilemma for Grade. He wants to make money, his friend Michael Green is worth £140m and is in *The Sunday Times Book of the Rich*. Grade cannot exercise the American option – that has closed for ever. So where does he go?

Yet, partly due to his own efforts, partly due to luck, he finds himself in a unique position: heading a channel whose future is certain. All around him the television world looks very insecure. 1996 will see the need for a new BBC charter and the ITV system is just recovering from the chaos induced by the franchise auction bids.

A few years ago, when Winston Fletcher interviewed a number of people about managing creativity, he found Grade much the most commercial of the people he spoke to. 'Isaacs was much more sympathetic and indulgent towards the creative people; Grade much tougher, less sympathetic.' Interestingly, Grade saw himself as a conductor, while Isaacs and Puttnam describe themselves as enablers and facilitators. It is an interesting distinction and goes to the heart of Grade at Channel 4. He would like to be the conductor of the creative talent there, yet he is not in philosophical sympathy with its creation. Graef can put the case against Grade well: 'I don't think he has understood the particular virtues of Channel 4. For two particular reasons. He has never been a programme maker, so therefore has never felt frustrated by the limitations of conventional television. Also, during the whole creation of Channel 4, he was against it. He was working for an ITV company that was trying to get Channel 4 as ITV 2. He has never felt the need for the channel as a programme maker or as an executive – that does make it harder for him to understand. It is not his private company.'

But he runs it like his private company, and though the storm over the golden handcuffs may lead to indignation and angry editorials, it cannot dent his position.

XII

JUST ANOTHER GRADE?

It's going to be a gentle descent, but it's inevitable
MICHAEL GRADE on the coming end of television's
Golden Age

IN JANUARY 1989 Grade was interviewed on BBC Bristol's egghead
series *Three Minute Culture* by Michael Ignatieff. The critics were
enthralled but, much to everyone's surprise, Grade presented a deso-
late picture of television, proclaiming that he was helping to preside
over the end of broadcasting's Golden Age. 'It's going to be a gentle
descent, but it's inevitable.' True, this was a bleak period for him,
both personally and professionally; his marriage to Sarah had
ended, and he was in the middle of the fight to secure Channel 4's
remit.

Today his words strike a chord. Viewed from the perspective of
1992, with the cries of the ITV chiefs as they scramble to save their
franchises ringing loudly, it does seem as if a television age, whether
it be considered a golden one or not, is coming to an end. And if the
dominance of television is really ending, then Grade may well be
seen as the last of the broadcasting executives who have appeared
larger than the medium they represent.

If so it would also chime with one of the most persuasive theories
about the media presented by television's resident intellectual, Brian
Wenham. His theory is that every new medium enjoys a fifty-year or
so span of attention and dominance. At the turn of the century and
continuing through to the First World War *media* meant newspapers, producing such giants as Northcliffe and Beaverbrook. Then
the novelty wore off, newspapers became much more accepted as
part of the environment, and while they continue to be produced
and new ones emerge, the print media has since produced nobody to
match Northcliffe or Beaverbrook in public prominence. In the
inter-war years and for a time after the Second World War *media*
was sound radio, with personalities such as Reith towering over the
medium and almost symbolising it. Since the mid-fifties it has been

television. Television's Golden Age has run for almost forty years now and, if Wenham is right, then it too is due to decline, just as newspapers and radio did.

This does not mean that television is likely to be replaced by some other medium in the way that it replaced newspapers and radio. What it means is that the importance of certain TV channels may change. Both in America and in the UK the post-war rise of television has seen the medium become dominated by a small number of companies. In the United States it has been the three major networks: NBC, CBS and ABC.

During the Vietnam War Walter Cronkite, the newsreader on nightly prime-time television, became, in effect, the conscience of the nation. Opinion polls in America showed that he was more trusted than any other public figure and he himself began to assume the role of a sort of guardian, concluding the news with a comment that was meant to be at once reassuring and a pithy moral lesson. The United Kingdom has not produced any such figure, although, in their own ways, Richard Dimbleby, Sir Alastair Burnett and Sir Robin Day have come close. As the UK television market fragments and the BBC and ITV duopoly breaks up, the chances of such figures emerging become increasingly remote. In America the networks are important but do not quite dominate viewing time as they did. Once, ninety per cent of all US viewing was provided by the big three; now it is down to sixty per cent and falling. In the UK, the decline may be less steep but just as definite. In such a situation no one single company can claim dominance and no one single individual, be he presenter or television executive, can claim to be really crucial to the future of television.

Where does this leave Michael Grade? Opinion as to where he deserves to rank varies considerably. Some, like Bill Cotton, rate him on a par with Reith. And even if this seem understandably partisan from a man who looks upon Grade as his younger brother, it is backed by the more independent assessment of the television critic Mark Lawson, who feels that Grade is one of the three giants produced by post-war British television, Sir Dennis Foreman and Jeremy Isaacs being the other two. His detractors, and their number is legion, treat such a suggestion almost as sacrilege.

Nobody presents the anti-Grade position more succinctly than Cotton's old colleague Aubrey Singer. 'Bill Cotton is absolutely bonkers. That is one agent talking of another agent. Michael basically has an agent's cast of mind, looking to buy and sell, or strip *Wogan* across the board at 7.30 p.m. It is not a great original mind, it is a deal-making mind. He may have been a great scheduler when he scheduled on BBC 1 but what has he done on Channel 4? Damn all. He has abdicated that role, given it to Liz Forgan, and she does not know anything.'

Singer echoes a criticism made by many: the man himself is likeable at the personal level but he deserves no great plaudit for his television work. 'Michael is a very nice chap, full of charm, gregarious, very pleasant, but I don't think there is much intellect there. It is a lot of surface, and a fairly floating surface at that. Examine his career and you find it is littered with disasters of one sort or another. He never takes a stand and keeps to it. His career is full of reversals.'

Interestingly, Singer and Grade do agree on one thing: both worry that television is declining, but Singer sees Grade's rise as part of that decline. 'He is,' says Singer, 'typical of this period in British television. It says something about British television which is not very flattering. I think we are becoming a trivial nation, I just feel we are slipping.' This may seem a high mandarin view of Grade; indeed, Singer has been described as a BBC mandarin, although, like Grade, he did not go to university but, crucially, made his reputation by producing science programmes including the highly regarded *The Ascent of Man*.

Grade, of course, is keenly aware of not having been to university, so keen that he sometimes gives the impression of having a chip on his shoulder about it. Mark Lawson has noticed that nearly all his speeches include the line about being educated at the *Daily Mirror* sports desk. But Lawson is convinced there is more to Grade than that: 'He is a very interesting mix of intellect, commercial flair and intellectual feeling for television, with a belief in the freedom of television. The English tend to talk of brilliant minds but what is the use of a brilliant mind if you do not have good instincts and are not pretty bright? Grade is far more intelligent than most executives in the BBC. Milne was terribly clever but proved pretty useless. He was very intelligent but his intellect did not work on television. Michael Grade reads widely but the only reason people disregard his intelligence is because he did not go to university. He believes a work should reach an audience. His weakness is that he can be attracted by stars like Bruce Forsyth; that was the biggest disaster in his whole career.'

But can this explain the criticisms Grade generates from such established television people as Singer and others? To an extent Singer's views reflect the general scorn that television programme makers have for those who have never made any programmes. Grade, as one of the

few executives who have risen to the top without making a single programme, is almost a ready target. Those outside television who do not
share such prejudices take a very different view. Carmen Callil who, as
non-executive director of Channel 4, played an important role in
appointing Grade, has had no reason to doubt her judgement since. 'I
am a great admirer of Michael Grade. He is very funny. He brings great
joie de vivre to things. I think he has performed wonderfully.'

Where Singer thinks Grade has abdicated, Callil is enchanted by his
management style. 'I think what he also brought to the channel is absolutely magnificent management. He is a great delegator, what the channel needed, so somebody like Liz has been able to shape the editorial
side. The programmes are getting better.' Not having perceived Isaacs
as a great intellectual Callil finds little to choose beteen Grade and
Isaacs. 'They are both intelligent. I don't think there is much between
him and Jeremy in programming.' Callil, who became a non-executive
director in the middle of Isaacs's regime, has enjoyed Grade's reign far
more. 'Jeremy had an affliction, Edmund Dell. With Jeremy it was his
company; Michael has made it much more open, more democratic,
more people have their oars in.'

That a public figure should attract such contrary views is not
unusual, but it is rare for anyone who is not a politician to generate
such violent contrasts. The fact that Grade does arouse such passion
indicates how much like a politician, albeit a television politician, he is.

Before Callil met Grade she was convinced he would be 'a yobbo,
this is what people tell you of this vulgar sort of family. When he got the
Channel 4 job he was presented as a dumbo.' It came as a pleasant surprise to her that he was very far from that. 'You only have to spend two
minutes with him to realise he isn't like that. You can have marvellous
conversations with Michael.' This surprise has led to such delight that
Callil almost purrs with pleasure as she talks about Grade: 'Michael
has been absolutely enchanting to work with. He is a pleasure. I think
he has done a better job on the political front than Jeremy would have
done. Jeremy is like me, he finds it difficult to put up with people. Jeremy does not suffer fools gladly; Michael is not as impatient.'

Some of the empathy Callil feels for Grade arises from the fact that,
being Australian, she, like Grade, is an outsider. 'I feel a tremendous
sense of being an outsider. This can be a very painful place to be an
outsider in, they are very brutal on outsiders here.' But she attributes
Grade's yobbo image to sheer English snobbery. 'There is a lot of
snobbery, unnecessary snobbery here. All this talk that he is show-biz

or that he didn't go to Oxbridge. This country works on networking. It is very English to think you can be only one thing, a person of culture or a populist. In publishing you can either produce popular fiction or serious novels, not both. If you try and do both you get rubbished. Michael has been portrayed as the cultural yobbo in charge of Channel 4.'

Even the language used by some of the Grade critics betrays this English dismissal of him as the outsider. Thus Singer talks of him having no 'bottom'. (Not that many people in television have 'bottom', according to Singer. Not Birt but, interestingly, Milne, who despite forcing him to leave the BBC remains a friend. Checkland has it. Wenham, too, says Singer, has 'bottom' but a 'shifting bottom'.) If not having bottom is the ultimate English put-down, then so is being considered an American, and Grade, as Rees-Mogg puts it, is not merely the American in British television but has 'a Californian cast of mind'. (To this Callil responds by saying, 'Coming from Rees-Mogg that is a compliment'.)

Callil may be pitching it a bit strongly in saying that Grade suffers from English snobbery but there is something in the argument that the British chattering classes have a curious view of television. They may have lost the arrogance they exhibited towards the medium in the fifties and sixties when it was fashionable for them to declare, 'We don't have a set', but it is astonishing how many television policy makers still have to acquire a set when they are appointed to a top television job. The list includes BBC governors and Edmund Dell, who had to get one when he was made chairman of Channel 4. The chattering classes may happily pontificate about television and reaily perform on it but they refuse to believe that the greatest mass medium ever invented has any role to play in shaping British society. In the mid-seventies Noel Annan chaired the Annan Committee on the Future of Broadcasting which made far-reaching recommendations. One of these led to the creation of BARB, the unified body to measure television ratings which has proved an essential crib for Grade the scheduler. Yet in 1990, when Lord Annan published his book *Our Age*, about the post-war generation that shaped modern Britain, he referred to television only twice, once when talking about Mary Whitehouse trying to clean it up, and again British television becoming the best in the world. In a book of 611 pages which is seen as 'an intellectual, social and political history of modern England', television, the most important medium in that age, gets no more than three lines from Lord Annan, the man who has dictated the cultural tastes of the elite of Britain for half a century.

Grade has broken another rule of the British chattering classes: that sport and arts do not mix. He may have overcome his lack of university education and lack of an Oxbridge network, but what he cannot overcome is that his early grounding was in sports journalism. It is a curious feature of British culture that while organised sports play a crucial part in almost everyone's life, British letters ignore it. Kingsley Amis may be as great a fan of cricket as Philip Roth is of baseball, but it is inconceivable that Amis would ever write a novel built around cricket as Roth did with baseball in his *Great American Novel*, which is centred round a character straight from the *Mirror*'s sports desk. So while cricket has an extensive library, it has never inspired a novel in the way baseball has done. Bernard Malamud's *The Natural* was not only a bestseller but it became a film; even when David Putnam sought to make a film about *Bodyline* he found himself confronted by insurmountable problems. Ring Lardner could become one of America's finest short-story writers, having started as a baseball reporter, and while his baseball background earned derision from Scott Fitzgerald, it did not stop him from making his mark on American fiction.

In Britain sports writers who aim at something more find they are not taken that seriously by the literary world. Brian Glanville, who is not only one of our best soccer reporters but a considerable novelist, has found that even in his own paper, *The Sunday Times*, his writ rarely runs beyond the sports pages. There he may be essential; in the literary pages he is an oddball: a soccer writer who aspires to be a novelist.

The British chattering classes can, of course, distrust people for the most extraordinary reasons. So the distrust of Janet Street-Porter, another figure who in her own way excites as much interest as Grade, boils down to, says Mark Lawson, 'nothing more than that people hate her voice. When you ask what it is people don't like about her, the answer you get is: it's that voice. Nothing more grounded or valid than that. Similarly with Michael Grade. There is the feeling that he is associated with the Grade dynasty which is associated with show business tackiness. ATV was regarded as a very bad ITV company and you cannot divorce him from all that.'

Lawson believes that 'the Grade family has never been liked in this country. Lew Grade has always been a bit of a joke. They are associated with glitz.' But is there more to the anti-Grade feeling than that? Lawson is sure there is. 'The Grades are associated with Jewishness. I don't think you can ever root out anti-semitism in this country.'

When Lawson covered politics he was amazed to find how many Tory backbenchers referred to Edwina Currie as Edwina Cohen, her maiden name, which is also a more recognisably Jewish-sounding one. In 1985, when for the first time the Pope's Easter message was not broadcast, one BBC governor approached Lawson, held up his finger to his nose to suggest the caricature Jewish nose and said, 'What do you expect with Michael Grade there?' 'There is no doubt,' says Lawson, 'that there is anti-semitism there and Michael Grade has suffered from it.'

Grade, says Lawson, 'has that problem that Jews of his generation have. They are not Jewish by observance but they are by tradition. Nigel Lawson is an example of that.' While Mark Lawson himself is neither a relation of Nigel Lawson nor Jewish, he appreciates that 'any Jew, even if he does not observe, would be sensitive to anti-semitism. The number of people who talk about the Jewish mafia is astonishing. I don't think it is easy being Jewish in this country. I don't think it is easy being anything other than white Oxbridge educated. Michael Grade suffers from not being in that category.'

Singer may dismiss such views as 'a common sort of paranoia' but the crucial test is that those who are Jewish are well aware of what it means. Paul Fox has never made any bones about the fact that he felt he could never become Director General of the BBC because he was Jewish and Grade was proud of the fact that when the BBC appointed him controller he was the first Jewish person from outside to be appointed to such a position.

Grade can play up his Jewishness when it suits him and nearly always makes a joke about his Jewish origin to defuse a situation. At Cambridge, during the fracas about the golden handcuffs he had negotiated with Attenborough, his speech was replete with jokes about Olga and his Jewish ancestry, but when the laughter died down it was evident that the jokes hid a deep anxiety, a certain defensiveness.

The anti-semitism neatly reinforces the feeling that Grade really belongs to the London Palladium and this makes his critics label him in all sorts of extraordinary ways, the most extraordinary being that he is too American. In television terms this is a nonsensical charge. Grade genuinely hates American television, but his critics use the label 'American' as a short-hand to describe un-British behaviour. Before the war, the nation's image of America may have been shaped by Henry James and rich American heiresses coming to London looking for noble lords to marry, like the heiress from Minneapolis who married Lord Curzon, the self-proclaimed superior person. In post-war Britain, being an American means being a person who is a bit too competitive, a bit too aggressive, a bit too brash and a bit too eager for money.

That Grade is competitive goes without question. But it is not an American kind of competitiveness, more of the type that English public schoolmasters display.

A Channel 4 commissioning editor describes a dinner he attended at Grade's request at the Grosvenor House Hotel for the Cancer Research Award. 'We had to buy a table to contribute to the charity, something like £2,000. There was a quiz and Michael chose people who could answer questions in the different categories. That is where his competitive spirit comes out. He wanted the Channel 4 table to be staffed with people who could answer questions on literature, sport, etc., and win the quiz. One of the literary questions was, 'Fill in the blank: "I must go down to the seas again, etc." One of the commissioning editors immediately said, " 'I must go down to the seas again, to the lonely sea and the sky, and all I ask is a tall ship and a star to steer her by.' John Masefield." Grade was very impressed. "You know all this shit?" he said in some awe. "Yes," said the commissioning editor. "I learnt it at school." "Fantastic," purred Grade like a master whose house was competing in a quiz programme.'

Grade himself knew all the film answers and although Channel 4 came only seventh out of fifty-two competitors, British Telecom emerging as the winners, his channel was the top-ranking television company and that meant a lot to Grade. He told his team, 'We beat the BBC in intellect. That is what matters.' People, says the commissioning editor, get him wrong when they see him as an American. 'He hates America and the way they do things. But he likes competition, he likes to win, he likes awards, he likes to show off.'

Such a competitive spirit is hardly unique to Grade. Birt can be extremely competitive when he organises his football matches but he has a rather British sense of proportion – off the field he can hide his competitive instincts in long memos – and owlish glasses suggesting a bookish diligence – which do his reputation no harm. Grade hates memos, preferring nothing more than a couple of hand-written sentences.

Grade has not helped his American, outsider image by having his own speech writer. In 1990 Mark Lawson was at a meeting of the Edinburgh Television Festival committee when the discussion turned to who should be selected to give the prestigious McTaggart Lecture. Somebody suggested Grade. Forgan immediately pointed to Lawson and said, 'You might as well get Mark to do it, he writes all Michael's speeches.'

As the laughter died down, Gus McDonald said darkly, 'So he has a speech writer. That explains a lot.' This was a bit unfair, as Lawson has written only two speeches for Grade, but, as Lawson himself admits, that 'has created a situation where every time Michael makes a joke people say Mark Lawson has scripted it.' The incident also made Lawson realise the 'sheer resentment Grade generates, in his style really. People seem to be pleased to attribute all his jokes and thoughts to his speech writer, which is completely unfair.'

This view of Grade is not helped further by the fact that he does seem to command a quite amazing publicity machine. Grade has featured in the *Celebrity Cookbook*, sharing the spotlight with Cilla Black and Glenys Kinnock, and is almost a regular in the 'Kindred Spirits' feature of the *Daily Telegraph* magazine. Here, every week, disparate people are shown sharing a common interest or experience. Grade has been shown having an interest in foreign languages, making him a kindred spirit of Gary Lineker (Lineker mentioned Spanish, Grade Yiddish), and having suffered bullying at school, which made him a kindred spirit of Willie Whitelaw, Kenny Everett, Julian Clary and Frank Bruno. Grade's publicity machine never seems to stop. It can be so prolific that when in June 1990 the IRA bombed the Carlton Club, Grade, as we have seen, got into the act with the result that ITN had a newsflash within half an hour of the event, while the BBC had to wait a further hour. What is more, Grade's 'scoop' also featured in the Peterborough Diary column of the *Daily Telegraph*.

Much of this explains the vehemence of the charge now being articulated that Grade is destroying Channel 4. The main charge against Grade, made by many of the independent producers, is that he has taken the channel downmarket, pumping it full of American imports. That is debatable; Isaacs also used American soaps to build up his schedule – *I Love Lucy* leading to the much acclaimed *Channel 4 News*, for instance. In any case, Channel 4 needed to change from the Isaacs days.

One commissioning editor, by no means an uncritical admirer of Grade, says, 'I don't think Michael has deliberately taken it downmarket, it would have happened anyway. There was a definite need to rationalise documentaries: too many of them and many of bad quality.

Most producers are documentary producers. Now that it has been rationalised they can't flood the channel with their crap. True, Grade would have considered it a success if he could have made Johathan Ross a Michael Aspel and got audience figures. That hasn't happened but to say he has taken it downmarket is extreme.'

The criticisms of independent producers also need to be treated with care because by the very nature of things they are always dissatisfied. They are a bit like freelance journalists who can never be happy with the work they are given: 'I submitted six ideas to the BBC and Channel 4 and they turned all of them down' is a common, persistent complaint. It existed even during Isaacs's regime. The very system of independent producers creates paranoia – an idea submitted by an independent producer might be done by somebody else – but the charges against Grade go beyond that.

A more serious charge is that Grade is failing as a manager, the very area he had marked out as his own special contribution to the channel. His supposed managerial competence was the quality that attracted John Gau to Grade as he and the other Channel 4 directors sat discussing Attenborough's dark horse. That is the quality that makes Callil gush about Grade: 'He runs as excellent ship, is a very, very good manager. Michael has done very well in moving Channel 4 to new areas, managing the beastly Act. I particularly like the way he has allowed colleagues to develop their own tastes and what they want to do at Channel 4.'

Yet as the row over the golden handcuffs shows, Grade's very managerial competence is now being questioned. Good managers are not supposed to create waves. Grade has done so with his handcuffs. Indeed, the affair calls into question whether the channel needs quite the sort of management style that Grade provides or even the management structure he has created. Anthony Smith's fear that he would bureaucratise the channel and destroy its purpose looks like coming true.

Channel 4 by its very nature needs to be an editorially led channel. Its editorship is peculiar. It is not like the national newspapers or other channels; the editors need to be idiosyncratic, not representative. In a sense it is the *Spectator* of television or perhaps Kingsley Martin's *New Statesman* where it was said the editor did not know what the back of the publication, the literary pages, looked like. Martin took little interest in them, confident that such was the style of the *New Statesman* that whatever was printed would be readable.

Channel 4, being a complementary channel, has a similar inter-
pretative role.

This is a difficult responsibility that devolves a heavy burden on the
commissioning editors. It is inconceivable that the BBC sports editor
would not bid to show football or cricket or Wimbledon, but for the
Channel 4 sports editor it is important to show American football or
kabbadi or women's netball. As one commissioning editor puts it,
'What you are brought here to do is to interpret the world according to
yourself and put on something you believe is complementary to the
mainstream, is innovative in content, and should definitely have a
minority audience. That makes it imperative for the chief executive to
discuss this interpretation with each commissioning editor, to give him
or her the kind of budget, programme plan, encouragement in the
schedules he or she needs to interpret in that way.'

But Grade has conspicuously failed to do this. He is no philosopher
and is proud of the fact. As he told his Cambridge audience while trying
to defend the golden handcuffs deal, he could not say what programmes Channel 4 would deliver in 1993 or 1998. 'Prescription seems to
be the envy of inspiration.' But in a channel built on inspiration this is a
dangerous stance to adopt. Unlike Isaacs, Grade has not been involved
in programming and while Isaacs watched a lot of programmes,
discussed things with the commissioning editors and gave the impression he knew about everything that was going on, Grade leaves it all to
the controllers he has appointed.

One commissioning editor describes the Grade strategy thus:
'Grade sees most things but only when it has gone out. He makes a
summary, a quick but sharp remark on it, and passes on. Grade's basic
idea is: in the schedule there must be that much entertainment, that
much fun, that much looking forward to things and he will move
heaven, earth, reputation and personnel to get it.'

The Grade hallmark is that he is the competent manager who
delivers. This works fine as long as he delivers. When he does not, then
this very hands-off approach of good delegation and good management seems like abdication.

The only two areas of the channel where Grade is hands-on are
budgets and schedules. Yet it is in budgets that he has come unstuck,
getting the board to award him and his fellow executive directors large
sums of money at a time when the budgets have been cut. To add to his
problems, news of this leaked just after the channel lost £5 million which
it had deposited in the Bank of Credit and Commerce International,

just a few days before it was closed. When that happens the question 'What price managerial competence?' becomes urgent.

What one Channel 4 commissioning editor would like is a chief executive who is a daddy figure. 'I would like him to say, "I have seen your programmes, let's talk about your philosophy." Michael has never done that. Jeremy would ask you what you wanted. Michael says, "Talk to your controller." He is quite happy to let the controller decide what the philosophy of entertainment and factual programmes should be. He does not set the philosophy. He doesn't have the idea. Isaacs would have had an idea. I may not have agreed with the idea. But we would have discussed things.'

Worse still, for all his charm and bonhomie, as far as commissioning editors are concerned Grade is not approachable. 'He only wants to know,' says one, 'who he want to know and what he wants to know. He has not said, "My door is always open. Come down, I will solve your problems, it will be immediately done." There is no demonstration that anybody can place any great faith in him for anything at all. If you have a problem, you solve it yourself, or you go to John Willis, the controller.'

In contrast, Isaacs could be approached. 'He would listen to your problem very carefully. Grade thinks he has dealt with the problem by appointing you as commissioning editor. You are not a person with a problem, you are there to solve it. His philosophy is, "I have hired you to do some work." So if I throw the television set out of the window he will say, "I hired him to do it, the television needed throwing, the window needed breaking."' This means Grade provides his commissioning editors with loyal support, but he does not inspire and while this is fine as long as managerial competence lasts, when it does not, the whole thing comes apart.

Isaacs created an atmosphere where everything seemed possible. It was easy for Isaacs, the channel was like a child learning new things every day. Now it is a strapping teenager, Grade has tried to create an atmosphere where the important things are budgets and schedules. But when, as in the golden handcuffs crisis, it becomes clear Channel 4 is like any other corporation, then there is no way out for Grade.

Had this book been written in 1987 when Grade was at the height of his powers at the BBC, looking ahead to succeeding Cotton as managing director and dreaming of the time he might become the next Director General, it would have ended on a positive note. One could point to the fact that his success with *EastEnders* had meant that he had produced a soap to challenge *Coronation Street*, no mean feat in British television, given that nobody had managed it before. He had also knocked on the head the conventional wisdom that summer was a dead time for television.

But since his stewardship of Channel 4, Michael Grade's abilities do not look quite so brilliant. In any case, since his supporters see him as one of the three great men of post-war British television, he needs to be judged by the highest standards. And by those standards he comes over as a man with no views; worse, one who often changes his views. If he has a concept of television it is that the television status quo as created in the immediate post-war years, the BBC–ITV duopoly, should be preserved. He supports this with jokes and a nice repartee.

The jokes, it must be said, are good, very good. When a multicultural programme about Muslim women, called *Immaculate Conception*, was delayed by production hassles Grade asked what the problem was. The commissioning editor explained that this was because the last leg of the programme being filmed in Surrey had been held up because of a lack of eunuchs. Grade's face lit up. 'No eunuchs in Surrey. Wonderful! Why don't you make that the title of the programme? Much better than *Immaculate Conception*.' The budget meeting collapsed in mirth.

But when the laughter dies there is not much else. Strip away the jokes and there is little left. Indeed, while some of Singer's assessments may be harsh, he is surely right in describing Grade as *nebish*, a lovely Yiddish word meaning 'a bit naïve'.

In the first three years of his Channel 4 reign Grade's lack of beliefs was an asset. Then he was arguing with politicians to secure the remit. 'For politicians in their forties,' says Mark Lawson, 'Michael Grade is an extremely attractive figure. Grade at the BBC was not thought to have "bottom", that word the British use to mean an intellectual theory of television. That counted against him then, it counted against him at Channel 4 in his battles with Michael Kustow. But these very qualities helped him with the government. The thing they were most suspicious of in television was cynical people, people they regarded as elitist broadcasters. They just couldn't pin that on Michael Grade.'

He is, as Tim Bell, Mrs Thatcher's public relations adviser, says, 'an entrepreneur working effectively in the public sector, a very English style of entrepreneurship. Michael understands that if you are successful, however much they may not like you, they have to acknowledge your success. He is a populist but the problem is the populist in the television system we have, dominated by the BBC, is not popular. He is perfectly capable of occupying whatever job he gets, but he belongs to the private sector. He would have been better in the commercial world.' Bell believes Grade would have loved to have privatised Channel 4. 'He said it should be privatised and went back on that but that was in public.' Bell is sure that 'if Grade had gone to Mrs Thatcher with a plan for the privatisation of Channel 4, he could have got it through. Mrs Thatcher was not really interested in the channel, she was more concerned with marginalising the BBC, and if somebody had come to her with a workable plan and said this is how we privatise Channel 4, she would have accepted. But he didn't.'

That may well turn out to be Grade's biggest mistake. Bound by the terms of his appointment to prevent the privatisation, he is now caught between the commercial success he seeks and the system that cannot provide such success. British television can provide material rewards but, despite the changes wrought by Mrs Thatcher, it does not provide scope for a television mogul to emerge, like a Bill Paley or a Ted Turner, Americans who might have been role models for Grade. So he is left with being another, weaker edition of Lew. As Charles Denton says, 'There can only be one Lew. He was an original.'

In that interview with Ignatieff, Grade had taken care to present his best television image, discarding his red braces for blue so that they matched his blue eyes, but, as Brenda Maddox noted, 'what came across was no fair-haired whizz kid, just a younger version of his uncle Lew. The eyes glittered, the lips curled and the cigar was poised, waiting for the main chance. And when it came, he grabbed it.'

That night on television he did. But as subsequent events have shown Michael Grade may have missed his real big chance. He is never likely to become Director General of the BBC, the highest post public service television can provide, and while Channel 4 may seem like the next best substitute, its future secure, removed from the hurly-burly that has convulsed the rest of television, it is not quite what Grade's entrepreneurial skills demand. Or the channel deserves.

One question remains: What can tempt Grade away? Temptation will certainly come, for he remains the most charismatic figure in our television world. Less than six months after his private and public life seemed to have collapsed, he was back on centre stage, flaunting his new affair with royal designer Lindka Cierach like a coltish young man. It's entirely in keeping with the Grade story that he should do so.

SELECTED BIBLIOGRAPHY

Noel Annan, *Roxburg of Stowe*, London 1965

Helen Baehr and Gillian Dyer (eds.), *Boxed In: Women and Television*, London, 1977.

Joan Bakewell and Nicholas Garnham, *The New Priesthood*, London, 1970.

Anthony Bianco, *Rainmaker: The Saga of Jeff Beck*, New York, 1991.

Stephen Brook, *The Club: The Jews of Modern Britain*, London, 1989.

Hunter Davies, *The Grades*, London, 1981.

Bernard Delfont, *East End, West End*, London, 1990.

David Docherty, *Running the Show*, London, 1990.

D. J. Enright, *Fields of Vision*, London, 1988.

Quentin Falk and Dominic Price, *Last of a Kind: The Sinking of Lew Grade*, London, 1982.

Rita Grade Freeman, *My Fabulous Brothers*, London, 1983.

Lew Grade, *Still Dancing*, London, 1988.

Andrew Goodwin and Garry Whannel (eds.), *Understanding Television*, London, 1990.

Stuart Hood, *On Television*, London, 1980.

Jeremy Isaacs, *Storm Over 4*, London, 1989.

Michael Leapman, *The Last Days of the Beeb*, London, 1987.

Alasdair Macdonald, *Stowe School*, London, 1977.

Tim Madge, *Beyond the BBC*, London, 1989.

Alasdair Milne, *DG: The Memoirs of a British Broadcaster*, London, 1988.

Howard Thomas, *With an Independent Air*, London, 1977.

Michael Tracey, *A Variety of Lives*, London, 1983.

Ian Trethowan, *Split Screen*, London, 1984.

Ernie Wise, *Still on My Way to Hollywood*, London, 1990.

INDEX